The Power of
CREATIVE REASONING

The Ideas and Vision of John Garang

Lual A. Deng

All rights reserved. It is illegal to reproduce, duplicate or transmit any part of this book in either electronic means or printed format. Recording of this publication is strictly prohibited. No part of this publication may be reproduced, stored in a retrieval system, or transmitted, in any form, or by any means, electronic, mechanical, photocopying, recording or otherwise, without the prior permission of the publishers.

Copyright © 2025 Lual A. Deng

9781763873490 (Paperback)
9781763873438 (Hardcover)
9781763873421 (E-Book)

This book is sold subject to the conditions that it shall not, by way of trade or otherwise, be lent, re-sold, hired out or otherwise circulated without the publisher's prior consent in any form of binding or cover other than in which it is published and without a similar condition including the condition being imposed on the subsequent purchaser.

Cover design, typesetting and layout: Africa World Books
Unit 3, 57 Frobisher St, Osborne Park, WA 6017
P.O. Box 1106 Osborne Park, WA 6916

Contents

Preface	*v*
Chapter One: Introduction	1
Chapter Two Reflections on Leadership	12
Chapter Three: Revisiting the Ten Powerful Ideas	41
Chapter Four: The Vision of New Sudan — Progress and Challenges	113
Chapter Five: Political Developments Since 2013	170
Chapter Six: A Review of the Application of 'Garangnomics' Since 2013	188
Chapter Seven: Lessons Learned and Future Directions	236
Chapter Eight Conclusion	290
Bibliography	*297*
Index	*305*

Preface

In the ever-evolving landscape of leadership and governance characterized by pervasive fragility, we must revisit John Garang's concept of creative reasoning. Therefore, the purpose of this second edition is not only to offer a fresh perspective but also to enhance our constructive engagement with Dr. John Garang's comrades, associates, and students regarding the ideals of the liberation struggle. We aim to enrich the dialogue surrounding the themes explored, encouraging critical thinking and inspiring further inquiry. Every page is designed to provoke thought, ignite passion, and foster a deeper appreciation for the intricacies of *Garangism*, which is defined as **the art of creative reasoning**.

Since the first edition's publication in 2013, we have witnessed a resurgence of political recklessness and factional conflicts within the Sudan People's Liberation Movement (SPLM). The rise of social media and advancements in telecommunications have hindered our progress toward establishing a new South Sudan marked by sustainable peace, economic growth, and poverty eradication. Amidst factional struggles within the SPLM over state power and national resources, the voices of practitioners, scholars, civil society, and communities insist on being heard, demanding that the SPLM reflects on the creative reasoning of its founding leader to effectively address the needs of a diverse and dynamic new nation. This second edition serves as a testament to the potency of creative reasoning, incorporating updated insights, contemporary examples, and diverse perspectives that underscore the relevance and urgency of our inquiry in the 21st century.

As we embark on this new phase of constructive engagement within the South Sudanese policy community, let us take a moment to acknowledge the invaluable contributions of those who have shaped this edition. We are deeply grateful to the scholars and practitioners whose pioneering work has informed our revisions and to the readers whose feedback has guided our reflections. To those who have partnered with us in this journey, your insights and encouragement have been crucial. This collective effort emphasizes that knowledge is not a solitary endeavor but a tapestry woven from shared experiences and insights.

We hope you find inspiration and challenge on every page of this revised journey. Thank you for being part of this endeavor and for your commitment to fostering a deeper understanding of John Garang's ideas and vision, grounded in the art of creative reasoning and critical thinking. Together, may we continue to serve our people and humanity through problem-solving and path-goal strategies in honor of this great leader and thinker, John Garang de Mabior.

Chapter One

Introduction

"Seventy-two percent of the population of South Sudan is under thirty years of age. It is this young generation that must utilize Dr. John's power of creative reasoning underpinning his ideas and vision in creating a new South Sudanese identity that is inclusive of all its nationalities. This calls for a nation-building project that looks beyond our tribes and geographical locations on the map of South Sudan. They must focus on the unifying factors of the people of South Sudan, not on what divides them." [1]

We start this second edition with the above passage from the book's first edition. The passage encompasses the essence of a vision, a trait that defined John Garang's life and work. It delves deeply into one specific aspect of his legacy: **creative reasoning**. John Garang was not only an economist, a soldier, and a revolutionary thinker but also a dedicated family man. In this second edition, we aim to provide

---

[1] From Chapter One of the first edition of this book.

readers with an updated exploration of the ideas and themes that defined the first edition.

Since its initial publication, significant developments have occurred in the socio-political landscape, both in South Sudan and Sudan, which confirms one of his ten ideas – that is, Sudan would never be the same again. This edition revisits John Garang's influential thoughts, highlighting their continued relevance in today's context.

John Garang was a visionary leader whose contributions to the struggle for freedom and equality resonate deeply in our current conversations about nation-building, social justice, and reconciliation. His ideas were not just historical artifacts; they offered valuable insights into contemporary issues faced by societies around the globe, particularly those grappling with the legacies of conflict and the quest for unity and dignified sustainable livelihoods. In this edition, we reflect on the changes that have transpired since the first edition, analyzing the impact of Garang's philosophies on emerging movements and their aspirations for democracy and human rights. By revisiting these concepts, we hope to inspire a new generation of readers in the two Sudans to engage critically with Garang's vision and consider how his ideals can be embraced in today's ever-evolving world.

This introduction sets the stage for a deeper exploration of Garang's contributions. It invites seasoned scholars and casual readers to appreciate the enduring significance of his legacy. As we journey through this second edition, let us seek to understand how Garang's insights can guide us in building a more just and inclusive society in the two Sudans. Those who ignore his ideas do so at their peril.

The members of a generation of South Sudanese envisaged in the first edition of the book to internalize Garang's ideas are now in their fifties. They have passed the age of revolutionary zeal and pursuit of new ideas to internalize *Garangism*, especially concerning our place in history. We would, nevertheless, remind them that the might and glory of the ancient kingdom of Kush could be restored to the present two Sudans. This is possible through the power of ideas of a courageous and visionary leader, such as John Garang, with a sense of mission to serve his people by rescuing them from a vicious circle of ignorance and injustice. He made some of us understand our history and who we are by showing where we came from.

Knowing where we came from evaded many Southern Sudanese leaders who came before John Garang. It continues to evade those who came after him, evidenced by the pervasive crises of leadership and governance.

Why is this? We argue that because his point of departure was the Sudanese commonality, which places the Kushites at the center of Sudanese heritage and being. This consciousness and awakening about our place in human history has demolished the wall of ignorance about who we are. This view is elucidated by Derek Welsby in the following passage:

> *"Consideration of the Kushites alongside such giants of the ancient world as the Greeks, Romans and Egyptians is justified on account of the longevity of the kingdom and of its size, if for no other reasons. At the time when Rome was a small village on the banks of the Tiber and the Greek city states held sway over minuscule territories, the Kushites ruled an empire stretching from the central Sudan to the borders of Palestine. The Kingdom of Kush outlived the Greek city states and the period of Macedonian hegemony over vast traces of the ancient world, and co-existed with the rise, heyday and much of the period of decline of the Roman Empire."* (1996, 8-9)

Two decades after John Garang's untimely passing, many Sudanese have yet to fully grasp the significance of understanding our historical context. Therefore, it is essential to reflect on the enduring legacy of the Kingdom of Kush, which provides valuable insights for both Sudan and South Sudan today. In this regard, we would like to highlight five critical features of the Kingdom of Kush's historical legacy.

1. Cultural Heritage

The Kingdom of Kush brilliantly exemplified the blending of diverse cultures. Its strategic location between Africa and the Middle East enabled it to absorb influences from various civilizations, creating a rich tapestry of traditions, languages, and practices. This teaches us about the strength that diversity can bring to a nation. In this regard, the passage from Derek Welsby illustrates how the Kushites thrived alongside some of the most influential civilizations in history. This highlights the importance of recognizing and valuing Sudan's rich cultural heritage, which should inspire national pride and unity in both Sudans. That is, the people of two Sudans must embrace this commonwealth, which John Garang calls Sudanese commonality.

In January 2025, a significant event unfolded that tested the idea of Sudanese commonality. The Sudan Armed Forces (SAF) successfully recaptured Wed Medeni, the capital of Aljazeera State, from the control of the Rapid Support Force (RSF). This military victory, however, was marred by shocking incidents of violence. Reports emerged that certain factions within the SAF, identifying themselves as Islamic militants, committed heinous acts against innocent civilians. Several South Sudanese individuals who were present in the town and its outskirts became targets of these brutal assaults, leading to the slaughter of numerous innocent citizens.

The horrifying nature of these incidents quickly spread across social media platforms, igniting outrage and dismay among the South Sudanese population. In response, a surge of anger rippled on the evening of 16th January 2025 through the capital city of Juba and various other states within South Sudan. What followed was a chaotic mob reaction; shops and businesses owned by Sudanese nationals were targeted and looted overnight, reflecting the deep-seated animosity fueled by the recent violence. This descent into mob action highlighted the fragility of peace in the region and the profound impact of the SAF's actions on ethnic and national relations in and around South Sudan.

The Government of the Republic of South Sudan (GRSS) took prompt and responsible measures in response to the outrage of the South Sudanese population. It prioritized the restoration of law and order while ensuring the safety and protection of Sudanese traders operating throughout the country. In a significant address to the nation on January 17, 2025, President Salva Kiir Mayardit emphasized the deep historical and cultural ties between the people of South Sudan and Sudan. He remarked, "**It is a known fact that South Sudanese still consider Sudan home; likewise, many Sudanese citizens consider South Sudan home. This is due to our shared history. Therefore, the government of Sudan is oblidge** (sic) **to protect South Sudanese citizens trapped in war zones under its control.**"

The President's statement highlights the imperative of mutual protection and cooperation between the two nations, underscoring the government's commitment to addressing the vulnerabilities of its citizens and fostering resilient cross-border relationships. The statement by President Salva Kiir Mayardit is a compelling testament to the strength of creative reasoning in leadership. It reflects his deep comprehension of *Garangism*, a philosophical framework derived from the ideals of John Garang, which has remained elusive for many of his former associates and students. Kiir's interpretation highlights the nuances and complexities of Garang's vision, showcasing his ability to grasp and articulate concepts that others may overlook.

This insight reinforces Kiir's leadership credentials and emphasizes the enduring legacy of Garang's thoughts on governance and nation-building. We revisit this point in Chapter Two, which discusses leadership reflections.

2. Strategic Resilience

Despite facing numerous challenges, including invasions and resource scarcity, the Kingdom of Kush demonstrated remarkable resilience. Its ability to adapt and thrive amidst adversity offers a powerful lesson on the importance of perseverance and unity in the face of current challenges in Sudan. For instance, the ancient Kushites were renowned for their impressive architectural achievements, including the construction of pyramids and temples. These structures showcased their advanced engineering skills and reflected their deep spiritual beliefs. The enduring legacy of the Kushite kingdom serves as a powerful testament to the importance of resilience and adaptability in ensuring survival and fostering growth.

As mentioned in the preceding paragraph, the Kushite civilization faced numerous challenges throughout its history, including environmental changes, economic fluctuations, and foreign invasions, yet it thrived for centuries. This historical narrative provides valuable lessons for the people of the two Sudans, both in the north and south, as they navigate the complexities of contemporary issues in the 21st Century.

By examining the strategies that enabled the Kushites to innovate and endure, Sudanese communities can cultivate a mindset geared toward overcoming present-day obstacles. Nurturing the creativity, collaboration, and perseverance of the Kushite community serves not only to honor our rich ancestral legacies but also empowers us to craft a more sustainable future, both on an individual level and as a collective society.

Hence, by embracing and celebrating the artistic innovations and problem-solving skills of the Kushites, we can draw inspiration from their historical achievements and values. This approach encourages us to work together, harnessing our diverse talents and perspectives to tackle contemporary challenges. Furthermore, by cultivating these qualities, we can ensure that our practices are sustainable, fostering an environment where future generations can thrive while staying connected to their cultural roots. In doing so, we create a bridge between the past, the present, and the future, promoting resilience and progress within our communities.

3. Territorial Influence and Political Savvy

The Kingdom of Kush exemplified shrewd diplomacy and strategic alliances, navigating complex relationships with neighboring kingdoms. This aspect of their history highlights the necessity of diplomacy and cooperation in achieving sustainable peace and development in today's geopolitical climate.

The expansive empire of Kush, for instance, serves as a historical reminder that geographical prominence can significantly enhance a nation's power and influence. Kush was a vital center for trade, linking sub-Saharan Africa with the Mediterranean and the Near East. The flourishing commerce of the Kingdom illustrates the significance of economic collaboration and the mutual benefits that can arise from engaging with neighboring regions. In this regard, the newly established countries arising from the former Sudan have the opportunity to capitalize on their strategic locations in Northeast, Central, and Eastern Africa. That is, by fully leveraging their unique geographic advantages, these nations can foster stronger economic relationships and deepen diplomatic ties with neighboring countries.

This cooperative approach could increase regional stability and prosperity, allowing for a more integrated and collaborative economic landscape. With fertile lands and abundant resources, the two Sudans hold considerable potential to emerge as the agricultural heartland, or the "breadbasket," of Africa and the Middle East. By focusing on agricultural development and trade, they could not only ensure food security for their populations but also position themselves as key players in regional and global markets.

4. Coexistence and Diplomacy

The Kushites, who thrived in the ancient region of Nubia, showcased an impressive ability to coexist with surrounding powers, including Egypt and other neighboring civilizations. This historical precedent illustrates that through effective diplomacy and collaboration, societies can achieve mutual benefits and foster stability. In the modern context, the two Sudans—South Sudan and Sudan—can draw valuable lessons from this ancient practice. By actively engaging in dialogue, both internally and with neighboring countries, they can work toward establishing robust partnerships that prioritize peace, trade, and cultural exchange. Such efforts could not only enhance regional stability but also promote economic growth and social progress in the communities involved, fostering a spirit of unity and cooperation in a diverse and often fractured landscape.

5. Learning from Decline

The decline of the Kushite kingdom and the subsequent partitioning of Sudan into two separate nations present an important historical lesson. These events highlight the critical need for effective governance and the active participation of citizens in the political process. A lack of cohesive leadership and failure to engage various societal groups can exacerbate internal divisions and conflicts, ultimately threatening the stability and unity of a nation. This serves as a cautionary tale for contemporary states, emphasizing that addressing issues of governance, fostering civic involvement, and promoting social cohesion are essential for maintaining national integrity and preventing the type of fragmentation witnessed in the past.

By revisiting the above five elements/characteristics of the Kingdom of Kush, Sudanese people today can draw essential lessons from the past, fostering a deeper understanding of our identity and shaping a more unified and prosperous future for both Sudans. By thoughtfully examining both the remarkable achievements and the significant challenges experienced by the ancient kingdoms, the Sudanese people in both Sudan and South Sudan have the opportunity to develop a forward-looking perspective that is firmly grounded in their shared history. This reflective process can enable them to recognize the lessons learned, appreciate their cultural heritage, and understand the complexities of their past. In doing so, they can cultivate a mindset that not only honors their traditions but also embraces the possibilities ahead.

By fostering such a united approach, the citizens of these two countries can work toward building a more prosperous future characterized by collaboration, mutual respect, and a commitment to overcoming obstacles together. Through this collective effort, they can lay the foundation for stronger, more resilient nations that thrive in harmony and development. At this juncture, we would like to walk the reader through what is coming in the remaining part of this edition of the book.

The second edition of the book has been significantly expanded, now comprising eight comprehensive chapters, in contrast to the four chapters found in the first edition. This increase in content allows for a deeper exploration of John Garang's ideas and vision, providing readers with more detailed insights and a broader range of topics to engage with. Each chapter builds upon the previous one, offering a more thorough analysis and enhancing the understanding of the overall framework underpinning Garang's ideas and vision of the New Sudan.

Chapter Two is a new chapter that focuses on leadership by comparing Garang's leadership style with that of current leaders. In Chapter Three, we revisit the ten powerful ideas of John Garang. The ongoing conflicts and complexities in Sudan and South Sudan have highlighted the relevance and intricacies of the ten powerful ideas in the book's first edition. Each one offers a lens through which to understand the challenges and opportunities in the region. Here, the second edition provides a comprehensive evaluation with new perspectives based on the current situation.

Chapter Four examines the vision of New Sudan. It assesses the vision since 2013, discusses progress made toward the ideals underpinning the vision articulated by Garang, and explores the current challenges facing the realization of this vision. Chapter Five is a new chapter that looks at the recent political developments since the first edition's publication and assesses their impact. An overview of significant political changes in South Sudan and Sudan is briefly discussed. Moreover, the analysis of peace agreements, conflicts, and political unrest since 2013 is undertaken in light of the role of Garang's ideology in navigating these challenges.

Chapter Six is also a new chapter. It examines socio-economic developments. It reviews economic changes and their alignment with Garang's ideas on development, followed by evaluating progress in education, health, and infrastructure, as well as the ongoing struggle against poverty and marginalization. Chapter Seven looks at lessons learned and future directions. It highlights key takeaways from the past decade since the book's publication, makes recommendations for leveraging Garang's ideas moving forward, and charts a vision for the future leadership of South Sudan and its implications for regional stability.

In Chapter Eight, we conclude the book with final reflections on John Garang's enduring legacy, the importance of creative reasoning in shaping the future of the two Sudans, and a call to action for readers to engage with Garang's vision.

Chapter Two

Reflections on Leadership

"I and those who joined me in the bush and fought for more than twenty years have brought to you the CPA in a golden plate. Our mission is accomplished. It is now your turn, especially those who did not have a chance to experience bush life. When time comes to vote at referendum, it is your golden chance to determine your fate. Would you like to vote to be second-class citizens in your own country? It is absolutely your choice." [2]

John Garang was engaging in an open dialogue at a public rally in Rumbek, the capital of Lakes State, on May 16, 2005. He conveyed the accumulated anger of Southern Sudanese stemming from years of marginalization, struggle, and conflict, highlighting their profound desire for independence from the North. Garang's leadership style was participatory, fostering a sense of ownership among the people and empowering them

---

2   From a speech by Dr. John Garang de Mabior on 16th May 2005 on the occasion of the 22nd Anniversary of the SPLA Day and quoted in the first edition, page 26.

to determine their destiny at the most opportune moment. This is what we refer to in this book as John Garang's path-goal strategy or strategic plan. He advocated for dialogue and collaboration around this strategy, which became essential in the struggle for independence.

However, today's political landscape presents substantial challenges for those inspired by Garang's vision. Current leaders frequently confront entrenched ethnic rivalries, which threaten to undermine national cohesion, and a striking lack of sustainable infrastructure underpinned by corruption, which hampers development efforts. These challenges have sometimes led to disillusionment and skepticism among the populace regarding their leaders' intentions. Nevertheless, amidst these adversities, there have been notable advancements that echo Garang's dedication to fostering a united South Sudan.

Recent initiatives to foster peacebuilding and reconciliation serve as a testament to this commitment. While the leaders spearheading these efforts often face scrutiny, they embody an understanding of the foundational principles laid out by Garang. These principles emphasize not just political independence but also social harmony and economic resilience. If effectively harnessed by visionary leadership, they hold the potential to guide South Sudan toward a more prosperous and unified future, embodying the spirit of the aspirations that paved the way for the historic referendum in 2011.

Reflecting on the leadership of the past, we must remember that Garang did not solely advocate for freedom and liberty; he envisioned a South Sudan where all voices could be heard, irrespective of tribal affiliations. This ideal is increasingly becoming important today in a world dominated by social media as leaders navigate the intricate web of loyalties that define the nation. The present generation must learn from the tapestry of Garang's leadership, striving to cultivate a political environment that prioritizes dialogue over discord.

Ultimately, as South Sudan continues to evolve, the reflection on Garang's legacy serves as both a guiding light and a cautionary tale. It challenges leaders to embody the values of integrity, humility, and commitment to the common good. The path to realizing Garang's vision will demand resilience, innovative thinking, and an unwavering focus on the principles of justice and inclusivity. As we honor the memory of Garang, we must also commit to fostering a leadership style that can unify the nation and pave the way for a brighter future for all South Sudanese.

In comparison, many current leaders wrestle with the balance between power and democratic governance. Some have fallen into autocratic tendencies, sidelining key stakeholders and exacerbating divisions that Garang sought to mend. This divergence reflects not merely individual character but also the complex socio-political dynamics at play in South Sudan today. Despite this divergence, there have been successes worth noting.

For instance, Salva Kiir Mayardit Kiir embarked immediately after he inherited the leadership of the SPLM and the presidency of the Government of Southern Sudan (GoSS) on initiatives aimed at peace-building and reconciliation within the southern house, echoing Garang's path-goal strategic plan. His focus then was on the referendum date stipulated in the Comprehensive Peace Agreement (CPA), signed on January 9, 2005, which was the path to the goal of self-determination.

Kiir understood that the CPA had laid the necessary conditions for the referendum on January 9, 2011. He was not willing to take any reckless action that could derail our march toward that date. Leaders who take the helm of such initiatives are often met with skepticism. Still, they demonstrate an understanding of the underlying principles of Garang's teachings—principles that paved the way for the peaceful conduct of the referendum on time as stipulated in the CPA.

On January 9, 2011, a pivotal event unfolded in the annals of

Southern Sudan's history as millions of citizens ventured to polling stations to cast their votes in a landmark referendum. This referendum was not merely an electoral exercise; it represented a decisive step toward self-determination and independence for a region scarred by decades of conflict and political strife. The journey to this historic moment began on May 16, 1983, and was profoundly influenced by John Garang's leadership style.[3] Notably, his path-goal strategic plan, which exemplified a unique approach to governance and community engagement. The strategic plan consisted of a series of tactical maneuvers (e.g., the idea of making unity attractive), all geared to the ultimate goal being pursued.

On 16 May 2005, the 22nd Anniversary of SPLA Day, Garang unambiguously envisaged the outcome of the vote. This demonstrates that Garang's leadership style was deeply rooted in logic and critical thinking, the cornerstone of his creative reasoning. His ability to articulate a vision of New Sudan resonated powerfully with the ordinary Sudanese citizens, who had long nurtured a collective anger stemming from years of marginalization and violent struggle against oppressive regimes in Khartoum.

The emotions encapsulated in the response to the referendum reflected a yearning for political self-determination and a fervent

---

3   This is not to say that we have ignored numerous armed resistances to foreign rule throughout history. In addition to the Torit Uprising on 18th August 1955, two major flash points of resistance against colonialism preceded the Torit Uprising, which deserve to be mentioned here. The first was the Aliab Dinka Uprising of 1919– 1920, which started on 30th October 1919, when about 3,000 spearmen of the Aliab Dinka of Yirol attacked Minkaman, where a police station was located. The second is the Ngungdeng-led Uprising of the Lou Nuer against the British colonial rule that ended with the killing of his son Guek on 8th February 1929 with the use of the Royal Air Force. It is to be noted that the use of air power was unnecessary since the patriotic villagers were only armed with spears and sticks.

aspiration for social and economic autonomy. Through participatory leadership, Garang instilled a profound sense of ownership among the people, empowering them to shape their own destinies at a critical juncture in their history. Garang did this by managing the anger of his people. His son, Mabior Garang de Mabior, has recently articulated this point further by talking about what he calls "**disorganized anger**" in the following passage:

> *"The best response is not disorganized anger, which can easily be hijacked by opportunistic politicians for their own selfish ends. We must be organized and focused for the sake of future generations so that our children can understand our historical struggle and inherit a viable and united nation. The political elite in our young republic do not care about the future of our country. They are only concerned with their relentless hunger for power, willing to do anything to satisfy it."* [4]

The above passage from Mabior Garang de Mabior underlines the fact that **leadership matters**. Leadership plays a crucial role in addressing significant issues that shape a nation's destiny. Leaders must effectively mobilize their constituents and cultivate a shared vision around the overarching objective. John Garang and Salva Kiir both confronted distinct forms of anger to manage in a highly turbulent environment characterized by varying objective conditions on the ground.

Garang, in particular, faced the challenge of managing and transforming what he described as "angry mobs!" Bona Malwal Madut

---

4   From WhatsApp Discussion Group managed by the SPLA/SPLM Veterans' Foundation

Ring asked John Garang: Why are you recruiting our people to be communists? Garang responded that they were managing an angry mob. The enraged mobs were composed of frustrated individuals and communities about the marginalization that successive governments in Khartoum subjected them to. They came from urban centers and rural communities. He successfully channeled this widespread discontent through his exceptional leadership skills into a powerful, organized military force that became the Sudan People's Liberation Army (SPLA). This transformation was not solely about military might; it involved the fundamental ability to inspire a diverse group of people toward a unified purpose.

Simultaneously, Garang recognized that his political framework, the Sudan People's Liberation Movement (SPLM), was intentionally designed to remain relatively weak at its inception. This was a strategic choice aimed at fostering grassroots participation and ensuring that the movement's growth was organically tied to the aspirations and needs of the people it represented. As a result, despite its initial vulnerability, the SPLM eventually evolved to support the military efforts of the SPLA, aligning political objectives with the realities of the conflict-stricken landscape and achieving at the peace talks the goal of self-determination.

Fundamentally, Garang's path-goal strategy emphasized open dialogue and collaboration. His approach was instrumental in uniting diverse communities around a common goal, especially in a region rife with divisions and ethnic tensions. Unlike many contemporary leaders who often grapple with reconciling authority and democratic principles, Garang sought to inclusively engage key stakeholders and mitigate the fractures that had historically plagued society. This focus on unity and collective decision-making established a framework that many current leaders in South Sudan have sought to emulate.

Salva Kiir, on the other hand, faced the daunting task of navigating the implementation of the Comprehensive Peace Agreement (CPA) amidst a backdrop of "disorganized anger" stemming from a faction of discontented elites within the Sudan People's Liberation Movement (SPLM). This environment required Kiir to exhibit a nuanced leadership style as he responded to various incidents instigated by these disgruntled elements within the ruling party, the SPLM.

One notable incident was the Yei standoff in October 2004, which threatened to escalate into a bloody confrontation between the late Chairman, Dr. John Garang, and his Deputy, Commander (Cdr.) Salva Kiir. Recognizing the gravity of the situation, Cdr. Kiir took the crucial step of engaging in dialogue, encouraged by voices from various societal segments, particularly community leaders from Rumbek. This decision to heed the counsel of the populace was pivotal, ultimately paving the way for the successful signing in Nairobi, Kenya, of the CPA on January 9, 2005, which marked a significant milestone in the quest for peace and, eventually, independence of South Sudan.

In September 2005, a pivotal moment arose for Salva Kiir, the new leader of SPLM, as he faced a significant decision regarding the political landscape of Sudan. In the face of fierce resistance from elements within the party, Kiir strongly advocated for the SPLM to join the Sudan Government of National Unity (GoNU), a crucial entity formed per the CPA. This recommendation was particularly controversial given that the National Congress Party (NCP), the dominant party in Sudan's government then, had violated established rules and procedures surrounding selecting and allocating cabinet portfolios, as stipulated in the CPA.

Despite these transgressions, Kiir's determination to participate in the GoNU was rooted in a broader strategic vision aimed at stabilizing the region and ensuring the sustainability of the peace agreement. His decision was instrumental in preserving the CPA, a fragile framework governing the relationship between the North and South of Sudan. By engaging in the GoNU, Kiir aimed to foster cooperation and dialogue, counteracting the potential fallout that could arise from a splintered political landscape. He predicted correctly that such behavior from the NCP would make unity unattractive and lead our people to vote for separation on January 9, 2011.

Had the SPLM opted out of this arrangement, it is widely believed that the delicate fabric of the CPA would have unraveled, plunging South Sudan back into a protracted struggle for independence. Such a scenario would have undermined the progress made toward peace and jeopardized the aspirations of millions of South Sudanese who longed for stability and self-determination. Kiir's strategic choice thus marked a critical juncture toward achieving lasting peace and independence for South Sudan.

In April 2012, Kiir made a contentious decision to order the Sudan People's Liberation Army (SPLA) to withdraw from Panthou, also known as Heglig. The SPLA had prematurely taken control of the area without orders from the President. At the time, there was a lack of understanding within the SPLA leadership that only the President of South Sudan, with the approval of the National Legislature, had the authority to declare war against any sovereign state. Although this withdrawal was met with dissatisfaction from the South Sudanese populace, Kiir's decision was prudent, especially in light of strong international opposition and pressure from South Sudan's allies. It also demonstrates how Kiir has been managing the "disorganized anger" underpinned by recklessness from within the SPLM.

Under Salva Kiir's leadership, a significant development occurred in February 2015 with the SPLM's Arusha Reunification Agreement (ARA) signing. This landmark agreement addressed the deep divisions that had emerged within the SPLM. These divisions seem to have been triggered by cumulative "disorganized anger" since September 2005. The ARA focused on promoting unity among the various factions of the SPLM, recognizing that such cohesion was essential for achieving lasting national stability and peace. By advocating for a unified front, the agreement sought to strengthen the party's political structure and enhance its ability to govern effectively, ultimately aiming to reconcile differing interests and restore trust among its members.

In August 2015, a pivotal decision was reached by signing the Agreement for the Resolution of Conflict in the Republic of South Sudan (ARCSS). This agreement marked a significant milestone in the quest for peace in a country suffering from profound divisions and violent conflict. Despite facing opposition from certain factions within President Salva Kiir's Cabinet, the ARCSS established a comprehensive framework aimed at fostering peace, stability, and national reconciliation. This framework sought to address the root causes of the conflict, promote dialogue among various stakeholders, and lay the groundwork for a more inclusive government. The challenge of uniting a fractured society would be immense. Still, the agreement was crucial to rebuilding South Sudan and creating a more sustainable future for its citizens.

One of the most significant moments in Salva Kiir's leadership occurred on July 8, 2016, during a violent clash at the Presidential Palace, widely known as J1. This incident erupted amidst escalating tensions between the SPLA and the forces loyal to Dr. Riek Machar, the First Vice President and Kiir's principal political rival. As chaos reigned and gunfire rang out, both sides found themselves engulfed in a deadly confrontation that threatened to plunge the nation into further conflict.

Amid this turmoil, Salva Kiir faced an urgent and critical decision: to pursue revenge or to choose a path of reconciliation. Demonstrating remarkable composure under pressure, he opted for a course that would ultimately favor peace. Kiir decided to spare Dr. Machar's life despite the overwhelming aggression surrounding them. This act of clemency saved Machar and sent a powerful message about Kiir's commitment to avoiding a resurgence of violence and prioritizing stability in South Sudan.

By choosing mercy over retribution, Kiir exhibited an essential quality of effective leadership, particularly at a time when many leaders might succumb to the primal urge for vengeance. This decision was pivotal, as it reflected Kiir's understanding of the dire consequences that might arise from further bloodshed and the importance of fostering dialogue and cooperation among South Sudan's fractured political landscape. In doing so, he reaffirmed his dedication to the peace process, striving to steer the nation away from the brink of yet another civil war.

In a significant effort to foster national unity and reconciliation in South Sudan, Kiir initiated the South Sudan National Dialogue in December 2016, with a formal launch in May 2017. This dialogue represented a crucial step in addressing the deep-seated divisions and conflicts that had plagued the country since its independence. Notably, Kiir made the unconventional decision not to assume the role of patron for the dialogue process. He stepped back from a leadership position to enhance the initiative's independence, transparency, and credibility.

This choice was pivotal, as it allowed for transparency and a more inclusive platform where diverse voices and perspectives from various segments of South Sudanese society could be represented and heard. The dialogue sought to engage not only political leaders but also ordinary citizens, civil society groups, and marginalized communities, thereby promoting a more holistic approach to peacebuilding and national reconciliation in South Sudan. However, the resolutions of the National Dialogue have not been implemented due to the usual "disorganized anger" from those of the SPLM who were not included in the process.

In 2017, President Salva Kiir made a significant decision to remove the military barricade around the residence of General Paul Malong Awan, the former Chief of General Staff of the SPLA. This action was crucial in preventing a potentially disastrous confrontation that could have escalated tensions within the country's already fragile political landscape. By lifting the barricade, Kiir demonstrated his dedication to preserving stability in South Sudan, prioritizing dialogue over conflict in a situation that threatened to spiral out of control.

However, Kiir's decision was met with resistance from certain factions within the security sector, who believed that keeping the barricade in place was necessary for maintaining order and safeguarding national security. These opposing elements were concerned about the implications of Malong's influence and the potential for unrest, reflecting the complex dynamics and divisions within the military and political spheres at that time. Despite the opposition, Kiir's choice ultimately highlighted his leadership approach, emphasizing the need for reconciliation and peace amid ongoing challenges.

On September 12, 2018, Kiir signed the Revitalized Agreement on the Resolution of Conflict in South Sudan (R-ARCSS) in Addis Ababa, Ethiopia. This renewed peace agreement created a conducive environment for pursuing sustainable peace and reconciliation among all stakeholders, including political parties. The subsequent Pretoria Declaration, ratified by seven groups of South Sudanese political parties in April 2019, underscored a collective commitment to fostering peace and stability in a nation yearning for unity and prosperity.

Every decision made by Salva Kiir reflects the intricate dynamics of his leadership approach. It highlights the significant challenges he faces while guiding South Sudan toward enduring peace amidst a landscape fraught with both internal strife and external pressures. We have intentionally selected these nine pivotal decision points to demonstrate how Kiir has navigated the nation through tumultuous times, striving to realize the vision of a brighter future despite the pervasive "disorganized anger" that often arises within the ranks of the Sudan People's Liberation Movement (SPLM).

Amid these challenges, Kiir has retained key elements of John Garang's leadership philosophy, mainly focusing on overarching goals and the "big picture." This aspect of his style is crucial, as it allows him to steer discussions and decisions toward long-term objectives, even when faced with the short-term chaos and discord that characterize the political landscape of South Sudan. By continuously realigning his strategies with this broader vision, Kiir seeks to foster unity and resilience in a country still healing from the wounds of conflict.

John Garang and Salva Kiir have been at the forefront of managing the affairs of our people during some of the most challenging and turbulent periods in our history, a remarkable journey spanning 42 years. Their unwavering commitment and leadership have culminated in a significant achievement: the establishment of our beloved nation, the Republic of South Sudan. We owe them a tremendous debt of gratitude for this monumental gift, which we accept with heartfelt appreciation.

However, as we approach the pivotal moment of voting in the upcoming general elections scheduled for December 2026, the leadership landscape in South Sudan may shift. The populace is likely to cast their votes in favor of leadership that demonstrates a genuine commitment to pursuing a developmental state that prioritizes progress and improvement for all citizens. This envisioned developmental state would be built upon three foundational pillars: morality, institutionalism, and constitutionalism. These principles are essential for fostering a just and prosperous society.

Reflecting on the wisdom of John Garang, we might paraphrase his message for the people of South Sudan to internalize it before they go to the polls in December 2026. This is paraphrased as follows:

> *When the time arrives to participate in the upcoming general elections, you will have a golden opportunity to shape your own destiny. Will you choose to continue living as impoverished citizens in your own homeland? The decision rests entirely in your hands.*

It is reasonable to expect that the Sudan People's Liberation Movement will heed the profound message conveyed by Garang in this context. John Garang dedicated 21 years of his life to the struggle and development of the Sudan People's Liberation Army/Sudan People's Liberation Movement (SPLA/SPLM). Tragically, he passed away just 21 days into his presidency of the Government of Southern Sudan. His legacy will reach a poignant milestone in July 2026, marking 21 years since his passing. This anniversary serves as a reminder of his enduring influence and his aspirations for our nation. We must honor his vision by making informed choices in our upcoming elections.

Translating noble ideals of the liberation struggle into practical reality has proven to be an arduous task laden with numerous challenges. The country's political landscape is characterized by deep-seated rivalries entrenched over decades, often rooted in historical grievances and ethnic divisions. These rivalries complicate efforts to foster collaboration and mutual understanding among different communities.

Moreover, the socio-economic obstacles are equally daunting.

Widespread poverty, inadequate infrastructure, and limited access to education and healthcare are significant barriers to progress. These factors contribute to a cycle of fragility, disappointment, disenfranchisement, and unrest, thus perpetuating instability in the two Sudans.

As a result, these ongoing challenges frequently escalate into conflicts that undermine John Garang's principles. The realities on the ground continually test his quest for unity, nation-building, state formation, sustainable peace, economic growth, and poverty eradication. Thus, the journey toward achieving these ideals is not only ambitious but also fraught with complexities, requiring visionary leadership, creative thinking, persistent effort, dialogue, and commitment from all stakeholders involved.

Nevertheless, John Garang's enduring legacy continues to galvanize new generations, inspiring them to aspire to the lofty ideals he promoted. His ability to articulate the people's aspirations resonates strongly, even amidst the country's significant adversities. Garang's philosophies, supported by creative reasoning and critical thought, remain central to discussions surrounding governance, leadership, identity, and human rights in Sudan and South Sudan.

As the region evolves continuously, grappling with new challenges and opportunities, Garang's influence will likely endure. His teachings and ideals will undoubtedly remain a crucial reference point for current and future leaders, shaping the policies and actions to achieve the peace, unity, and prosperity he envisioned for these nations. The dialogue he inspired about fundamental goals of sustainable peace, economic growth, and poverty eradication will continue to be relevant as society navigates its path forward. In this regard, our role in the service of our people is to provide them with a brief overview of the types of leadership from which they can choose when the time comes to do so.

It's the Leadership, Stupid!

We start the brief with, "It's the leadership, stupid!" James Carville, campaign strategist for Bill Clinton's 1992 American presidential race, coined the phrase, "It's the economy, stupid!" Carville depicted the inability of President George H. W. Bush to revitalize the American economy, which was going through a painful recession, and made it the focus of Clinton's campaign. Bill Clinton won the race and subsequently fixed the economy. We have rephrased Carville's catchphrase (1992 campaign slogan) to illustrate the systematic inability of early leadership to correctly identify the root causes of the Sudanese crisis of state and identity. Some scholars have concluded that one of the root causes of the Sudanese crisis was the "huge cultural gap" between the North and the South. This viewpoint is elucidated by Philip Bowring (2011) below:

> *"It was not so much a question of Muslims versus Christians and others or even Arabic speakers against others. Problems were exacerbated but not created by Islamist strictures. After all, back in 1964, Islamic intolerance was not an issue. Abu Jamal beer was brewed at the Blue Nile Brewery on the banks of the Nile in Khartoum. Ordinary weddings saw vast consumption of the lethal local liquor, and red-light districts were easily identified. But the huge cultural gap was as evident, then and now, whether the issue was music or sexual mores. To it has been added the lure of oil."*

We would, despite the above-stated view, argue that the pre independence leadership was myopic, evidenced by its use of culture as a tool for marginalization instead of being an instrument for inclusiveness, that is, by constructing a Sudanese identity through a combination of cultures of various nationalities that have interacted throughout the history of Sudan since time immemorial. A constructed Sudanese identity would have then united the Sudanese people around a shared national identity and destiny. Culture is often understood as a way of life. To this extent, it is a powerful vehicle for any nation-building project that aims at developing the basis of political life, national identity, and shared destiny.

However, the quest for a shared destiny determines the national identity as its driving force, a product of the cultures of all the elements embedded in a nation-building project. So, the problem in Sudan has not been, per se, the enormous cultural gap. Instead, the leadership of the nation-building project could not recognize cultural diversity as an element of strength, not weakness. Hence, it is poor leadership that led to institutional failure underpinning public policy and associated development strategies of post-independent Sudan. The consequences of the failure of the Sudanese leadership to implement a nation-building project have been violent conflicts over identity and the vision of governing Sudan.

The ongoing conflict in *Al-bilad Al-*Sudan represents a profound continuation of the struggle over the nation's identity and the vision for its management and governance. This struggle is deeply intertwined with the historical and political narrative of Sudan, where issues of national unity and statehood have long fueled tensions. In contrast, the conflict within the newly independent South Sudan centers on the critical task of establishing a robust developmental state. This state is envisioned to ardently pursue the ideals that emerged from its liberation struggle, aiming for social and economic progress that can uplift the lives of its citizens.

The foundational premise of this book posits that tackling the current leading issues of development in South Sudan could benefit significantly from a visionary and competent leader—much like John Garang—who understood the complexities of the Sudanese malaise. Such a leader would not only be capable of diagnosing the root causes of the country's challenges but would also provide actionable solutions and a clear prescription to address these issues sustainably. The call for effective leadership is echoed in the aspirations of ordinary South Sudanese citizens, which require guidance that can spearhead the creation of a development-oriented state.

A state built on a foundation of political morality and ethics, robust institutions for effective governance, and a commitment to the rule of law must be established through a constitutional framework that reflects the contributions of all segments and nationalities of South Sudan. However, it is imperative to recognize that such a state will not materialize spontaneously or be created for us by neighboring countries and allies. Instead, we must actively engage in a consensus-driven dialogue to build it.

In our commitment to fostering a collaborative and consensus-based dialogue, we aim to equip political parties with the insights and tools necessary for their dedicated pursuit of a development-oriented state. To achieve this, we will delve into the rich tapestry of leadership experiences from countries both near and far—particularly those that have effectively faced and overcome comparable challenges. By examining a diverse range of case studies and historical examples, we can generate a comprehensive summary highlighting successful governance and state-building strategies and practices.

This exploration will not only reveal valuable lessons learned from past endeavors but also illuminate pragmatic pathways that can guide current political leaders in their efforts to cultivate effective governance structures and promote sustainable development within their nations.

Through this process, we aspire to foster a deeper understanding of the complexities involved in leadership and to inspire innovative solutions tailored to the unique contexts of our own political landscapes.

Leadership is paramount, both in contemporary society and throughout historical contexts. A pertinent example is Malaysia, which encountered circumstances analogous to those of Sudan at the time of its independence. Malaysia benefited from the presence of visionary leaders who adeptly navigated cultural diversity and promoted social cohesion, ultimately establishing a solid foundation for the nation's advancement.

A comparative examination of the leadership achievements in countries such as Ghana and Malaysia during the early years of their independence offers valuable insights into the significance of effective leadership in national development. Countries in Africa and Asia that gained independence around the same time shared broadly comparable initial conditions. Nonetheless, the interplay of robust institutions and competent leadership has played a crucial role in determining these nations' varying levels of development. For instance, Malaysia attained its independence from Great Britain in 1957, coinciding with Ghana's independence in the same year and just one year after Sudan's independence.

However, Malaysia has by far reached a higher level of development relative to these two African countries. The ability of the Malaysian leadership has enabled the country to be where it is today on the development ladder and consequential political stability. The leadership conceptualized delicate social integration arrangements between its three nationalities: Malays, Chinese, and Indians. This then created a solid foundation for forming its national identity, which it effectively utilized in forging a common national destiny.

Both Sudan and Malaysia had multi-ethnic/racial groups with

a combination of ethnic and religious tensions at independence. A federated arrangement was conceived in both countries as a practical framework for power-sharing, social harmony, and economic development. Malaysia was lucky to have had visionary and effective leadership of its nation-building project at independence in the person of Tunku Abdul Rahman. He forged a multi-ethnic identity/nationalism through a robust power-sharing arrangement, essentially a social contract enshrined on three essential ingredients: compromise, consensus, and reciprocity among Malays, Chinese, and Indians. This social contract was erected on the three pillars of Malaysian institutions.

That is, the working rules of collective action of the three ethnic groups/nationalities, Malays, Chinese, and Indians. These working rules of collective action were sufficiently used in the restraint, liberation, and expansion of individual action(s) of the three nationalities toward a common national destiny. Although Malays were the majority, they did not impose their culture on the other nationalities. In other words, Malays did not make themselves what Al-Baqir al-Afif Mukhtar (1999) calls the center of identity. Instead, Chinese and Indians were given equal opportunities in the political landscape that enabled them to effectively participate in the country's national affairs while retaining their languages, economic power, religion, and cultural institutions.

The ability of early leadership to construct a cohesive national identity enabled Malaysia to endure the ethnic violence that occurred during the first half of the 1960s. Subsequent Malaysian leaders, including Dr. Mahathir Mohamad, have effectively utilized Tunku Abdul Rahman's established national identity to implement policies that translate this vision into tangible outcomes, as evidenced by Malaysia's significant economic development. I have visited Malaysia six times, and I continue to be impressed by the robustness of their social integration model, which undoubtedly serves as the foundation for their economic progress.

On the other hand, the Sudanese nation-building project was never formulated in a manner consistent with the theory of identity, which guides such a project (nation-building).[5] Attempts to build consensus and compromise around a common national destiny (goal of the nation-building project) and its associated national identity were frustrated since the Juba Conference of 1947 by Northern Sudanese cultural and political elites. Why the Northern Sudanese elite? It is simply because they were more educated than their Southern counterparts were at the high-policy forum in which the critical questions of state and identity were discussed. For instance, the Northern delegation to the Juba Conference consisted mainly of academically qualified persons, such as legal experts (Shingeiti), teachers, administrators, and so forth.

On the other hand, the Southern delegation was primarily composed of "uneducated" traditional chiefs (for example, Lolik), though with a strong sense of human dignity and justice in the service of their people. These quality differentials in education notwithstanding, the Southern traditional chiefs were more visionaries than their educated Northern brethren. It took eighteen years for the South to learn the tricks of politics when the Southern Front (SF) adopted self-determination at the Roundtable Conference of 1965 as a strategic goal for Southern Sudanese to pursue. This marks the beginning of the rise of Southern strategic thinking with respect to Sudanese politics.

---

5   See Al-Baqir al-Afif Mukhtar (1999) for an excellent analysis of the theories of identity in "The Crisis of Identity in Northern Sudan: A Dilemma of a Black People with a White Culture," a paper presented at the CODSRIA African Humanitarian Institute at Northwestern University in Evanston, Illinois (United States of America)

The South, and for that matter, the country, had to wait another forty years for the strategic goal to be reformulated as a strategic vehicle for carrying Southern Sudanese to a decision point enshrined in the Interim Constitution of Sudan. The decision point at which Southern Sudanese were to choose between the unity of Sudan or secession was January 9, 2011. This was made possible by the SPLM/A under the guidance of a competent leader, John Garang de Mabior. This point is the topic of chapter four of this second edition.

What, then, distinguishes effective leadership in such contexts? This question invites a deeper exploration into the qualities and characteristics that define successful leaders. Attributes such as vision, charisma, resilience, empathy, and the ability to foster inclusivity are vital for leaders who aspire to guide their nations through periods of turmoil and transition. Therefore, understanding what makes a leader effective is not merely an academic exercise; it is essential for shaping the trajectory of nations striving for peace, stability, and development.

A literature review of leadership theories by J. Rodney Turner and Ralf Muller (2005) found that "**an appropriate leadership style, and the competence and emotional intelligence of the leader, delivers results**." We would argue that an appropriate leadership style is a function of the leader's competence and emotional intelligence. Competence and emotional intelligence are among the key qualities that enable a leader to choose an appropriate way of managing the affairs of her or his organization or country.

A competent leader would, for instance, assess the situation at hand and then take a relevant course of action (or actions), reflecting the leadership style. Intelligence would be reflected in this case by the right choice of the course of action (or actions) derived from the assessment exercise. Moreover, assessment of the situation is contingent on several factors, such as technical knowledge, the surrounding environment (physical, social, cultural, and so forth), risk-taking, and self-confidence of the leader about the envisaged outcome of her or his decisions.

Risk-taking does not feature explicitly in the leadership theory literature as one of the traits of effective leaders. Nevertheless, it was one of John Garang's key qualities. How do you explain his leaving Rumbek secondary school in the second year and joining the first war of liberation before the Sudan African National Union (SANU) leadership persuaded him to go back to school in Tanzania and subsequently to Grinnell College in Iowa, United States, for his undergraduate studies? In 1969, he was admitted into graduate studies at the University of California Berkeley, but again, he opted to return to the liberation struggle.

He was a doctorate holder, deputy director of the Military Research Directorate of the Sudanese People's Armed Forces (SAF), and lecturer of economics at the University of Khartoum when he opted to lead a rebellious Battalion 105, comprising Any-Nya forces that were absorbed into the SAF in accordance with the 1972 Addis Ababa Accord, into the bush. These three actions indicate, in our view, that John Garang was a risk-taker, though well-thought-out.

We now turn to Turner and Muller's literature review, which elucidates the relevance of the following six schools of thought on leadership in our quest to understand the attributes of effective leaders. We encourage all the South Sudanese political parties to study them carefully before the next general elections.

1. The Trait School
The trait school of leadership theory posits that effective leaders are inherently born rather than cultivated through experience or education. This perspective asserts that leadership qualities are innate traits, suggesting that individuals possess specific characteristics—such as charisma, decisiveness,

confidence, and intelligence—that naturally predispose them to take on leadership roles. According to this view, these intrinsic qualities cannot be developed or taught, meaning that leadership is primarily a matter of personal attributes one is either endowed with or lacks.

Proponents of this school argue that identifying these traits can help select leaders and understand their potential effectiveness in guiding others. This approach highlights the significance of assessing individual characteristics to predict leadership success, emphasizing the idea that great leaders emerge from their fundamental nature rather than through external influence or training.

2. The Behavioral or Style School

The behavioral or style school of thought in leadership posits that leaders are not born but are made through experience and learning, focusing primarily on how their behaviors and actions influence decision-making processes. A significant contribution to this theory comes from Kurt Lewin, a pioneering psychologist who, in 1939, proposed a framework that classifies leadership styles into three distinct categories:

2.1. Autocratic Leaders

This type of leader makes decisions independently and tends to dictate the direction of the team without seeking input or suggestions from colleagues or subordinates. This style can create an environment with clear expectations and swift decision-making. Still, it may lead to a lack of motivation and creativity among team members, as they are not given an opportunity to contribute their perspectives.

2.2. Democratic Leaders

Unlike autocratic leaders, democratic leaders prioritize collaboration and inclusiveness in their decision-making processes. They actively seek out the opinions and ideas of their team members, encouraging participation and fostering a sense of ownership and commitment to the final decision. This approach can enhance team morale and generate innovative ideas; however, it may also result in longer decision-making times due to the need to consult and consider multiple viewpoints.

2.3 Laissez-Faire Leaders

This leadership style is characterized by a hands-off approach. Leaders provide minimal guidance and allow their teams considerable autonomy in decision-making. While this can empower team members and promote creativity, it can also lead to ambiguity and a lack of direction if team members are not sufficiently skilled or motivated to work independently.

The literature suggests that the laissez-faire leadership style may sometimes emerge when a leader is disengaged or distracted by external factors, such as personal challenges or lifestyle choices, which can manifest as a lack of investment in the team's objectives or performance. This can negatively impact the cohesion and effectiveness of the group, as team members may feel unsupported or uncertain about their roles and responsibilities. Understanding these styles can help organizations better identify leadership potential and develop leaders who can adapt their approaches to meet the needs of their teams.

3. The Contingency School

The Contingency School of thought emphasizes that effective leadership is inherently linked to the specific circumstances and context in which a leader operates. This approach suggests that there is no one-size-fits-all method to leadership; rather, the best strategies and actions depend significantly on the unique factors present in each situation. To successfully analyze these varying situations, a leader must possess a diverse set of competencies. Key attributes include not only intelligence and technical knowledge relevant to the field but also strong critical thinking skills and emotional intelligence. These qualities enable leaders to assess challenges accurately and respond with strategies that are most suitable for their particular environment, ultimately leading to more effective leadership outcomes.

4. The Visionary or Charismatic School

The visionary or charismatic school of thought emphasizes the importance of key qualities that drive effective leadership and create a thriving environment. Central to this approach are attributes such as motivation, which ignites passion and purpose among individuals; inspiration, which encourages creativity and innovation; and trust, which fosters strong relationships and collaboration.

Leaders within this framework are characterized by their energy, maintaining a dynamic presence that galvanizes others to engage and participate. Integrity plays a crucial role as well, as it establishes a foundation of credibility and ethical behavior that inspires confidence and loyalty. Overall, this school champions the idea that effective leadership is not merely about managing tasks but also cultivating an enthusiastic and principled community where everyone feels empowered to contribute and succeed.

5. The Emotional Intelligence School

The significance of emotional intelligence is that it is a fundamental characteristic of effective leadership. It posits that a leader's ability to understand and manage their own emotions, as well as the emotions of others, plays a crucial role in fostering a positive and productive work environment. While emotional intelligence is considered the cornerstone of successful leadership, the school recognizes that it must be complemented by other essential traits, such as strong communication skills, decisiveness, adaptability, and integrity.

Hence, our political parties must explore the nuances of emotional intelligence, learning how to cultivate these qualities alongside other leadership attributes to inspire and motivate their teams and cadres effectively. The aim is to develop well-rounded leaders who not only excel in emotional insight but also possess the skills to navigate the complexities of their roles in various organizational and governance contexts.

6. The Competency School

Effective leadership is defined by three key characteristics: intellectual ability, emotional stability, and managerial skills.

Intellectual ability encompasses critical thinking, analytical skills, and the capacity to understand complex concepts. Leaders must be able to process information quickly and make informed decisions that drive the organization forward. Emotional stability refers to a leader's capacity to manage emotions and remain calm under pressure. This trait is essential for creating a positive work environment, building strong relationships, and handling crises with poise. Emotionally stable leaders inspire confidence and trust within their teams.

Lastly, managerial skills involve the practical abilities necessary for planning, organizing, and executing tasks efficiently. This includes strategic thinking, resource management, and the ability to motivate and guide team members toward achieving common goals.

These three characteristics form the foundation for effective leadership, enabling leaders to navigate challenges and foster a productive and collaborative environment.

It is evident from a brief look at the above-stated six schools of leadership theory that their focus is on the attributes of an effective leader. Political parties in South Sudan should know that the search for the virtues of effective leaders goes back as far as Aristotle and Chinese Confucius. A cursory look at the literature review by Turner and Muller indicates that a successful leader has both managerial and motivational (or emotional) functions. Managerial functions entail an institutional setting where a leader operates (for example, making decisions, monitoring their implementation, and evaluating the impact of such decisions). Barnard (1938) envisaged the managerial functions of a leader to include "**guiding, directing, and constraining choices and actions.**" An effective leader would nevertheless expand choices and actions by institutionalizing creativity and innovation or through what John R. Commons (1934) calls "**liberation and expansion of individual action.**"

The motivational functions of an effective leader include setting goals around which he or she develops trust and dedication (or a sort of social contract) for achieving them. For instance, John Garang used emotionally driven terms, such as "marginalization" and "oppression," to effectively define the vision of New Sudan that motivated millions of Sudanese to support the SPLM/A. The call for the creation of New Sudan became analogous to what Barnard (1938) termed a "**larger moral purpose**," which is beyond individual self-interest. This larger moral purpose energized many Sudanese to demand the ending of marginalization in the whole of Sudan, not only in Southern Sudan. John Garang also applied symbolic logic, which became a powerful tool beneath his creative reasoning, to persuade many Sudanese to join the SPLA/SPLM.

The actions mentioned in the preceding paragraphs are consistent with the path-goal theory of leadership effectiveness by R. J. House (1971), which states that a leader "**must help the team find the**

path to their goals." The goal and the path were first defined and constructed in our case. Then, Southern Sudanese were shown and directed to the roadmap for the promised land. That is, John Garang defined the goal first in his letter of January 1972, from which we have shared a passage earlier in this chapter. It articulated and then constructed a strategic path to the goal through the liberation struggle (1983-2005).

In addition to the survey of the six schools of thought on leadership, Shelley A. Kirkpatrick and Edwin A. Locke (1991) identified six key traits of effective leadership: drive and ambition, the desire to lead and influence others, honesty and integrity, self-confidence, intelligence, and technical knowledge.

How many of our leaders (past and present) would meet the above attributes of effective leadership? We leave that for the vigilant reader to find the answer for herself or himself. But the following long passage, which summarizes the work of Kirkpatrick and Locke (1991), could aid the reader:

> *"The study of leader traits has a long and controversial history. While research shows that the possession of certain traits alone does not guarantee leadership success, there is evidence that effective leaders are different from other people in certain key respects. Key leader traits include drive (a broad term that includes achievement, motivation, ambition, energy, tenacity, and initiative); leadership motivation (the desire to lead but not to seek power as an end in itself); honesty and integrity; self confidence (which is associated with emotional stability); cognitive ability; and knowledge of the business. There is less clear evidence for traits such as charisma, creativity,*

and flexibility. We believe that the key leader traits help the leader acquire the necessary skills, formulate an organizational vision and an effective plan for pursuing it, and take the necessary steps to implement the vision in reality."

We conclude this chapter by stressing that the literature on leadership emphasizes that while possessing certain characteristics is not a definitive pathway to success, effective leaders exhibit distinct attributes that set them apart. John Garang and Salva Kiir are not exceptional in this view. History will judge their leadership during more than four decades of turbulence. Such an assessment should be based on key traits such as drive, leadership motivation, honesty, self-confidence, cognitive ability, and business knowledge, which contribute significantly to a leader's effectiveness. These traits not only enhance a leader's ability to gain essential skills but also empower them to craft a compelling organizational vision and devise strategic plans for its realization.

In Chapter Two, we explored the fundamental qualities essential for effective leadership. While charisma, creativity, and adaptability are significant, foundational qualities are paramount for achieving success. These fundamental qualities serve as the bedrock that informs both current leaders and those aspiring to leadership positions as they endeavor to inspire and influence others. By recognizing and cultivating these essential traits, leaders can effectively guide their political parties toward a progressive and developmental future for South Sudan.

Chapter Three

Revisiting the Ten Powerful Ideas

"In failed societies, there are a thousand fools for every wise mind and a thousand foolish words for every thoughtful one. The majority always remains foolish and constantly outnumbers the wise." [6]

As we embark on this updated chapter, our objectives are twofold: first, to honor the legacy of John Garang by reflecting on how his ideas can inform present-day leadership and its strategic approaches to policy formulation and implementation. The second is to engage a new generation of thinkers and doers who can contribute to the ongoing discourse surrounding South Sudan's path toward a developmental state of stability and prosperity. Through this exploration, we hope to inspire deeper engagement with Garang's vision and show that we are not a failed society like the one articulated by Anton Chekhov in the above passage.

---

6   Quoted from: https://oblongmedia.net/2024/07/01/the-nature-of-a-failed-society/ and attributed to Anton Chekhov (1860 - 1904), a renowned Russian writer.

This chapter is, therefore, about ideas and their power in shaping the fate of societies. It aims to rekindle interest in his ten ideas shared in the first edition. In revisiting the ideas and vision of John Garang, Anton Chekhov's statement is a powerful reminder of the foundational ideas that have shaped the discourse around leadership, governance, nation-building, and the struggle for freedom and liberty. Garang's commitment to a vision of public service and equality for all the people in the two Sudans remains profoundly relevant today. His emphasis on self-reliance, cultural identity, *Sudanism*, and social justice provides an enduring framework for addressing contemporary challenges.

The enduring framework of ideas of John Garang is grounded firmly on conviction, courage, and consistency (the three Cs) in whatever he did. We view these attributes – conviction, courage, and consistency - as the glue that ties together the ten ideas explored in the first edition. The following passage informs his conviction of our place in history:

> ***"Around 5,000 years ago, a rich and powerful nation called the kingdom of Kush (also referred to as ancient Nubia) was a center of culture and military might in Africa. Ancient Nubia had a wealth of natural resources such as gold, ivory, copper, frankincense and ebony, but they also produced and traded a variety of goods such as pottery."*** [7]

The above quotation has elucidated the Sudanese commonality (i.e., *Sudanism*), which provides a strong foundation for our belief in

---

7   wysinger.hornestead.com/Nubians.htrnl

the correctness of the vision of New Sudan. It also demonstrates that **"Every great leap in human progress- from the printing press to the steam engine to the semiconductor- has been driven by ideas. But ideas do not emerge in a vacuum; they come from people."** [8] This is why the two Sudans could be a center (New Kush/Cush, for that matter) of culture and military might in the heart of Africa. And one cannot discuss the ideas of John Garang without, in his own words, **"historical context and contemporary realities."** [9] We will not discuss the historical context of *Garangism*, for the above quotation already illustrates it.

A key contemporary reality is this: South Sudan is endowed with natural resources (for example, oil, vast agricultural land, water, and critical minerals), but it is a landlocked country surrounded by six countries with a total land boundary of 5,413 kilometers (CIA Factbook, 2012). The countries are Sudan to the north (2,184-kilometer-long boundary), Ethiopia to the east (934-kilometer-long boundary), Kenya to the southeast (232-kilometer-long boundary), Uganda to the south (435-kilometer-long boundary), Democratic Republic of the Congo (DRC) to the southwest (639-kilometer-long boundary), and Central African Republic (CAR) to the west (989-kilometer long boundary).

This contemporary reality is composite, as it combines natural resource endowment with the geopolitical realities of a landlocked country. South Sudan's new membership in the community of sovereign states would require strategic thinking and rational behavior at three levels: regionally (with its six neighbors), continent-wide,

---

8   From Finance & Development Magazine of the International Monetary Fund (IMF), of March 2025, focusing on Human capital – The Economics of Talent

9   John Garang, *The Vision of the New Sudan: Questions of Unity and Identity,* 1997

and globally. We will return to this point later when discussing John Garang's idea of *tamazuj*.[10]

We would like to briefly examine the three Cs (conviction, courage, and consistency) before discussing John Garang's ideas and vision. We consider the three Cs to be the moral virtues inherent in these ideas.

On conviction, Dr. John (as our people call him up to now) articulated the concept of *Sudanism* (or Sudanese commonality) as the shared heritage, which is symbolized by the richness of our diverse cultural traditions and beliefs passed down to us from the Kush/Nubian ancient kingdoms. We want to illustrate this conviction with a quote from a message from my daughter Abiol to one of her sisters:

> *"I wish you could have been with me when I went to the ruins of the Nubian kingdom in Sudan. We were born in this life with an advantage to so many other Africans. Not only do we know where we come from-we have an illustrious history. But our ancestors did not sacrifice, struggle, fight for us to be the way we are now."* [11]

John Garang affectionately referred to Abiol as the "SPLA baby." She was born on May 15, 1983, at 5 PM in Madison, Wisconsin

---

10 This is an Arabic word that Dr. John used in describing the Abyei area of the Ngok Dinka as a melting pot of African and Arab cultures that would be the hub of stability, tranquility, prosperity, and sustained peace for either a united New Sudan or new Sudans (two independent Sudanese states at peace with each other and within themselves).

11 An email message from Abiol Lual Deng to NuNu (aka Nyandeng) Lual Deng on April 27, 2011. Abiol visited in 2006 Jebel Barkal and Merowe in northern Sudan.

(USA), which was early May 16 in Bor, Sudan. This unique intersection of time and place highlights the dual heritage that Abiol embodies. This dual heritage, which is shown mainly through the above heartfelt message she conveyed to her sister, is strong evidence of *Sudanism*. Abiol eloquently articulated the legacy left by our ancestors, emphasizing that they bravely fought to secure a rich cultural heritage. This solid commonwealth empowers successive generations of Kushites to generate additional forms of wealth and creativity.

Her words not only reflect a deep-seated emotional connection but also resonate with Dr. John's steadfast belief in the shared identity of the Sudanese people. This shared conviction is fundamental to understanding the broader ethos of Garangism, which we have yet to explore fully. In this framework, a nurturing dimension exists that is often overlooked. At its core, Garangism is built upon what we refer to as the five Cs: conviction, courage, consistency, creativity, and compassion. However, this discussion will focus primarily on conviction, courage, and consistency.

These three Cs serve as essential pillars that guide leadership and inspire collective action. In Chapter Two, we have already discussed the two Cs—creativity and compassion— and analyzed how they further illuminate the principles of effective leadership within the Sudanese context. By exploring these concepts, we can gain a more nuanced understanding of how John Garang's vision continues to influence and inspire new generations.

A people without a traceable cultural heritage would not have a body of knowledge to create commonwealth and sustainable legacies for future generations. In this respect, throwing away the rich legacy of the Kushites, as some elements in South Sudan propose, would be an act of self-denial and social suicide. Our very being is our heritage bequeathed to us over five thousand years since the time of the Kush/

Cush kingdom. Dr. John's conviction is an evidence-based belief; biblical sources and archeological research findings support.

The book of Genesis (10:6) talks of Cush/Kush as the son of Ham, the son of Noah. Archaeological research has confirmed the Kush/Cush kingdom to be the first recorded kingdom in sub-Saharan Africa. Because of our lazy thinking, we have been unable to dig deep into our history. But Dr. John did that for Abiol's generation, a generation of dotcom and social media that will never betray his legacy for which he paid the ultimate.

Dan Morrison of the *National Geographic News* reported, "**The first recorded kingdom in sub-Saharan Africa, Kush was one of the first civilizations to take hold in the Nile River Valley.**" [12] Moreover, according to the University of Chicago archaeologist Geoff Embeling, the kingdom "**was unusual in that it was able to use the tools of power - military and governance - without having a system of writing, an extensive bureaucracy, or numerous urban centers.**"[13] The same team of Chicago archeologists working with Professor Geoff Embeling stated that:

> *"The team also excavated a cemetery where they uncovered burials with artifacts that suggest the region was part of the kingdom of Kush, which would have ruled an area much larger than previously believed. The discoveries thus indicate that the kingdom, the first in sub-Saharan Africa, controlled a territory as much as 1,200 kilometres in length.* [14]

---

12   Dan Morrison, "Merowe, Sudan," National Geographic News, June 18, 2007

13   Quoted from: http://www.afrol.com/articles/25907

14   Ibid

While we acknowledge the possibility that more archaeological research might eventually uncover evidence suggesting the Kush kingdom possessed a written language, such as the Meroitic language, it is also vital to recognize the significance of what we already know. Even without definitive evidence of a written script, we should take immense pride in our rich and illustrious history. The Kush kingdom, renowned for its remarkable contributions, is recognized as the birthplace of the iron industry, paving the way for advancements in metallurgy that influenced nearby civilizations.

Additionally, the sophisticated irrigation systems developed by the Kushites played a crucial role in agricultural practices, allowing for flourishing communities in the challenging deserts of Nubia. These innovations highlight the ingenuity of our ancestors and underscore the Kush civilization's profound impact on both regional and global scales.

The challenge we face today calls for a collaborative effort between South Sudanese historians and world-renowned archaeologists to uncover the intricate system of governance in ancient Kush. Unfortunately, this critical historical narrative has often been obscured by the pervasive racism and prejudices that have shaped scholarly perspectives. By confronting these prejudices and reevaluating the evidence, we can work toward a more accurate understanding of Kush's historical importance, recognizing it not merely in relation to Egypt but as a powerful and influential culture in its own right.

Dr. Timothy Kendall, one of the leading voices in this field, eloquently addresses this issue, highlighting a longstanding misconception in the study of Kush:[15]

---

15   See http://wysinger.homestead.com/Nubians.html

"Historians have long known about Kush, but relegated its importance to a vassal state of Egypt, significant only for its gold reserves. Early excavations in the Kush capital at Kerma suffered from the innate racism of the archaeologists. Fabulous grave goods, discovered in the 20th century, were thought to have belonged to Kush's Egyptian overlords. They didn't consider that a black African culture could have challenged Egypt's supremacy."

A more nuanced understanding of Dr. John's political philosophy and moral framework can be gleaned from the redistributive economic system of the ancient Kingdom of Kush. According to a Wikipedia article quoting scholar Derek Welsby, historians are currently debating the nature of the Kushite economy.[16] Some argue that it operated as a redistributive system whereby the state collected taxes in the form of surplus agricultural produce, which was then redistributed to the populace.

Conversely, others contend that a significant portion of society was self-sufficient, working the land independently and contributing little to the state in the form of taxes or services. Additionally, northern Kush was generally more productive and prosperous compared to the southern region, suggesting a disparity in resource distribution and management.

The Kushite governance system is a clear example of what philosopher John Rawls calls "distributive justice," contrasting sharply with the dominant monarchical structures of much of the ancient world. While it is well-documented that most monarchies historically

---

16   http://en.wikipedia.org/wki/kingdom_of kush#cte_ note-Welsby.2c_ Derek A 1998-1

depended on the labor and compliance of their subjects to maintain their power and wealth, evidence indicates that the Kingdom of Kush operated under a fundamentally different paradigm. In this context, the Kushite system emphasized fairness in the distribution of resources and opportunities, fostering a sense of social equity that significantly diverged from the often-exploitative nature of feudalism practiced in medieval Europe.

Feudalism, as defined by the New Oxford American Dictionary, was **"the dominant social system in medieval Europe, in which the nobility held lands from the Crown in exchange for military service, and vassals were in turn tenants of the nobles, while the peasants (villains or serfs) were obliged to live on their lord's land and give him homage, labor, and a share of the produce, notionally in exchange for military protection."** This definition highlights the inherent inequalities and burdens faced by the lower classes within the feudal system.

Peasants, often referred to as villains or serfs, were typically bound to the land and subject to the demands of their lords. This led to a social structure that favored the elite and perpetuated a cycle of exploitation. Their obligations were not only labor-intensive but also limited their autonomy and political power, resulting in a deep-seated divide between the classes.

In contrast, the Kushite approach to governance appears to have fostered a more integrated and reciprocal relationship between rulers and subjects. Instead of exploiting labor for personal gain, the Kushite system might have provided mechanisms for sharing resources and ensuring that the welfare of the populace was considered in the decision-making processes. This framework promotes a more equitable society and aligns with the principles of justice that Rawls advocated, where all citizens' well-being is prioritized, thus creating a more stable and harmonious social order.

Ultimately, the Kingdom of Kush's governance exemplified a leadership model that embraced the ideals of justice and equity, setting it apart from the oppressive feudal systems that marked much of Europe during the same period. This distinct approach not only challenges conventional narratives about ancient monarchies but also offers invaluable insights into alternative forms of governance that prioritize the needs and rights of all individuals.

In summary, the economic model of the Kingdom of Kush, with its emphasis on redistribution for the welfare of its people, offers a compelling contrast to the exploitative feudal systems of contemporary societies elsewhere. This aspect of Kushite governance aligns more closely with Dr. John's vision of justice and equity, signifying an alternative approach to wealth distribution that has largely gone unrecognized in historical discourse.

This conviction about our proper place in history, as evidenced by the Kush kingdom, has led the Sudan People's Liberation Movement (SPLM) to keep the name of Sudan for the new Republic of South Sudan. So we have two new Sudans out of the old Sudan as Dr. John envisioned. As discussed in the next chapter, he laid solid foundations for establishing a nation of which all the Sudanese would have been proud, irrespective of their gender, race, region, religion, political inclination, and/or socioeconomic status.

The failure to achieve a common Sudanese nation has created two Sudans for now. However, it could lead to the further disintegration of the two Sudans and the establishment of several nation-states, each providing a rallying point for groups that feel united by a common culture and destiny. Our discussion of the New Sudan Project in the next chapter will illuminate such possibilities.

The virtue of courage stands out clearly in *Garangism*. His call for a united Sudan on a new basis against the separatist inclination of most Southern Sudanese people illustrates it beyond doubt. We are reminded of Andrew Jackson's eloquent phrase, "**One man of courage makes a majority.**" [17] John Garang was such a man. Moreover, as if describing the courage of Dr. John Garang, John F. Kennedy articulates in his celebrated book, *Profiles in Courage*, the courage of President John Adams as follows:

> *"[B]ecause his desire to win or maintain a reputation for integrity and courage was stronger than his desire to maintain his office-because his conscience, his personal standard of ethics, his integrity or morality, call it what you will-was stronger than the pressures of public disapproval because his faith that his course was the best one, and would ultimately be vindicated, outweighed his fear of public reprisal." (Kennedy 1956, 218- 19)*

Courage is used here not to mean "standing firm in battle," as the Athenian General Laches understood. We are using "courage" here as Socrates provided in his counterexample to General Laches' understanding of "What is courage?" Socrates' counterexample runs as follows:

> *"[S]omeone might stand firm in battle, but simply out of foolish endurance, putting both themselves (sic) and others in danger. A genuinely courageous person knows both when to stand firm and when to retreat."*

---

17 John F. Kennedy, *Profiles in Courage*, 1956

John Garang knew when to stand firm in battle and when to retreat. For instance, he retreated from his position of a secular Sudanese state to that of a one-country-two-systems governance model for the interim period. This model subsequently paved the way for a peaceful secession instead of standing firm on the call for a united democratic and secular state as a prerequisite to any peace agreement.

Another example of "foolish endurance" would be, in our view, the call for separation by some Southern political elite without a clear strategy for achieving it. Here, the vision of New Sudan was a superb strategy, as we shall see in the next chapter. During his various discourses with his associates, Dr. John used to say, "**My Southern Sudanese separatists would have to come first with me to Khartoum for them to achieve their goal of an independent South Sudan.**" In the next chapter, we tell the story of his long march (to paraphrase Nelson Mandela) of twenty-one years to Khartoum.[18]

In this context, courage is not merely defined as "standing firm in battle," as Athenian General Laches might have understood it. Instead, we draw upon Socrates' insightful counterexample to Laches when addressing the question: "What is courage?" Socrates proposed that standing firm in battle could stem from mere foolish endurance, a reckless resolve that endangers the individual and their comrades. True courage, as Socrates articulated, involves the wisdom to discern when to stand firm and when to retreat tactically.

John Garang exemplified this nuanced understanding of courage throughout his leadership. He demonstrated the ability to navigate complex political landscapes, knowing when to make tactical retreats from the path-goal strategy and when to hold firm on this strategic

---

18   President Nelson Mandela's autobiography, *Long Walk to Freedom*, was published in 1995 by Little Brown & Company. We have used this title to describe how John Garang reached Khartoum after twenty-one years of the war of liberation.

path against adversity. For instance, Garang's decision to shift from advocating for a secular Sudanese state to endorsing a one-country-two-systems governance model during an interim period illustrates this wisdom. By doing so, he laid the groundwork for a peaceful secession, a strategy that ultimately proved more effective than rigidly insisting on a united democratic and secular state as an absolute precondition for any peace agreement.

On the other hand, consider the calls for separation that emerged from certain Southern political elites, which at times lacked a coherent strategy for execution. This scenario reflects a form of "foolish endurance"—an unwavering stance without a viable plan that could lead to tangible outcomes. In contrast, Garang's vision of a New Sudan represented a well-thought-out path-goal strategy to unify diverse factions under a common goal while addressing the aspirations for independence.

Dr. John often, as stated earlier, emphasized during his discussions with colleagues that for the Southern Sudanese separatists to realize their goal of an independent South, they needed to approach Khartoum together with him, symbolizing solidarity and a unified front. This was not just a battle for separation; it was about shifting the narrative and creating a sustainable future for Southern Sudan. In the forthcoming chapter, we will delve into the story of his arduous twenty-one-year journey to Khartoum, a long march that symbolized his commitment and determination. Ultimately, while the verdict on these historical events may remain in the hands of future generations, it is clear that, in our view, history has indeed favored Dr. John Garang and his vision.

Consistency is another enduring virtue of *Garangism*. Dr. John was consistent in his conviction of the vision of New Sudan, which he espoused in 1972 when he was a twenty-seven-year-old officer in the then-Anya-Nya guerrilla army of Southern Sudan. This enduring consistency has enabled the people of South Sudan to regain their dignity and liberty. He stayed focused on the message of the liberation struggle despite numerous attempted distractions. We have already discussed leadership qualities in Chapter 2, and consistency is one of his strengths that kept him leading and inspiring his people to follow him even at times of despair and temporary setbacks on the battlefields of the war of liberation.

Garang's path-goal strategy is driven by problem-solving, which integrates critical thinking with cultural consciousness and is a vital compass for today's leaders and activists. By embracing creative reasoning, we cultivate the flexibility needed to foster dialogue, inspire collaboration, and push the boundaries of what is possible in shaping a peaceful future.

We are now poised to delve deeper into fresh perspectives on his ten pivotal ideas, which resonate profoundly with today's socio-political landscape and the evolving quest for a developmental state erected on political morality and ethics, on robust institutions that serve as frameworks for collective action while also underscoring the Constitution as the definitive foundation of the rule of law. In this age of rapid transformation and multifaceted challenges, the significance of the ten ideas underpinned by creative reasoning cannot be overstated. As we navigate many global issues—from socioeconomic disparities to environmental crises—we must seek innovative approaches that effectively address these complexities.

Garang's path-goal strategy stands out as a beacon of problem-solving prowess, seamlessly blending critical thinking with cultural awareness. This synthesis not only informs effective leadership but also empowers activists, serving as an essential guide for those striving to influence change.

By embracing creative reasoning, we develop the adaptability required to engage in meaningful dialogue, inspire collective collaboration, and expand the horizons of what is achievable in our pursuit of a peaceful and just future. The ongoing conflicts and intricate dynamics in Sudan and South Sudan offer a stark illustration of the urgent need for these ten powerful ideas, which aim to provide insights and potential avenues for resolution in a context fraught with tensions and uncertainties. Each idea is a building block for understanding the complexities at play and reimagining a path forward that fosters healing, unity, and sustainable development. The ideas are:

1. Why Be Serious When It's Already Serious
2. We Say What We Practice and Practice What We Say
3. Disappointment Is a Function of Expectations
4. Peace Through Development
5. Collegial Presidency
6. Sudan Would Never Be the Same Again
7. You Must Finish What You Set Out to Do
8. Taking Towns to Rural Areas
9. Poverty Is a Function of Marginalization
10. The *Tamazuj* Zone

Each of the above ten ideas offers a lens through which to understand the challenges and opportunities in the region. However, we must reproduce some paragraphs from the first edition to refresh our memories. Here is a comprehensive evaluation with new perspectives based on the current situation, new perspectives, and developments related to each idea.

1. Why Be Serious When It's Already Serious

This idea highlights the absurdity of adopting a lighthearted demeanor in the face of severe circumstances. The gravity of conflict necessitates that leadership approach crises with pragmatism rather than frivolity.

Two years following the Addis Ababa Agreement, which ended the first civil conflict in Sudan, a pervasive sense of discontent had already begun to brew among the Southern Sudanese intelligentsia regarding the state of development in their region. Dr. John, a prominent figure in this discourse, emphasized the importance of strategic planning and maintaining a cool-headed approach. He firmly believed that the complexities of our situation demanded thoughtful consideration, not emotional reactions or what Mabior Garang is now calling "disorganized anger." According to Dr. John, our existing problems were critical enough; adding emotional weight could exacerbate them, especially without a well-structured plan of action to guide us.

He posited that the most appropriate response in a serious situation is not through disorganized anger but to resist the urge for quick fixes, instead prioritizing the search for sustainable solutions. This perspective aligns closely with John Commons' definition of institutions, where restraint emerges as a fundamental principle.[19] Dr. John's guidance fostered a spirit of self-discipline within us; he urged us to resist the temptation to hastily ignite the fires of the liberation struggle under the belief that immediate action was necessary due to the exigency of our circumstances.

Our movement toward liberation did not happen overnight; it required a dedicated nine years of strategic thought, planning, and preparation before Dr. John felt confident in allowing his associates to initiate the people's liberation struggle on May 16, 1983. This drawn-out process serves as a stark reminder of Robert F. Kennedy's powerful quote derived from Bonar Law: **"There is no such thing as inevitable**

---

19   John R. Commons defines institution as "working rules of collective action in restraint, liberation, and expansion of individual action."

war. If war comes, it will be from the failure of human wisdom." [20]

However, it seems that many in the Sudan People's Liberation Movement (SPLM) have not fully grasped this essential principle. This was painfully evident when, in January 2012, oil production was abruptly shut down without a thorough analysis of the potential repercussions. South Sudan continues to suffer until the time of writing this second edition (i.e., 2025) from that decision of January 2012. The controversial Panthou (Heglig) episode of April 2012 also illustrated similar miscalculations. These two examples illustrate vividly the consequences of responding to disorganized anger. Such a response is especially concerning given that many senior officers in the Sudan People's Liberation Army (SPLA) are well-educated in the foundational principles outlined in Sun Tzu's Art of War.

It raises an alarming question regarding where the principles underpinning "**the art of strategy**," as articulated by military historian Andrew Bacevich (2008, 165), have faltered within our leadership hierarchy.

Sun Tzu crucially advises that "**The art of war is of vital importance to the State. It is a matter of life and death, a road either to safety or to ruin. Therefore, it is a subject of inquiry which can on no account be neglected.**" [21] This statement underscores the gravity of military strategy and its profound implications for a nation's survival and prosperity. Given the significant stakes involved, it prompts a critical examination: Why do we, as a society, often approach such serious issues with a sense of levity or irreverence? When the consequences of our decisions can profoundly shape the future, it is essential to adopt a mindset that recognizes the urgency and gravity of the circumstances we face and, therefore, avoid any recklessness in our actions.

---

20   Robert F. Kennedy, foreword to Profiles in Courage, by John F. Kennedy

21   From the English version translated by Lionel Giles, 327-28

The Power of Creative Reasoning

As the Dinka people would advise, the idea of questioning the necessity of seriousness in serious times can be reframed as a call for restraint or **kon koc** (literally meaning wait a minute/moment). For members of the SPLM, this translates into a thoughtful consideration of their words and actions. We can cite two illuminating examples of this principle in practice:

The first example pertains to the conduct of SPLM members toward Southern Sudanese politicians, specifically individuals such as Uncle Bona Malwal Madut Ring. Those of us who were perceived as close associates to the SPLM chairman were urged to refrain from employing abusive or denigrating language or behavior toward any Southern Sudanese leader. Even when Uncle Bona embarked on a negative campaign against Dr. John Garang in his publication, the Sudan Democratic Gazette, our leadership emphasized the importance of restraint.

We were encouraged to leverage our historical political relationships with Uncle Bona from the 1980s to restore amicable social and political ties rather than engage in hostile exchanges.[22] Regrettably, due to unforeseen circumstances, we could not fulfill this mission before that unfortunate day in July 2005.

The second example of restraint can be seen in the peace process itself. When unresolved issues arose from the negotiations between the SPLM and the Government of Sudan (GoS), these matters were escalated to the principals for resolution. During these critical discussions,

---

22 The late Dr. Justin Yac Arop, late Elijah Malak Aleng, and I were supposed to travel to England to meet with Bona at his residence in Oxford to ascertain his grievances against the chairman. This is a Dinka way of doing things in that the chief/leader of the community reaches out for those in the community who are not happy with the state of affairs. For the record, Bona was ready to receive us and willing to phone the chairman, according to traditions, from his residence the day after our arrival.

I had the privilege of accompanying Dr. John during his meetings with Mr. Ali Osman Taha, the First Vice President of Sudan, focusing specifically on contentious issues surrounding wealth-sharing negotiations.

Our initial session was quite engaging. Dr. John commenced the meeting by breaking the ice with jokes. He opened a bottle of water and thoughtfully served it first to his counterpart, the First Vice President of Sudan. He lightheartedly quipped, "**You and I want an economist with one hand**!" In response, I interjected, "**Comrade Chairman and Mr. First Vice President, you are currently looking at two Wisconsin-educated economists with five hands**!" Our lighthearted banter instantly created a relaxed atmosphere, enabling a productive discussion on challenging topics such as land rights, oil revenues, and central banking—a prelude to a more constructive negotiation process.

El Fatih Ali Siddig, my counterpart, then delivered a comprehensive seventy-five-minute presentation on the GoS budget process with a resource envelope in which the national government in Khartoum was taking more than 95 percent of the oil revenues. I responded thoughtfully, fostering an environment where serious matters could be addressed with the depth and gravity they warranted. My response was very brief. I told the two leaders that our role as their respective economic advisers was not to burden them with figures but to advise them on the budgetary implications of their decisions. I told them that the budget was nothing but a mirror of society's social and economic choices.

The two leaders continued their hard bargaining and tradeoffs with civility and self-discipline. The result was a win-win outcome for the entire people of Sudan in the form of the Comprehensive Peace Agreement (CPA). Ustaz Ali Osman Mohamed Taha later described the Naivasha peace process as "an open Sudanese school" in which both sides of the Sudanese political divide developed mutual respect and acquired basic skills that would be used to sustain peace and address the legitimate aspirations of the Sudanese people.

We have a new perspective on why being serious when it is already serious. It could be explained in the two Dinka words of *kon koc*! Another way of expressing this is Mabior's disorganized anger, which he advises: do not respond to disorganized anger without a credible plan. We reproduce two sentences from what we have previously cited from Mabior Garang de Mabior:

"The best response is not disorganized anger, which can easily be hijacked by opportunistic politicians for their own selfish ends. We must be organized and focused for the sake of future generations so that our children can understand our historical struggle and inherit a viable and united nation."

Mabior will retain the right to challenge our interpretation of his concept of disorganized anger. However, we will utilize this concept to enhance our people's understanding of the various consequences that can arise from responses rooted in such disorganized anger. The press conferences held on December 6 and December 8, 2013, at the SPLM House, which involved factions within the SPLM leadership, epitomized these dynamics of disorganized anger. The fallout from these events culminated in a violent conflict on the night of December 15, 2013. This eruption of violence set off a chain reaction, leading to a series of armed conflicts that continue to affect the country today.

In conclusion, the exploration of disorganized anger reveals profound insights into the human experience. By confronting the origins and implications of unchecked emotions, we can better understand the chaos they create—and why Garang's profound statement, "Why Be Serious When It's Already Serious," resonates so deeply. This notion encourages us to recognize that a sense of futility can lead to a spiraling cycle of disillusionment and turmoil. Instead of succumbing to or dismissing our emotions, we should confront them head-on and strive for clarity and purpose. By cultivating this awareness, we foster a culture of emotional intelligence that empowers us to navigate life's challenges with grace and resilience.

In recognizing the gravity of our emotional landscapes, we can transform disorganized anger into constructive dialogue, paving the way for understanding and healing in our communities. Only then can we approach serious matters with the sincerity they demand, fostering a collective mindfulness that not only addresses the issues at hand but also promotes a healthier, more empathetic society.

2. We Say What We Practice and Practice What We Say

The idea of "We Say What We Practice and Practice What We Say" encapsulates the core principle of integrity within governance and society, particularly in the context of Sudan and South Sudan. This principle emphasizes the importance of political leaders aligning their words with their actions, thereby fostering trust and accountability among citizens and communities. In many instances, a gap between the rhetoric of political leaders and their actual actions has resulted in widespread distrust, leading to societal fragmentation. This issue is especially pronounced in the complexities of post-colonial Sudan, where the historical relationship between Northern and Southern political entities has been marked by mistrust and misunderstanding.

Dr. John Garang's leadership within the Sudan People's Liberation Movement (SPLM) sought to bridge this divide by establishing a new political framework that embraced inclusivity and a shared vision of governance. Historically, Northern political elites were accustomed to interacting with Southern leaders who advocated for separation and secession, often viewing Southern political movements through a lens of division. The SPLM's paradigm shift—advocating for a "New Sudan" rather than a divided one—was radical and not readily understood by these elites. This led to persistent inquiries such as, "What does John Garang want?" which reflected their confusion and skepticism toward the SPLM's intentions.

In response to these uncertainties, Dr. John firmly asserted the SPLM's commitment to integrity with his proclamation, **"We say what we practice and practice what we say."** This statement was not just a mantra; it reinforced the SPLM's dedication to transparent governance and principled leadership throughout their prolonged liberation struggle. The SPLM's vision was consistent in advocating for a federated unified Sudan based on principles of equality, justice, and participatory governance, which was crucial during a time marked by civil strife and division.

3. Disappointment Is a Function of Expectations

The rationale behind this idea is clear: by actively engaging communities in setting achievable goals and expectations, we significantly reduce the potential for disappointment when those goals are not met. Inclusive dialogues that specifically address local needs serve to align our aspirations with realistic outcomes.

We cannot expect to reap the benefits of what we have not sown. Many of us are currently enjoying the fruits of Dr. John's tireless efforts—even amid doubts about his vision during the long journey toward freedom, liberty, and human dignity. A fortune is often labeled 'luck' when it comes without labor or planning. However, even luck requires preparation, as emphasized by John C. Maxwell (2001). While many within the SPLM may be familiar with this concept, the degree to which it has been internalized remains uncertain.

We urge the SPLM rank and file to reflect on their own interpretations of the idea that disappointment stems from unmet expectations. In the following paragraphs, we will share our understanding of this idea. Internalizing this idea has the potential to reignite the revolutionary spirit and moral virtue of public service that SPLM/A embodies—qualities that the blood of our martyrs has transformed into a symbol of personal sacrifice and duty we must all strive to emulate.

Implicit in this idea is the understanding that expectation is fundamentally linked to responsibility driven by robust institutions, preparation, and resilience. In essence, this means that the core elements of this concept are embodied in personal sacrifices and a commitment to public service executed with integrity and dignity. Dr. John consistently reminded us that our expectations should be rooted in our own responsibilities and the institutions we have built to discharge our duties and obligations. When we take ownership of our actions, we eliminate the tendency to rely on others for our well-being and our destiny. In short, we hold the key to our own futures.

However, the SPLM leadership appears to have strayed from its long-established tradition of resilience and self-reliance. This point is articulated below by one of the friends of Sudan and South Sudan, a former British Ambassador to Sudan, Mr. Alan Goulty. He observed the following in his review in March 2013 of the first edition of this book:

> *"This short book gives an excellent summary of key elements of Dr. Garang's thinking and his plans for South*

> *Sudan, which were cut off by his tragic death in a helicopter crash in July 2005. (One suggestion that he was assassinated is unfounded and should not have appeared in this work).[23] It also provokes questions still relevant to the governance of South Sudan: why did Dr. Garang not succeed in mobilising SPLM cadres to support and continue his work, and why did governments in South Sudan not follow his blueprint for the development of the country? Lual Deng's insights provoke much thought and reflection - one test of a scholarly work like this. A must-read for all friends of South Sudan."*

The two questions from the review of the book by Ambassador Goulty were: **why did Dr. Garang not succeed in mobilizing SPLM cadres to support and continue his work, and why did governments in South Sudan not follow his blueprint for the development of the country?** These two questions represent the disappointment of South Sudan's friends. To bring the point home, Ambassador Goulty arranged the launch of my book on April 24, 2013, at the prestigious Woodrow Wilson Center for International Scholars, Africa Program in Washington, D.C. The launch was titled **A Crisis of Governance in South Sudan**. The outline of my presentation consisted of the following five points that we thought were the drivers of a crisis of governance in South Sudan:

1. Weak Institutions,
2. Pervasive Corruption,

---

23   Our assertion is based on what President Museveni said on August 5, 2005, after viewing the body of Dr. John in Yei, Central Equatoria State, that there were hands behind the death of this man! Those hands are the assassins in our view.

3. Poor Economic Management,
4. Absence of Cohesive National Identity, and
5. Insecurity.

Furthermore, avoiding disappointment hinges on meticulous strategic planning, which we prefer to refer to simply as preparation. Dr. John Garang was known for his prudence; he never made public statements with potential long-term repercussions for our people without careful strategic consideration and preparation. Sadly, it seems that the SPLM leadership has not fully internalized this foundational principle established by its founding fathers.

Disappointment is often said to arise from a gap between expectations and reality. This is especially poignant in South Sudan, where the absence of a coherent national identity has led to widespread disillusionment among its citizens. In a nation still grappling with the aftermath of conflict and fragmentation, individuals' expectations for their government, institutions, and society often clash with the harsh realities they face.

The quest for a cohesive national identity in South Sudan has been fraught with challenges. With a rich tapestry of ethnicities, languages, and cultures, the country is a vibrant mosaic that remains at odds with the need for a united front. While a strength in many respects, this diversity has often been exploited to foster division rather than unity. Consequently, many South Sudanese find themselves navigating competing loyalties that dilute their sense of belonging to a single nation. This lack of a shared identity creates an environment rife with misunderstanding and mistrust, ultimately fueling disappointment as people look to their leaders for direction and vision.

Expectations of governance and social cohesion among South Sudanese are high. Dreams of freedom, prosperity, and unity marked the nation's struggles for independence. These aspirations inspired hope and set the stage for expectations that the government would prioritize inclusive policies and foster a sense of belonging among all citizens. Unfortunately, reality has often fallen short. The absence of a coherent national identity leaves citizens feeling unrepresented, as political leadership tends to cater to specific ethnic interests rather than embrace the nation's collective aspirations.

When leaders fail to recognize the importance of cultivating a strong, unifying national identity, they inadvertently foster an atmosphere of disappointment. South Sudanese citizens expect their leaders not only to articulate a vision for the future but also to take concrete steps toward realizing that vision. However, the deep-seated political fragmentation and lack of accountability have led to a failure to deliver on these promises. Citizens watch as their expectations remain unfulfilled, disillusioned, and disheartened by the persistent conflicts and inadequate governance.

Moreover, the absence of participatory governance compounds this disappointment. When people are not actively engaged in decision-making processes, their hopes for a better future are quickly dashed. When citizens feel excluded from governance and policy-making processes, their ability to invest in their country wanes. This disengagement further exacerbates the divide, reinforcing the cycle of disappointment that stems from unfulfilled expectations.

To break this cycle, leaders in South Sudan must prioritize the establishment of a coherent national identity that reflects the interests and needs of all citizens. This requires a strategic shift toward inclusivity and accountability, where citizens are not merely passive observers but active contributors to the nation-building process. By fostering dialogue among different ethnicities and communities, leaders can help cultivate an environment where shared values and common goals take precedence over "tribal" affiliations and urban-based community associations.

Only by aligning actions with the expectations of the populace can the South Sudanese leadership begin to mitigate the disappointment that plagues their governance. The formation of a cohesive national identity is not merely a political necessity; it is a moral obligation that can help restore faith among the citizens. Ultimately, when people see their hopes reflected in the actions of their leaders, they are more likely to engage positively with the institutions that govern them, moving the nation closer to the dream that many South Sudanese continue to hold for a united country and prosperous future.

The expectations of the ordinary South Sudanese people are clear: they seek tangible actions from the SPLM that fulfill their aspirations, not merely lofty statements. A disorganized and ill-prepared SPLM risks failing to deliver on these promises, leading to profound disappointment among the millions of people who supported it during the liberation war. The five drivers of a crisis of governance in South Sudan are further discussed in the rest of the chapters of this Second edition.

We must, nevertheless, state that insecurity in South Sudan is deeply interwoven with the critical challenges of weak institutions, pervasive corruption, poor economic management, and the absence of a cohesive national identity. The crisis of governance cannot be viewed in isolation; instead, it is a complex web that is exacerbated by insecurity, which erodes public trust and hampers developmental efforts.

As will be discussed later in Chapter 4, weak institutions are among root causes of the crisis of governance in South Sudan. That is, insecurity is a function of institutional weakness to provide the stability and support necessary for governance. Insecure environments often lead to heightened factional fighting, not only within the Sudan People's Liberation Movement (SPLM) but also among various political groups and inter- and intra-communal conflicts.

This fragmentation results in a vicious cycle where insecurity undermines the very foundations of governance, evidenced by the recent events (March 2025) in the Nasir County of Upper Nile State. The politically engineered barbaric killing of Gen. David Majur Dak Thel by the so-called White Army is a testimony to our statement.

The perception of institutional effectiveness is paramount for maintaining public trust and social order. When individuals witness their institutions, such as the South Sudan People's Defence Forces (SSPDF), fail to uphold their responsibilities, particularly in critical moments like rescuing encircled military personnel, it breeds disillusionment, disappointment, and erodes faith in leadership.

The SSPDF's inability to rescue its general and his men from the siege in Nasir serves as a glaring example of a broader issue: a breakdown in state authority. This situation illustrates that when a governing body cannot fulfill its primary function of safeguarding its citizens and forces, it signals a lack of control and competency. Such failures not only exacerbate public cynicism but also encourage chaos and instability.

As the social contract between the state and its citizens weakens, we see a ripple effect—people start questioning their institutions' legitimacy and overall power. Suppose citizens feel that their government and military are unable to protect them. In this scenario, they may turn to alternative power structures or groups, such as the White Army and *Gelweng*.

This shift can lead to an environment where lawlessness prevails, further complicating efforts to restore order. For a society to function cohesively, there must be a shared belief in the efficacy of its institutions. Therefore, the SSPDF's failure in this instance not only highlights a critical moment of weakness but also poses significant long-term ramifications for the stability and future governance of South Sudan. Restoring faith in such institutions is crucial for preventing further disintegration of authority, and it is clear that immediate action and reform are needed to regain public trust. Corruption thrives in conditions marked by insecurity.

When institutions lack accountability and transparency, those in power may exploit their positions for personal gain, further alienating citizens and heightening feelings of disenfranchisement. This pervasive corruption, coupled with insecurity, creates a breeding ground for disillusionment among the populace. Citizens who feel abandoned and unrepresented are less likely to engage with the institutions that should serve them, leading to a further erosion of effective governance structures.

Poor economic management exacerbates insecurity by limiting the population's access to resources and opportunities. When the economy falters, it fuels desperation and increases the potential for unrest. Unemployment, especially among the youth, and poverty serve as catalysts for insecurity, leading individuals to join armed groups or engage in violence as a means of survival. In this context, economic stability is not just an aspiration; it is a fundamental requirement for peace and security.

The absence of a cohesive national identity also plays a pivotal role in driving insecurity. When citizens do not identify with a unified national narrative, they may prioritize ethnic or factional loyalties over national interests. This fragmentation can lead to conflicts that are rooted in mistrust and historical grievances, making it challenging to forge a path toward sustainable peace. A cohesive identity, grounded in shared values and goals, is crucial for fostering national unity and reducing insecurity.

4. Peace through Development

In the annals of history, few leaders have wielded the transformative power of development as a means to achieve lasting peace as effectively as John Garang, the founder of the Sudan People's Liberation Movement (SPLM). Garang's philosophy and vision centered on the idea that sustainable development is essential not only for economic growth but also for resolving conflicts within societies. His assertion that "peace through development" should guide national policies highlights a profound understanding of the interconnectedness of development and peacebuilding.

At the heart of Garang's ideology is the realization that poverty, ignorance, and lack of infrastructure are primary catalysts for conflict. When basic human needs are unfulfilled, frustration and desperation can lead individuals and communities to resort to violence as a means of expression and survival. Dr. John recognized that in a society where people are unable to provide for their families due to economic stagnation and underdevelopment, the seeds of unrest are sown. Therefore, his approach sought to tackle the root causes of conflict by addressing these issues head-on through comprehensive development initiatives. The following passage further illuminates this line of thinking:

> *"Little else is requisite to carry a state to the highest degree of opulence from the lowest barbarism but peace, easy taxes, and tolerable administration of justice: all the rest being brought about by the natural course of things."* [24]

---

24   Adam Smith on the need for "peace, easy taxes, and a tolerable administration of justice" (1755), from https://oll.libertyfund.org/quotes/436

Garang's concept of development extended beyond mere economic measures, as illustrated by the above passage from Adam Smith. It encompassed social, political, and cultural dimensions as well. He understood that for development to be meaningful, it should cultivate an inclusive environment where all citizens have access to education, healthcare, and economic opportunities. This egalitarian approach aims to unify disparate communities by fostering a sense of shared purpose and collective identity, which is essential in multi-ethnic societies often plagued by division and mistrust.

By building a national narrative centered on shared values and commonwealth, John Garang sought to align the aspirations of diverse groups, reducing the inclination toward factionalism that often hinders peace efforts. Furthermore, Dr. John emphasized that sustainable development must be participatory. Development cannot be imposed from the top down; rather, it requires the involvement and commitment of the people it aims to serve. Garang's approach fosters ownership, accountability, and empowerment by engaging communities in the development process.

When individuals feel they are active contributors to their society's progress, they are more likely to invest in peaceful resolutions to conflicts, as they see themselves as stakeholders in a joint endeavor. For instance, efforts by the New Sudan Council of Churches (NSCC) that brought together Dinka and Nuer Traditional Authority leaders in Wunlit Conference in 1999 and two other places in Jonglei - Waat and Liliir - are examples of empowering the society to manage inter- and intra-communal conflicts. Such a model could be applied to resolving the current crisis in Nasir County of Upper Nile State through the idea of "peace through development."

Real-world examples further illustrate the viability of John Garang's vision. Nations that have successfully pursued peace through development have often experienced remarkable transformations. For instance, post-conflict countries that prioritize rebuilding infrastructure, investing in education, and creating job opportunities can mitigate tensions that might lead to a resurgence of violence. Through development initiatives such as community rebuilding projects, vocational training, and investments in farming households and healthcare, societies can cultivate resilience against the forces that drive conflict.

In the heart of South Sudan, the vision of John Garang echoes like a beacon in the dark, illuminating the path toward peace through development. His philosophy resonates not only within the borders of his homeland but also serves as a clarion call for policymakers around the globe. Countries emerging from the ashes of conflict often find themselves at a crossroads, grappling with the daunting task of rebuilding. Garang's insights remind us that peace is not a finite destination—it is a continuous journey marked by an unwavering commitment to nurturing human potential and strengthening the social fabric of society.

The lessons are stark and urgent as political turmoil unfolds in places like Nasir. South Sudanese leaders stand at a pivotal moment, tasked with reinforcing the fragile social contract between the state and its citizens. The recent unrest has exposed vulnerabilities, but Dr. Francis Mading Deng always reminds us that where there is a crisis, there is also opportunity. Engaging groups like the White Army and *Gelweng* in constructive, community-oriented projects offers a pathway to counteract dissent and foster trust.

Imagine a bustling scene where citizens unite around communal efforts in group ranching and sustainable farming. The fields of Nasir transformed into vibrant patches of collaboration and productivity, as former adversaries work side by side, herding cattle and cultivating not only crops but also a renewed sense of hope. In this collaborative landscape, citizens begin to see the government not as an abstract entity but as a protector—a force committed to their welfare.

By investing in these cooperative initiatives, South Sudanese leaders can help dismantle the appeal of alternative power structures. When individuals feel the tangible support of their government and military, their reliance on armed groups tends to diminish. They will perceive a state that prioritizes their needs, a military that protects their lives and properties, and a community that promotes peace through collective purpose.

In this vision of the future, peace is fully realized not through the mere cessation of conflict but through society's active engagement in its own recovery and growth. Garang's enduring legacy challenges us all to embrace this reality: that forging a peaceful society requires constant effort, dedication, and a shared investment in the human spirit. As nations reckon with their histories, let South Sudan be a testament to the transformative power of development in the service of lasting peace.

In conclusion, John Garang's idea of peace through development remains a compelling and relevant philosophy for contemporary society. Investing in social equity, economic opportunity, and participatory governance can break the cycle of conflict, paving the way for a more peaceful and prosperous future. Garang's legacy serves as a reminder that development is not merely a means to an end but a foundational pillar upon which true and lasting peace can be built. In pursuit of a harmonious society, the imperative is clear: development is not just beneficial; it is essential.

5. Collegial Presidency

The idea of a collegial presidency was prominently integrated by the framers of the Revitalized Agreement on the Resolution of the

Conflict in South Sudan (R-ARCSS). Specifically, Article 1.5 outlines the organizational structure of the executive branch of the Revitalized Transitional Government of National Unity (RTGoNU). In contrast, Article 1.9 meticulously delineates the powers, functions, and responsibilities shared among the President, the First Vice President (FVP), and the four Vice Presidents (VPs). This structure emphasizes the necessity of continuous consultations and mutual agreements among these leaders. Article 1.9.1 articulates this collaborative governance framework clearly:

> *"The RTGoNU is founded on the premise that there shall be collegial collaboration in decision-making and continuous consultations within the Presidency, encompassing the President, the First Vice President, and the four Vice Presidents. This is essential for ensuring effective governance during the Transitional Period."* [25]

The adoption of a collegial approach among key leaders is not just a strategy; it is essential for fostering a collaborative environment where shared decision-making can truly flourish. In the context of Sudan and South Sudan, this cooperative model is not merely beneficial but crucial for the long-term stability and progress of the two Sudanese nations.

However, the stark reality remains that both countries have experienced the severe ramifications of power struggles. These conflicts not only disrupt the collaborative spirit needed for effective governance but also actively undermine the very foundation of collective leadership.

---

25   See page 12 of the Revitalized Agreement on the Resolution of the Conflict in the Republic of South Sudan, Addis Ababa, Ethiopia, 12 September 2018

When leaders become enmeshed in rivalries, it creates an environment of distrust, division, and inefficiency. As a result, fragmentation within the government occurs, crippling its capacity to function optimally.

This fragmentation has profound implications for the populace, as critical issues—such as security, infrastructure, agriculture, and healthcare—go unaddressed. The pressing needs of the citizens are overshadowed by the pursuit of power and control, leading to a cycle of neglect and disillusionment. To break free from these detrimental patterns, leaders in both Sudan and South Sudan must embrace a collaborative ethos, prioritizing the needs of the people over personal ambitions. Only then can they establish a government capable of addressing the myriad challenges they face and fostering a brighter future for all.

Furthermore, it is crucial to establish robust conflict resolution frameworks within the leadership structures to foster a more productive and harmonious leadership dynamic. Such frameworks can provide clear protocols for addressing disputes and promote a culture of collaboration and understanding. Additionally, equipping leaders with negotiation and mediation skills through targeted training programs can significantly mitigate the rivalries that may emerge. This proactive approach can enhance unity among leaders, ultimately leading to a more stable and effective governance system during the challenging Transitional Period.

6. Sudan Would Never Be the Same Again

This acknowledges the irreversible changes in political and social structures caused by conflict. Sudan's breakup into two nations showcases the lasting impact of civil strife.

Sudan would never be the same again, and this truth is underscored by the profound and irreversible changes that civil strife has wrought on its political and social fabric. The breakup of Sudan into two countries – Sudan and South Sudan - is a stark evidence of the enduring consequences that conflict can unleash, reshaping identities and power dynamics in ways that resonate for generations. In light of this reality, it is paramount that we adopt a new perspective on governance—one that emphasizes adaptability and evolution. By embracing a model of adaptive governance, we can create institutions that are flexible enough to respond to the intricate socio-political landscape that emerges from such transformative upheaval.

The ongoing conflict between the Sudan Armed Forces (SAF) and the rebel Rapid Support Forces (RSF) further complicates an already fragile situation in Sudan. With the potential for the violence to escalate, there are concerns that the country could face additional fragmentation. The historical context of Sudan's breakup into two countries illustrates how internal conflict can alter the geopolitical landscape dramatically. If the current violence continues unchecked, it is plausible that regions within Sudan might seek greater autonomy or independence, leading to the emergence of new national entities.

John Garang's vision, which emphasized public service and a comprehensive approach to governance, can serve as a guiding framework for Sudan and South Sudan during this tumultuous period. Garang advocated for a political solution that encompassed inclusivity and respect for diverse identities. By revisiting Garang's ideals, both countries could promote dialogue and reconciliation among varying factions, addressing grievances that have historically fueled conflict.

Furthermore, Garang's emphasis on building strong, accountable institutions can be pivotal. For Sudan, creating a governance model that is responsive and adaptable to the ongoing changes can mitigate the risks of further division. For South Sudan, embracing these principles could foster stability and strengthen ties with its northern neighbor. Collaboration between the two countries, guided by shared interests and mutual respect, could lay the foundation for regional peace and sustainable development.

While the risk of further fragmentation remains a legitimate concern, adaptive governance and Garang's vision of unity, underpinned by political morality, can help both Sudan and South Sudan aspire to restore peace within their borders. It can also cultivate harmonious relationships with neighboring countries.

This approach not only acknowledges the complexities of our new reality but also fosters resilience within our institutions, allowing them to thrive amidst challenges. As we look to the future, it is essential to recognize that while the past has indelibly changed Sudan, reforming institutions and strengthening governance structures can evolve to meet these new demands, ultimately paving the way for a more stable and prosperous society. John Garang has provided the path-goal strategic plan, and what is required is for the leaders of the two Sudans to implement it to avoid further fragmentation and disintegration.

Our governance structures are not static; they are dynamic frameworks capable of transformation to meet the pressing demands of today – the quest for a developmental state erected on political morality, resilient institutions, and the rule of law. By embracing adaptability and innovation, we can create systems that are not only functional but also responsive to the aspirations of our diverse populace. This evolution is crucial not just for overcoming the immediate crises at hand but for laying the groundwork for a stable and prosperous society in both countries.

Indeed, as we look toward the future, we must harness the potential of our reformulated institutions as agents of change. A commitment to robust governance, transparency, and inclusive participation will cultivate an environment where citizens feel empowered and invested in their collective destiny. When the voices of the people are recognized and embraced, the path to sustainable peace, economic growth, and poverty eradication becomes clearer.

Moreover, fostering resilience within our governance structures sets a powerful precedent. It signals to national and international observers that the two Sudans are not defined solely by their respective challenges but also by their unwavering commitment to growth and renewal. By proactively addressing weaknesses in our governance, we can build a foundation of trust and integrity that enhances the social contract between the government and its citizens. For South Sudan, the quest for a developmental state is imperative for achieving the noble objectives of the liberation struggle.

Ultimately, this transformative journey, driven by the ideas and vision of John Garang, is not just a response to our historical challenges; it is a bold affirmation of our commitment to creating a brighter future. The potential for a stable, prosperous society is within our grasp, and we must act decisively to achieve it. Let us work together to reshape our institutions and governance frameworks, ensuring they are resilient, responsive, and reflect the values we cherish. Together, we can lay the foundation for a thriving South Sudan, where every citizen has the chance to contribute to and benefit from a shared vision of progress.

7. You Must Finish What You Set Out to Do

John Garang's philosophy firmly emphasized the importance of commitment and perseverance in the pursuit of political and social goals. He believed that once a vision or mission is established, it is paramount to see it through to completion. This tenacity is especially crucial in the context of countries like Sudan and South Sudan, which have faced significant challenges and disruptions.

Garang championed a holistic approach to governance that prioritizes inclusivity and honors society's myriad identities. He believed that true progress could only be achieved by embracing diversity and ensuring that all voices are represented in decision-making processes. Central to his vision was the imperative for leaders to remain resolute in their commitments, navigating challenges and barriers to bring about meaningful and sustainable change.

Dr. John's emphasis on perseverance and follow-through in governance is particularly relevant when examining Sudan's historical context, especially during its transitional periods. The ousting of Omar al-Bashir in 2019 marked a pivotal moment in Sudan's history, as millions of citizens rallied for change after decades of authoritarian rule. The transitional government that emerged faced immense challenges, including economic crises, ethnic tensions, and lingering security issues. During this period, leadership prioritized stability and institutional strength while engaging diverse communities and addressing their varied needs. There was a general agreement on the path-goal strategic plan.

However, the transitional government's commitment to this clear roadmap, which included reforms in governance and the establishment of a more inclusive political landscape, was quickly derailed. The consequence is the ongoing conflict between the Sudan Armed Forces (SAF) and the rebel Rapid Support Forces (RSF). Hence, the urgency for engaging with civil society and ensuring representation within the political framework opened channels for public participation, thus laying the groundwork for a resilient and cohesive nation.

Similarly, South Sudan's journey since its independence in 2011 highlights the severe consequences of leadership faltering on commitments. The civil conflict that erupted shortly after independence was exacerbated by a lack of consistent governance and failure to implement peace agreements. Leaders often fail to prioritize accountability, leading to deep mistrust and continued violence. The International Crisis Group lamented in its 2021 report that without steadfast dedication from leaders to uphold their promises, hopes for lasting peace collapsed, plunging the country further into chaos. This cycle of broken promises and lack of commitment to governance illustrates the critical need for unity and perseverance in leadership to build a sustainable future.

Examining other African contexts, Rwanda's recovery after the 1994 genocide provides a compelling example of the transformative power of committed leadership. The Rwandan government's unwavering resolve to implement developmental initiatives—such as enhancing education, infrastructure, and reconciliation—has propelled the nation to remarkable economic growth and stability. This determination not only rebuilt trust but also inspired collective national efforts toward resilience and unity, cementing Rwanda's position as one of Africa's fastest-growing economies.

Globally, Germany's post-World War II experience further emphasizes the importance of perseverance in governance. The implementation of the Marshall Plan, aimed at rebuilding the war-torn economy and infrastructure, was characterized by a long-term commitment to recovery. This steady course of action facilitated Germany's emergence as a leading economic power in Europe, underscoring that consistency and dedication in governance can yield extraordinary outcomes.

These historical examples—from Sudan and South Sudan to Rwanda and Germany—demonstrate that enduring commitment is essential in fostering trust among the populace and ensuring sustainable development. Leaders in these contexts who emphasize perseverance and follow through on their initiatives create a sense of shared purpose, guiding their communities toward resilience amid governance challenges. Ultimately, the legacy of stability and growth hinges on leaders' ability to see through their commitments, reflecting John Garang's vision for effective governance.

By maintaining a steadfast course, whether in Sudan, South Sudan, or elsewhere, leaders can foster trust among the populace and inspire a collective sense of purpose. This ultimately steers their communities toward resilience and sustainable development, setting an example for others to follow. Such an enduring commitment is essential in creating a legacy of stability and growth amid the challenges of governance

In light of the preceding narratives, leaders in Sudan and South Sudan are called upon to embrace Garang's ideals by committing themselves to the long-term vision of peace, stability, and prosperity. By upholding this principle, they can work toward bridging divides within their respective countries, mitigating conflicts, and ultimately fulfilling the hopes and aspirations of their citizens. In doing so, they honor his legacy and create a sustainable pathway for the future of both nations.

8. Taking Towns to the People in Rural Areas

It is payback time! This phrase resonated deeply with the thousands of New Sudanese who warmly welcomed Dr. John during his month-long tour across the five regions of New Sudan in June and July of 2004. During these gatherings, he seized the opportunity to convey vital messages of peace and reconciliation to the masses. Dr. John articulated the six protocols of the Comprehensive Peace Agreement (CPA), taking the time to apologize on behalf of the Sudan People's Liberation Movement/Army (SPLM/A) for the hardships endured by the people during the two decades of the liberation struggle. His heartfelt commitment to this cause reflected a genuine belief that it was time to compensate all who had participated in the war of liberation in various capacities.

At the core of his vision was a sustainable development package that primarily focused on rural development, underscoring the importance of uplifting the communities most affected by conflict. Complementary to this vision was Dr. John's passionate advocacy for agriculture as the driving force behind the nation's economy during its early stages of development. He emphasized that agriculture as an engine of the economy could be effectively powered by the country's oil revenues, which should be strategically invested in building the necessary infrastructure to support agricultural productivity and rural livelihoods.

He wanted to take towns to the people in the rural areas of Sudan, then and of the two Sudans now. Food security is the binding framework of Dr. John's two ideas: taking towns to the rural areas and making agriculture the engine of our economy in the early stages of development and state-building.

Dr. John had passionate and professional convictions about rural development. Several factors - he was born and brought up in rural Southern Sudan, attended high school in rural Tanzania of Julius Nyerere, and finished college education (Bachelor of Arts, Master of Science, and Doctor of Philosophy, all three degrees in economics) in the American Midwest - had a cumulative effect on Dr. John in the development of this idea of taking cities to the rural areas. Madam Rebecca Nyandeng de Mabior (widow of John Garang de Mabior) successfully applied this idea during the liberation war. She built a mini-rural city popularly known then as New Site in the heart of Tapoza land in Kapoeta County of Eastern Equatoria State.

The New Site provided an intellectual sanctuary for the SPLM leadership and peace talk teams during the critical days of the Sudan peace process (2002- 2005). Some of us were proud of this model, which enhanced our image as people who could develop and manage their own development. The New Site has been abandoned, but we hope it can be recreated as one of the historical sites of the liberation struggle.

How do you take cities to rural areas? The founding father of the SPLM and New Sudan was not thinking about the *Ujamaa* model, which he studied in the early 1970s. The pattern of traditional human settlement in most of rural Southern Sudan was not to be tampered with. Instead, a rural city is expected to grow and develop through the provision of basic social services and core economic infrastructure. The people would come to these services at their convenience during the day and return to their homesteads at the end of the day. The challenge lies in designing feeder roads to facilitate the movement of people, goods, and services between homesteads and rural cities. This rural city was to start initially as a community resource center at every *Payam*[33] with the following six facilities/blocks:

1. An administration complex that houses the *Payam* government, executive, legislature, and judiciary, including traditional chief courts.
2. Education complex, including schools and vocational training facilities for various trades such as bricklaying, blacksmithing, carpentry, and plumbing.
3. Primary healthcare complex, including public toilet facilities, potable water, and other essential amenities.
4. A cultural complex, including sports facilities, a theater, and a TV viewing/video hall, would also be used for town/village hall meetings and other civic/community activities.
5. The agricultural complex comprises crop and veterinary extension services, as well as a refrigerated mobile dairy unit.

6. The economic complex comprises a microcredit clinic (or village bank), a shopping center, a village cybercafé, telephony services, a small business development unit, a telecommunications unit (including Starlink and VSAT), a solar/windmill power station, and a water supply facility.

Taking towns to rural areas was one of the projects included on the list of programs to be initiated during the first 180 days of John Garang de Mabior's presidency of Southern Sudan.[34] We then assumed the total number of *Payams* to be one thousand, including those in Abyei, Nuba Mountains, and Funj. The GoSS was to make an initial contribution of $250,000 to jump-start the six components of a typical community resource center in each of the 1,000 *Payams*. This would translate to $250 million, approximately one-fourth of the projected share ($1.1 billion) for GoSS from oil revenues in 2005. By way of illustration:

1. The initial capital for a microcredit scheme was to be
2. $10,000
3. A TV satellite dish and a hall for $5,000
4. A solar energy set for $40,000
5. A hand-operated water pump for $10,000
6. A brickmaking machine for $15,000
7. A primary healthcare facility for $50,000
8. A four-classroom building for $50,000
9. A VSAT for $10,000
10. An administration block for $30,000
11. An agricultural complex for $30,000

The communities were expected to shoulder operating costs, provide labor, and offer other vital in-kind contributions, showcasing their dedication to sustainable growth. The beneficiary communities' commitment to actively engaging in their development is not just a necessity but a powerful testament to their resilience and determination. However, this effort was not meant to stand alone. We recognized then the vital role played by nongovernmental organizations (NGOs), United Nations (UN) agencies, and the international donor community, who were eager to invest in rural development schemes.

The Government of Southern Sudan (GoSS) was tasked with coordinating these generous contributions through a coherent framework anchored in Dr. John's two key ideas: bringing towns to the people in rural areas and making agriculture the engine of the economy.

This vision of communal compensation through 'payback-time' schemes was precisely the transformative approach envisioned to commence with the start of the Interim Period stipulated by the CPA. The strategy was to pave the way toward sustainable peace, economic growth, and poverty eradication by harnessing the strengths of both local communities and international partners. The initiative was not just about financial assistance; it was about inspiring a culture of collaboration and shared responsibility, ensuring that the benefits of development truly resonate within the heart of our communities. The silent motto was: Together, we can build a brighter, more equitable future for all.

The Revitalized Transitional Government of National Unity (RTGoNU), led by the SPLM, took two decades to revisit and embrace these critical ideas. In a landmark move, the RTGoNU allocated 11.9 percent of the FY2024/2025 budget, amounting to around SSP250 billion, for public investment in the agricultural sector. Several compelling factors drove the push to revive this vision, but we will highlight only one.

The SPLM was preparing for general elections, which were

anticipated to take place at the end of the transition period in December 2024. This necessitated that some of us revisit several of the SPLM's programs and ideas formulated toward the end of the war of liberation. Our point of departure was to ask: **Where is the compass of our political morality after the war of liberation?** This is one of the foundational questions we sought to answer before launching a new program for the upcoming elections.

Our country, we stressed, is facing a food crisis in a land of abundant resources (e.g., land, water, etc.). This is mainly due to greed and selfishness, underpinned by arrogance and ignorance, in the management of these resources. Therefore, the leadership decided to revisit the two ideas with food security as a binding framework for achieving the objectives of sustainable peace, economic growth, and poverty eradication. This strategic focus on agriculture, underpinned by political morality, would reduce our people's reliance on international humanitarian assistance and restore their human dignity. It would also make us realize the potential of becoming the breadbasket of Africa.

As Professor Bromley reminds us, **"Gifting is bad for the soul over the long run. It creates dependence on the part of the recipient, and dependence is always accompanied by a loss of self-esteem."** [26] We can contextualize Professor Bromley's advice in that South Sudan's total surface area is approximately 644,329 square kilometers, with a population of 12.5 million.

Yet, statistics reveal a stark reality: only about 4 percent of arable land is utilized for agricultural production. That is, around 573,300

---

26   Cited from "Toward sustainable livelihoods in South Sudan: the necessary institutions of governance" a paper by Daniel W. Bromley presented at the conference **"A New Start For South Sudan: Building Resilient Institutions and Effective Governance"** held in Juba, Republic of South Sudan, February 13-15, 2014, organized by the World Bank and Ebony Center for Strategic Studies

square kilometers—or about 89 percent of the surface area is suitable for cultivation, yet only 4 percent of this vast potential is used. To fully appreciate this potential, one must consider the country's diverse agroecological zones, each offering unique advantages for agricultural activities. Researchers have identified seven main ecological zones in South Sudan:[27]

1. **The Ironstone Plateau**: This zone covers much of Bahr el-Ghazal, west of the River Nile, and is characterized by its iron-rich soil.
2. **The Central Hills**: Located along the Nile, north of the Green Belt, these hills offer diverse agriculture opportunities due to their varied topography.
3. **The Green Belt**: Encompassing the southern regions of Eastern Equatoria, Central Equatoria, and the western parts of Western Equatoria, this area benefits from two rainy seasons and has the most fertile arable land in the country.
4. **The Imatong Mountains**: Situated along the Uganda border, this zone offers unique microclimates that can support various crops.
5. **The Flood Plains**: These areas, including the vast Sudd region, are critical for aquatic and semi-aquatic agricultural practices.
6. **The Nile-Sobat Corridor**: This zone, along the banks of the River Sobat from Ethiopia, is vital for irrigating and transporting agricultural products.
7. **The Semi-Desert Area**: Found in the extreme southeast, this area poses challenges for agriculture but may be suitable for drought-resistant crops.

---

[27] See for instance, Michael Roberto Kenyi Legge and Betty Achan Ogwaro: Revitalizing Agriculture and Local Economic Integration, a paper presented to the First National Economic Conference, 4 – 8 September 2023, Juba, South Sudan

By strategically tapping into these ecological zones and prioritizing investment in infrastructure and sustainable practices, South Sudan could significantly enhance its agricultural production, promote food security, and foster economic development in rural areas. Dr. John's vision, rooted in reconciliation and commitment to progress, remains a beacon of hope for the future of agricultural development in South Sudan. This is because in the vast land of South Sudan lies a profound opportunity to transform the lives of millions of rural households through a sustainable homestead model. This progressive approach facilitates a crucial shift toward food security and economic self-sufficiency.

The sustainable homestead model is more than just a theoretical construct; it is a call to action that resonates deeply within the fabric of South Sudanese society. By empowering smallholder farmers, the government is addressing food insecurity and actively participating in creating resilient communities capable of thriving in an evolving agricultural landscape. Through unity, innovation, and sustained investment, the government can revitalize the two ideas of taking towns to the rural areas and of making agriculture the engine of economic growth and sustainable livelihoods.

The sustainable homestead model aims to enhance agricultural productivity in South Sudan significantly. Ambitious targets include increasing cereal yields from the current 454 kilograms (kg) per feddan to a remarkable 1,000 kg per feddan. Achieving this dramatic increase is not just an aspirational target but a concrete goal that necessitates urgent and decisive government action. The time to initiate this transformative process is now.

In response to these pressing needs, the government announced in January 2024 a comprehensive restructuring of the Agricultural Bank of South Sudan (ABSS), recognizing it as the most fitting institution to spearhead the implementation of the sustainable homestead model. A new Board of Directors was appointed, composed of members who thoroughly understand two pivotal concepts: bringing urban resources and services to rural populations and positioning agriculture as the cornerstone of economic growth and sustainable livelihoods within the nation.

To bolster the bank's efforts, the new Board has prioritized not only the capitalization of the institution but also the initiation of a pilot project founded on the Community-Public-Private Partnership (CPPP) framework. This innovative strategy empowers farming households by encouraging them to form cooperatives. By pooling their resources, such as sharing access to tractor services and other essential agricultural equipment, these cooperatives can operate more efficiently within a well-structured supply chain focused on value addition.

The rationale for implementing the CPPP framework stems from the fact that South Sudan has an abundant agricultural land resource, with 136.5 million feddans deemed suitable for cultivation; alarmingly, only a mere 4 percent of this land, as mentioned earlier, is currently being utilized. By harnessing these underutilized resources and promoting cooperative farming through the CPPP model, the government aims to stimulate economic growth, improve food security, and enhance the livelihoods of rural communities nationwide. This strategic initiative represents a pivotal step toward realizing the agricultural potential of South Sudan and fostering a more sustainable future for its people.

The investment model strategically prioritizes the traditional farming subsector, emphasizing its critical role in enhancing food security and promoting sustainable livelihoods. Approximately 60 percent of South Sudan's households, or 1.2 million households, are primarily engaged in subsistence agriculture, cultivating approximately 2.6

million feddans. These farms currently yield an average of 454 kilograms of cereal per feddan, highlighting the potential for increased productivity through targeted support and organization.

The model encourages the formation of farming households into clusters or cooperatives to enhance farming efficiency and facilitate effective communal resource management. Each household is envisaged to be allocated ten feddans of communal land, resulting in a substantial total allocation of around 12 million feddans dedicated to the 1.2 million farming households nationwide. Therefore, these households will be sustainable homesteads that are food self-sufficient and ready to supply their surplus to the market.

As a pilot initiative, a Community-Public-Private-Partnership (CPPP) framework will be established, initially involving a community of 1,000 sustainable and self-sufficient homesteads, encompassing 10,000 feddans of land. In addition, the scheme will include an extra 1,000 feddans earmarked for shared facilities and resources that cater to the broader needs of the farming community. These facilities will encompass essential services, including agricultural extension programs, demonstration farms showcasing innovative practices, storage facilities for crops, educational institutions, community governance centers, business hubs, artificial lakes for irrigation and aquaculture, industrial parks, rural electrification stations, and recreational sports facilities.

A distinguishing feature of the CPPP framework will be the establishment of a Rural Agro-Mechanical Tractor Hire Center (RAMC). This center will have five 75-horsepower tractors and a dedicated workshop, capable of cultivating at least 10,000 feddans per season. The RAMC will not only serve the communities involved in the CPPP but will also offer tractor services on a hire basis to traditional farming households opting out of the scheme. To ensure financial sustainability and recoverability, the investment in these tractors will be structured to cover operating costs fully, thus providing continued support for agricultural productivity and efficiency in the country.

The ABSS will establish a Joint Farm Management (JFM) entity to ensure the sustainability and effectiveness of utilizing the tractors underpinning the CPPP development model. This management body will consist of representatives from ABSS, the Military Production Unit (MPU)—referred to as "Tiger" in the initial CPPP scheme—along with local or state entities and community stakeholders. The JFM will be structured to promote collaboration among these key stakeholders, facilitating effective decision-making and resource allocation processes in a transparent and accountable manner.

ABSS will be responsible for appointing a qualified Farm Manager. The JFM will be led by a specialized team representing the interests of each of the three primary parties involved. This approach will require the Agricultural Bank of South Sudan (ABSS) to exercise creativity and innovation. To this end, the Bank will strategically tailor and enhance specific operational frameworks that have been successfully used in the oil and gas sector, adapting these models specifically for the agricultural domain.

Two well-established frameworks—the Exploration and Production Sharing Agreement (EPSA) and the Production Sharing Contract (PSC)—are used in the oil and gas sector. These models have demonstrated their efficacy in overseeing intricate and capital-intensive projects within the industry. By incorporating their principles into agricultural initiatives, the Bank can significantly improve its operational efficiency and overall project management of the CPPP schemes.

Adopting these contractual arrangements is intended to expedite the implementation process of the President's policy directives while safeguarding the Bank's interests. By utilizing the EPSA and PSC frameworks, the Bank aims to mitigate risks associated with operations, thereby reducing potential financial vulnerabilities and enhancing its operational resilience. This path-goal strategy will ensure that the Bank's initiatives are aligned with the government's objectives of cost recovery associated with the tractors and strengthen the Bank's position in becoming a robust development bank for the agricultural sector of our economy.

The PSC will meticulously outline the methodologies for calculating production costs associated with both capital expenditures and operational expenses, detailing how these costs will be deducted from the total revenue generated. Furthermore, the PSC will establish protocols for profit-sharing among stakeholders, ensuring transparency and fairness.

Through these carefully designed initiatives, the model aims to transform South Sudan's agricultural landscape, ensuring that farming communities are equipped to thrive while contributing to national food security objectives. More importantly, the model is a strategic approach toward taking towns to the people in the rural areas and making agriculture the engine of economic growth and sustainable livelihoods.

9. Poverty Is a Function of Marginalization

Dr. John saw poverty and the sense of marginalization as two faces of the same coin. Marginalization deepens poverty and exacerbates conflict dynamics. Disenfranchised groups in the two Sudans often lack access to resources and opportunities, which public policy must tackle through strategies that recognize this reality. By way of illustration, the SPLM and GoS were preparing a joint concept note on an Interim Poverty Reduction Strategy Paper (IPRSP) for Sudan in October 2004 when Dr. John instructed the SPLM team to persuade the workshop participants to adopt a joint national document under the name of Poverty Eradication Strategy Paper (PESP) instead of PRSP.

We did succeed. We based our approach on a three-phase strategy. Poverty alleviation is possible in the short term through a combination of operational measures that lay the foundation for tackling this age-old problem in the subsequent phases. The second phase, the medium term, is where poverty reduction strategies are applied. The final phase - long term - is the stage at which we, according to Anver Versi, "**harness our anger, our rage, our indignation, our hurt pride and direct it against the real enemies of our people: hunger, lack of clean water, disease and poverty**" (Anver Versi 2006, 13). The enemy of our people is underdevelopment, which manifests in four key dimensions: poverty, hunger, a lack of clean water, and disease.

Our firm conviction that our people can break out of the vicious cycle of underdevelopment if we acquire analytical tools embedded in the theory and practice of development influenced our return to school to pursue graduate degrees. For instance, the famine that struck the Horn of Africa in the early 1980s reinforced our professional conviction that poverty could be eradicated. Dr. John was at the final stage of his doctoral dissertation while I began my graduate studies in development economics. Hence, our minds were still fresh with ideas of the theory and practice of development. Dr. John returned to Sudan in February 1982, having obtained his doctorate in economics in December 1981.

The CPA created an enabling policy environment for the Sudanese leaders to address some of the consequences of the long and devastating civil conflict. Among these is pervasive poverty, which Dr. John conceptualized as a function of both marginalization and a sense of exclusion, prevailing throughout what was then Sudan. Dr. John envisioned that one of the cornerstones of the post-conflict economic recovery and development program would be to combat poverty and the sense of marginalization throughout the country. We referred to this as *Garangnomics*. This idea informs the post-conflict recovery program's key triple objectives: sustainable peace, economic growth, and poverty eradication.

Dr. John never liked the concept of poverty reduction, which he considered a defeatist approach. He said poverty eradication was possible in the post-conflict period, especially in light of Sudan's natural resource endowments (oil, water, and arable land). We shared this professional conviction with him and many other Sudanese economists.[28]

So, we were obliged to formulate a framework that differentiates between the three concepts of addressing poverty. We initiated a policy matrix as the most appropriate framework for tackling poverty. This was then the basis of the SPLM concept note on poverty eradication strategy (PES) with three strategic objectives corresponding to near-, medium-, and long-term development strategies. That is, the strategic objectives of the PES were to alleviate poverty in the near term (ranging from twelve to thirty-six months), reduce poverty in the medium term (ranging from thirty-six to seventy-two months), and eradicate extreme poverty by 2015, consistent with the Millennium Development Goals (MDGs).

These strategic objectives were to be within the post-conflict recovery and development framework. Hence, our approach to poverty

---

28   These were lead Sudanese economists like Professor Ali Abdel Gadir Ali of the Arab Planning Institute; Dr. Ibrahim Elbadawi of the World Bank (then); Professor Tahir Nur of Khartoum University; Professor Yongo Buro of Ketting University (United States); Professor Rashid Hassan of Environmental Economics and Policy Center for Africa in Pretoria, South Africa; Dr. Abdalla Hamduk with the Governance Center for Africa in Pretoria, South Africa (then); and so forth.

eradication was premised on a sound post-conflict recovery and reconstruction program, formulated with the triple objectives of achieving sustainable peace, promoting economic growth, and eradicating poverty.

We proposed broad policy measures to achieve the strategic objectives of PES, in light of the triple objectives of the SPLM approach to poverty eradication. These were categorized into three broad policy areas for strategic intervention, which we reproduced in a policy matrix format as Dr. John envisioned. The Policy matrix was a critical analytical tool through which Dr. John intended to tackle the underlying causes of poverty in Sudan, such as exclusion in all its dimensions and forms. The underlying premise here was his call for agriculture to be the engine of growth of the Sudan economy, propelled by the newfound oil.

During those days, the sky was the limit to our aspirations to liberate our people from marginalization and eliminate abject poverty.

SPLM Poverty Eradication Policy Matrix

Strategic Policy Measures	Strategic Objectives:		
	Alleviate Poverty (AP)	Reduce Poverty (RP)	Eradicate Poverty (EP)
1.0: Better governance[29] 1.1: Empowerment and social inclusion 1.2: Peace building and reconciliation 1.3: Effective administration of justice	1.2.1: Improve governance by incorporating ex-eluded groups in the traditions and institutions by which authority is exercised in the Sudan. 1.2.2: Create an enabling policy environment for the poor to reestablish their social capital through networks of civic/communal engagement.	1.3.1: Establish an inclusive political process through which all Sudanese citizens participate in the selection (appointment and removal) of governments without resorting to violent and/or unconstitutional methods. 1.3.2: Allow freedom to develop ideas/views, institutions, and personal autonomy apart from the state..	1.4.1: Ensure free religious institutions and private/ public religious expressions and protect the separation of state from the church/mosque. 1.4.2: Ensure gender equality, property rights, including communal land ownership, freedom of movement, choice of residence, choice of marriage, and size of family.

---

29   Daniel Kafumann et al. (2003) define governance as the "traditions and institutions by which authority in a country is exercised."

	1.2.3: Establish peace and reconciliation committees in all the counties. 1.2.4: Establish police units in all the counties.	1.3.3: Give full political rights to enable the poor to effectively participate freely in the Sudanese political process 1.3.4: Provide guarantees for full independence of the media. 1.3.5: Establish peace and reconciliation committees in all thePayams. 1.3.6: Establish police units in all thePayams.	1.4.3: Guarantee equality of opportunity, including freedom from exploitation, slavery, or dependency on landlords, employers, and so forth. 1.4.4: Establish peace and reconciliation committees in all the Bomas. 1.4.5: Establish police units in all the Bomas.

2.0: Macroeconomic measures 2.1: Fiscal measures 2.2: Monetary measures	2.1: Establish a social security system (for example, food stamps) for the poorest of the poor. 2.2: Establish a poverty eradication fund. 2.3: Establish pilot community-based microcredit institutions. 2.4: Formulate a pro-poor macroeconomic policy framework that ensures macroeconomic stability in the context of sustained peace.	3.1: Expand social security system to cover 60 percent of the poor. 3.2: Expand microcredit institutions to all the Payams and transfer full ownership and management to the beneficiaries. 3.3: Maintain a pro-poor macroeconomic policy framework that ensures macroeconomic stability in the context of sustained peace.	4.1: Provide social security to support all the citizens. 4.2: Establish microcredit to be managed by the beneficiaries themselves in all the Bomas. 4.3: Maintain a pro-poor macroeconomic policy framework that ensures macroeconomic stability in the context of sustained peace.

3.0: Sectoral measures	3.2: Support development of sustainable homestead model in randomly selected counties on pilot basis.	3.3: Implement sustainable homestead model in fifty counties.	3.4: Implement sustainable homestead model in all Payams.
3.1: Agriculture (livestock, forestry, fishery, and wildlife) 3.2: Infrastructure 3.2: Education 3.4: Health 3.5: Environmental protection	3.1.2: Establish community resource centers (CRCs) in fifty counties to provide agriculture extension services. 2.6: Support establishment of mobile veterinary clinics for pastoral communities. 2.7: Rehabilitate three thousand kilometers of roads that have direct impact on the poor. 2.8: Establish accelerated learning centers/facilities for adult education in all the counties. 2.9: Support the establishment of primary schools in all the Payams.	3.1.3: Expand CRCs, when successful, to all the counties. 3.5: Enhance regulatory frameworks for livestock markets. 3.6: Encourage development of livestock cooperative groups. 3.7: Encourage development of fishery cooperatives. 3.8: Support development of cooperative groups in establishing solar/wind-generating rural electricity in a sample of Payams. 3.9: Expand adult education centers to all the Payams.	3.1.4: Establish CRCs in all the Payams. 4.5: Enhance institutional capacities of the poor to manage forestry, fishery, and wildlife more sustainably. 4.6: Ensure access to power and telecommunication systems for all the population. 4.7: Establish distance learning centers in all the counties with the view to eliminate adult illiteracy rate.

	2.10: Establish vocational training centers in all the counties.	3.10: Establish primary schools in every Boma to achieve universal and compulsory primary education by the end of the interim period of the peace agreement.	4.8: Support the establishment of secondary schools in all thePayams.
	2.11: Support communities to establish a primary health care unit (PHCU) in every Payam.		4.9: Establish states universities/ colleges in all the states.
	2.12: Rehabilitate all the county hospitals.	3.11: Support communities to establish a PHCC in all the counties.	4.10: Support communities to establish maternal and child health centers (MCH) in all the counties.
	2.13: Assist states and counties to establish a primary health care center (PHCC) in all the counties and a select sample of Payams.	3.12: Assist states and counties to establish rural hospitals in a select sample of Payams.	4.11: Assist states and counties to establish rural hospitals in all the Payams.
	2.14: Ensure all development projects/ programs are environmentally sustainable and socially acceptable.	3.13: Ensure all development projects/ programs are environmentally sustainable and socially acceptable.	4.12: Ensure all development projects/ programs are environmentally sustainable and socially acceptable.

Targeted, inclusive policies that actively promote the economic and political inclusion of marginalized groups are essential for addressing the root causes of poverty. By focusing on empowering local communities through comprehensive capacity-building initiatives, we can create systems that are not only more equitable but also more resilient.

In line with this vision, the government has recently launched a strategic approach to food security, as outlined under idea number 8. This initiative aims to combat the interconnected challenges of poverty and marginalization, recognizing that food security is a critical cornerstone for sustainable development.

Furthermore, the SPLM PEP Matrix must be effectively utilized in conjunction with two key strategies: the initiative to bring essential services and economic opportunities directly from urban centers to rural communities, and the goal of positioning agriculture as a pivotal engine for economic growth and sustainable livelihoods. By prioritizing these strategies, the government can enhance food sovereignty, foster community resilience, and ultimately uplift the living standards of marginalized populations.

10. The *Tamazuj* Zone

Dr. John articulated this idea at his first press conference as Sudan's First Vice President (FVP), which marked the end of the first two weeks at the Republican Palace in Khartoum.

One of the journalists asked Dr. John what he thought about the report of the Abyei Borders Commission (ABC) and whether Abyei was a place of *altimas* (tangency) between the Ngok Dinka and Museerya Arab. The FVP's response was strategic yet straightforward. Abyei is the hub of the *Tamazuj* zone between the North and South of the country. Dr. John later explained to some of us the concept of the *Tamazuj* zone as the backbone of a viable Sudanese state, at peace with itself in the event of unity, or two viable Sudanese states at peace with each other and within themselves in the event of the secession of Southern Sudan.

We must put the idea of the *Tamazuj* Zone in context before analyzing the conditions for two viable Sudanese states. There are four dimensions of this context: (a) geography, (b) history, (c) economics, and (d) social capital.

Geography

A 2,184-kilometer-long border is between the two countries, a reality that policymakers in Juba and Khartoum cannot ignore. The *Tamazuj* zone accounts for approximately 40 percent of the arable land in the two Sudans. About 40 percent of livestock is found here, and 100 percent of the oil produced in the two countries comes from here. About 37 percent of the population of the two Sudans (43 percent of South Sudan and 36 percent of Sudan) are in this zone (see Table 1). This is more than a border. It is the real backbone of the two Sudans (Greater Sudan). It should, therefore, be handled with care, not only by the two Sudanese states but also by their immediate neighbors and the African and Arab worlds.

Hence, promoting intercommunal dialogue and cultural exchanges in the *Tamazuj* Zone is urgent. Such a dialogue would foster understanding and mitigate future conflicts. Celebrating diversity while finding common ground offers a pathway to coexistence.

Resolving border issues represents a critical and progressive approach to addressing the longstanding territorial disputes that have long troubled relations between South Sudan and Sudan. The two countries can foster a mutual understanding and a climate of cooperation through diplomatic engagement that prioritizes peaceful negotiation over conflict. Dialogue, as the cornerstone of this strategy, provides a platform for open communication, enabling the two countries to achieve the goal of two viable Sudanese States at peace with each other and within themselves.

Constructive engagement through diplomatic channels is essential to addressing and resolving the complex issues surrounding border demarcation, the Abyei referendum, and regional stability. This process requires sustained commitment, patience, and the unwavering support of the international community. Ensuring that all voices are heard, especially those of local communities in the *Tamazuj* zone directly impacted by border uncertainty, is paramount to achieving a comprehensive and enduring settlement.

Resorting to international legal frameworks and precedents, and facilitating discussions with experienced mediators, can further guide the talks toward a resolution that respects South Sudan's sovereignty and territorial integrity, while promoting regional harmony. Leveraging the principles of international law and conflict resolution, Juba and Khartoum can work toward delineating legally recognized and geographically sensible borders.

Table 1: Population and Land Area of the *Tamazuj* Zone States

State (South Sudan)	Population	Area (Square Kms)
Upper Nile	964,363	77,283
Unity	585,801	37,837
Warrap	972,928	45,567
Northern Bahr El Ghazel	720,898	30,543
Western Bahr El Ghazel	333,431	91,076
South Sudan	3,577,421	282,307
Blue Nile	832,112	45,844
Sennar	1,285,058	37,844
White Nile	1,730,588	30,411

Southern Kordofan	1,406,404	155,000
Southern Darfur	4,093,595	127,300
Sudan	9,347,757	396,399

Source: Constructed by the author from the 2008 population census of Sudan

The *Tamazuj* zone, which spans a 2,184-kilometer common border, is more than just a boundary; it links ten states, five on each side. On the Sudanese side (the new southern Sudan), the states are Blue Nile, Sennar, White Nile, Southern Kordofan, and Southern Darfur. Corresponding states on the South Sudan side (northern South Sudan) include Upper Nile, Unity (Western Upper Nile), Warrap, Northern Bahr el-Ghazal, and Western Bahr el-Ghazal.

Geography plays a pivotal role in shaping the economic development of both Sudans, and the case for the *Tamazuj* zone highlights its strategic importance. *Tamazuj*, spanning a region that includes parts of South Sudan and Sudan, presents unique opportunities that can leverage South Sudan's geographical situation to foster growth and stability.

Firstly, South Sudan, a landlocked country, faces significant challenges in accessing global markets. The *Tamazuj* zone, which constitutes 40.4 percent of its total land boundary, serves as a potential trade corridor connecting South Sudan with Sudan. Establishing robust trade relationships within the *Tamazuj* zone can enhance economic cooperation and create mutually beneficial opportunities for both countries.

Moreover, the geographical diversity of the *Tamazuj* zone, characterized by agricultural potential and natural resources, can become a cornerstone for economic development. By fostering agriculture, livestock rearing, and trade in this region, South Sudan can not only achieve food security but also generate income and employment opportunities for its population.

Another crucial aspect is the potential for fostering peaceful coexistence in the *Tamazuj* zone. Given the historical tensions and complex dynamics between South Sudan and its northern neighbor, promoting dialogue and collaboration in this area can build a foundation for peace and stability. Encouraging shared economic initiatives in the *Tamazuj* zone can help mend relationships and create a sense of interdependence among the border communities of the two Sudans.

Furthermore, by prioritizing development initiatives and infrastructure projects within the *Tamazuj* zone, South Sudan can enhance transport networks and accessibility. This will facilitate trade and enable the movement of people, goods, and services, thereby stimulating economic activity and integration between the two countries. Investing in the *Tamazuj* zone is not just a matter of economic necessity; it's an essential step toward ensuring stability and growth for South Sudan and its northern neighbor, the Sudan.

History

The Nilotic group in South Sudan shares a rich and profound common heritage that can be traced back to the ancient kingdom of Kush, known for its remarkable contributions to the region's history and culture. This ancient civilization, as mentioned earlier, thrived along the banks of the Nile River and was renowned for its monumental architecture, sophisticated society, and advanced trade networks, which connected it with various cultures across Africa and beyond. The legacy of Kush has left an indelible mark on the identity of the Nilotic peoples, influencing their traditions, languages, and social structures.

In addition to this ancient lineage, a shared colonial legacy has significantly shaped the contemporary dynamics of Sudan and South Sudan. The periods of colonial rule introduced new political structures and social institutions that impacted both governance and the relationship between various ethnic groups. As a result, the historical context of colonialism has fostered a complex interplay of cultures, leading to a shared set of experiences and challenges among the peoples and communities within the *Tamazuj* zone. Today, this intertwined heritage and colonial influence continue to inform the societal institutions within this zone.

From local governance systems to communal practices, the legacy of the ancient kingdom of Kush, coupled with the lessons learned from colonial history, plays a crucial role in shaping the current identity and aspirations of the populations within this zone. Through a collective memory of shared struggles and triumphs, these groups/communities are united in their efforts to navigate the present while honoring their rich past.

Economics

The *Tamazuj* zone, which spans five states in South Sudan, is characterized by significant economic interdependence with Sudan, particularly in the supply of goods and services. Prior to the onset of the SAF-RSF conflict, a staggering 80 percent or more of these goods and services were sourced from Sudan, underscoring the intricate and often precarious economic ties between the two nations.

In the realm of oil production, the **Tamazuj zone** is crucial, as it accounts for the entirety of oil extraction for both Sudan and South Sudan. This region is vital not only for its abundant oil reserves but also for the infrastructure necessary to bring this resource to market. However, the mid- and downstream facilities, which encompass essential processes like refining and distribution of oil, are predominantly located in the Sudan.

The only notable exception is the Tharjath oil fields in block 5A, located within South Sudan, where some level of processing can occur. This reliance on neighboring Sudan for critical processing and distribution capabilities adds another layer of complexity and vulnerability to the economic landscape of the ***Tamazuj* zone**, particularly amidst ongoing conflicts.

Social Capital

In the Tamazuj zone, local communities exhibit a paradoxical yet significant form of social capital that plays a crucial role in their social dynamics. Despite occasional conflicts over grazing rights and land use, these communities have established and maintained relatively robust civic and communal engagement networks. The foundations of these connections are steeped in a rich historical context, rooted in centuries of interactions that cultivate a profound sense of unity, mutual support, and shared identity among the residents.

Renowned political scientist Robert Putnam asserts that social capital is fundamentally rooted in norms of reciprocity and trustworthiness, which form the foundation for effective cooperation (Putnam, 2000). Within the *Tamazuj* context, this social capital is manifested through the strong and enduring relationships between local leaders and their respective communities. This interconnectedness underscores their collective capacity to collaborate for the common good, revealing how social bonds can play a transformative role in conflict resolution and community resilience.

An illustrative example of this phenomenon is the partnership between Babo Nimir, the paramount chief of Musserya, and Deng Majok, the paramount chief of Ngok Dinka. Their collaboration is a compelling case study of how social capital can facilitate peaceful coexistence and cooperation among diverse communities. Through shared initiatives and dialogue, they demonstrate that it is indeed possible for distinct groups to coexist harmoniously, promoting the idea that two viable states can thrive side by side. This partnership enhances community ties and stresses the critical importance of trust and reciprocal relationships, which are essential for fostering stability and peace in the region.

As we explore the call for two viable states that exist in peace with one another and within their own borders, it becomes evident that cultivating social capital is beneficial for sustainable development and lasting harmony in the *Tamazuj* zone and beyond. By nurturing these communal networks and fostering ongoing collaboration, communities can pave the way toward a brighter and more prosperous future.

The idea of a *Tamazuj* zone is opportune, as it provides a solid foundation for realizing the two viable states at peace with each other through a more effective process aimed at influencing Khartoum, Juba, and other major players. Therefore, we would state the necessary and sufficient conditions for the viability of the two Sudanese states. The necessary condition is for them to be at peace with each other, while the sufficient condition calls for them to be at peace within themselves. John Garang's idea of the *Tamazuj* zone would provide the political, legal, economic, and institutional framework for the viability of the two Sudans.

Such a process should be grounded on four fundamental binding constraints for the two Sudans to be at peace with each other. We prefer to refer to the two new Sudans as the Greater Sudan. The binding constraints are geography, history, economics, and social capital, which we have discussed in the preceding paragraphs.

We think that the first step in the process of encouraging Juba and

Khartoum to internalize the *Tamazuj* zone idea as the cornerstone of their peaceful coexistence is to urge them to agree on the shared vision, mission, and objectives of the conceptual framework for two viable Sudanese states at peace with each other and within themselves. These are stated below:

   a. **Shared Vision:** The two Sudans become a center of stability and economic might in the Greater Horn of Africa[46]. It is now absolutely clear to any rational policy analyst/observer that neither Juba nor Khartoum can be a center of stability and economic might alone. They need each other to restore the glory of the Kush kingdom.
   b. **Shared Mission:** The two Sudans jointly embark on the process of democratic transformation and establish institutions of coherent governance as prerequisites for their march on the steady-state path of stability, prosperity, and development. The leadership of the two Sudans must internalize the basic principle of sovereignty as a function of responsibility.
   c. **Shared Objectives:** The two Sudans enable each state to formulate and implement a development program that aims at sustainable peace, economic growth, and poverty eradication in the long term.

The shared vision, mission, and objectives articulated above form the foundation for a comprehensive roadmap that both Sudans can pursue in their effort to establish two viable, sovereign states that coexist peacefully both with each other and within their own borders. Achieving this ambitious goal will require the leadership in Juba and Khartoum to fully embrace and internalize the key elements of the *Tamazuj* zone. Essential prerequisites to ensure success include the following:

1. **Delineation and Demarcation of the Border**: The two countries must delineate and demarcate the 2,184-kilometer-long border, a crucial step for achieving long-lasting peace. By establishing a clear, agreed-upon border, both nations can facilitate a framework that promotes the seamless movement of people, goods, and services across this boundary, transforming it into what could be termed a "soft border." This will not only enhance cross-border trade but also foster stronger interpersonal connections among communities on either side of the border.

2. **Debt Relief and Lifting of Arms Embargo**: Once the border has been fully demarcated and accepted by both countries, it is crucial to write off Sudan's external debts and lift the arms embargo on South Sudan. This financial relief will provide the necessary foundation for economic growth and development in Sudan, allowing it to participate more fully in the regional and international markets.

3. **Establishment of the *Tamazuj* Zone Governors Forum**: A key governance structure must be implemented, including a *Tamazuj* Zone Governors Forum, consisting of representatives from the ten states, co-chaired by two Vice Presidents of the Greater Sudan. This forum will convene quarterly meetings, with the responsibility of hosting alternating between the ten states. These gatherings will serve as a platform for dialogue, collaboration, and addressing regional issues that require cooperative solutions.

4. **Creation of the *Tamazuj* Development Bank (TDB)**: To finance joint programs, initiatives, and individual projects within the ten states, the establishment of a *Tamazuj* Development Bank is essential. Ideally headquartered in Abyei,

the bank should also have branches in the capitals of each state and additional liaison offices in Khartoum and Juba. This financial institution will play a pivotal role in ensuring that resources are allocated efficiently to catalyze economic growth in the region.

5. **Engagement with International Partners**: It is vital to enlist the support of the Troika (comprising the United States, the United Kingdom, and Norway), alongside institutions such as the International Monetary Fund (IMF), the African Development Bank (AfDB), the World Bank, and Arab financial institutions. Their expertise and resources will be crucial in guiding both nations as they embark on a path of economic integration and reform, providing financial and technical support.

6. **Restoration of the Joint Integrated/Monitoring Unit (JIU/JMU)**: To ensure ongoing security and compliance along the North-South border, the restoration of the Joint Integrated/Monitoring Unit is necessary. This unit would be responsible for monitoring the border, with technical support from African Union (AU) forces, and would require funding from the Troika and Gulf States. This mechanism will help to build trust, prevent conflicts, and ensure that both nations adhere to mutually agreed-upon terms concerning border management and security.

By addressing the above-stated six critical areas, both Sudans can work toward a stable and prosperous future, fostering an environment where peace can thrive and the potential for economic collaboration can be fully realized. For the two Sudanese states to be viable, they must be at peace within themselves. A fundamental condition for each country to be at peace with itself is complete democratic transformation. The two Sudans can avoid the post-colonial African story by undertaking a genuine process of transforming their institutions of governance on the one hand and their economy on the other.

The reality is that the two Sudanese states are not at peace within themselves. The SAF-RSF strife is threatening the very existence of the remaining part of the old Sudan. We will return to this point in Chapter Five, which examines political development in the two Sudans since 2013.

Chapter Four

The Vision of New Sudan — Progress and Challenges

"There are only two possible ways for resolving the Sudanese crises: The birth of two nation-states out of the present (geographical) Sudan or political autonomy for both the South and the North (and/or any other part that so demands) in a federated United New Sudan. Political Autonomy in this usage means that the autonomous regions have adequate political power, in terms of armed forces, to protect the region against the encroachment by the federation or by one of the regions in the federation, and, furthermore, that a region retains the right to secede from the federation if its interests are not adequately served by the federation. (It must be clear to Southerners that the retention of the right to secede from such a federation must be guaranteed by the federal constitution and by the existence of a physical Southern Armed Forces.)" [30]

A journey backward through the history of modern Sudan would help us understand how the critical questions of destiny and identity were

---

30   John Garang de Mabior (January 24, 1972)

not sufficiently articulated as two sides (or faces) of the same coin—the Sudanese nation-building project. There was no clear identification of the overarching path-goal of the nation-building project around which all the nationalities or ethnic groups in the Sudan could have rallied and followed. How did Dr. John solve the Sudanese puzzle?

The above-cited quotation from John Garang's historic internal memorandum unambiguously captures the art of creative reasoning: *Garangism*. In our view, it vividly articulates the vision of New Sudan and the path to reach it. The period between January 24, 1972, and January 9, 2011, spans 39 years, during which the prophecy, as mentioned earlier, was fulfilled. John Garang was 27 years old when he conceptualized what became a viable exit strategy for Southern Sudan from the perpetual Sudanese crisis of identity and state. By the time he projected on May 16, 2005, the implications of the referendum on self-determination, he had reached the age of 60.

Therefore, Dr. John Garang was instrumental in ensuring that the Interim Constitution of the Sudan, which was in effect from 2005 to 2011, clearly articulated explicit guarantees for a referendum on self-determination. Southerners would have been trapped without such an exit strategy from Dr. Hassan El Turabi's Islamization project, in which conversion to Islam from Christianity was made while retaining the Christian name to disguise the conversion.

Moreover, the quoted passage articulates the centrality of leadership with a strategic vision in a nation building project. That is, the passage elucidates this leadership quality from a letter (essentially an internal memo) highlighting the negotiation guidelines prepared and signed by a then-Anyanya officer, John Garang. It was addressed to the Anya-Nya National Armed Forces (ANAF) commander-in-chief and members of the Southern Sudan Liberation Movement (SSLM) Negotiation Committee at the Addis Ababa Peace Talks.

This chapter aims to provide: a) a brief assessment of the vision of John Garang since the publication of the first edition of this book; b) progress made toward the ideals of *Garangism*; and c) the current challenges facing the realization of the vision of New Sudan in the two new countries of Sudan and South Sudan.

A. Assessment of the Vision Since 2013

This section of Chapter Four focuses on a brief assessment of John Garang's vision since the publication of the first edition of this book. We argue that the Comprehensive Peace Agreement (CPA) serves as a pivotal manifestation of Dr. John Garang's visionary framework, which provided the necessary and sufficient conditions for the birth of a new state in Sudan.[31] The CPA not only represented a formal cessation of hostilities but also embodied the ideals of unity, inclusivity, and coherent governance that Dr. John Garang championed.

Through this framework, Dr. John envisioned the creation of a new Sudanese nation-state, which ultimately materialized as South Sudan. However, some analysts have argued that South Sudan is not yet a state, though it is a nation with defined territory and people. We propose that a more fitting label for this nascent entity would have been the New Sudan,[32] as it would better reflect the transformative

---

31 Machakos Protocol of the CPA provides such necessary conditions, while the Security Arrangement Protocol provides the sufficient conditions for the secession of Southern Sudan from Sudan.

32 Or the Republic of Kush, as Professor Daniel Bromley of the University of Wisconsin-Madison suggested. Dan is one of my professors who spent some time at New Site (Kapoeta County) in 2004. He also had discussions with Dr. John on the sidelines of the peace talks at Naivasha in the same year and would have been one of the technical advisers of Dr. John Garang.

aspirations that Garang articulated for all the Sudanese people, irrespective of ethnic or regional affiliations.

A critical reading of the cited passage reveals that John Garang's call for the creation of two nation-states as a resolution to the Sudanese crisis is anchored on the concept of a state's viability, which is underpinned by morality (or the moral foundation), institutions (or the institutional foundation), and the rule of law (or the legal foundation) of state. We consider these three attributes to be the necessary pillars of a viable state at peace within itself and with its neighbors.

The Moral Foundation of the State

Morality is the foundational bedrock for any state seeking peace and stability. It encapsulates the ethical principles and values that guide the actions of both individuals and governmental institutions. When a society prioritizes moral conduct, it fosters an environment where trust, respect, and social cohesion thrive. This ethical framework is essential for resolving conflicts amicably and ensuring that citizens are treated with dignity and justice. It is elucidated by Dr. John's idea of "We Say What We Practice and Practice What We Say." Moreover, this ethical framework calls for what Dan Bromley considers the moral community (2021: 13-14):

> *"...that is able to acknowledge and respect the various interests and aspirations of everyone. A moral community allows for all voices to be heard, it encourages the asking for and giving of reasons, and it creates mechanisms and processes for the peaceful resolution of the inevitable differences of opinion."*

Examining the philosophical underpinnings of this idea, one can turn to John Locke's "Essay Concerning Human Understanding," where he discusses morality in relation to voluntary actions and the laws that govern them. Locke identifies three essential laws that shape our moral responsibilities, which would seem to us that they have not been understood and internalized by the SPLM. Consequently, the "**disorganized anger**" has made the SPLM dysfunctional through recurrent factional quarrels over power and wealth. These laws are presented below to enable readers of this second edition to assess how the SPLM is practicing the moral foundation of the New Sudan vision as conceptualized by John Garang.

1. The Law of Nature
This law is rooted in reason and dictates that individuals should seek peace, preserve themselves, and respect the rights of others. It sets a foundation for mutual respect and cooperation, which is vital for societal cohesion. Hence, it serves as a fundamental principle that underscores the intrinsic relationship between reason, human behavior, and the rights of individuals within a society. This law is often regarded as a moral compass guiding individuals toward the pursuit of peace, self-preservation, and respect for the rights of others.

At its core, the Law of Nature emphasizes the importance of seeking peace. In this regard, the SPLM cadres must know that human beings, by nature, thrive in environments where harmony prevails. They must understand that the quest for peace is not merely an individual endeavor but a collective one that fosters cooperation and understanding among members of society. When individuals prioritize peaceful coexistence, conflicts are reduced, and the potential for constructive dialogue increases, paving the way for collaboration on shared goals and aspirations of the liberation struggle, in which we lost millions of precious souls.

Preservation of oneself is another key tenet of the Law of Nature. This instinct concerns not only physical survival but also maintaining one's dignity, well-being, and sense of identity. Our people exhibited these attributes during the war of liberation. A society that recognizes and upholds the right to self-preservation cultivates an atmosphere where individuals feel safe and valued. When people are empowered to care for themselves, they are better equipped to contribute positively to their communities, creating a virtuous cycle of support and growth. This is how social capital is formed.

Furthermore, the Law of Nature inherently respects the rights of others. Acknowledging and upholding the rights of individuals is essential for fostering mutual respect. This principle enforces the understanding that for anyone to thrive fully, others must also be afforded their rights and freedoms. Respecting the rights of others instills a sense of moral responsibility that binds people together, encouraging a culture where cooperation reigns over conflict. The World Bank acknowledges that the new country began with a binding narrative of triumph and freedom:

> *"On July 9, 2011, the Republic of South Sudan celebrated its independence. The country began its life with significant natural resources and a binding narrative of triumph and freedom, but with a legacy of over 50 years of conflict and an extremely low level of physical, human and institutional development."* [33]

---

33   Interim Strategy Note (FY 2013–2014) for the Republic of South Sudan. Report No: 74767-SS]

The above passage critically articulates the initial conditions at the historical point from which, in July 2025, the people of South Sudan must take a backward journey. This journey would reveal that South Sudan started the process of state formation with the necessary compass—a **political morality**—in which the "**binding narrative of triumph and freedom**" was embedded.

Hence, these elements of the Law of Nature establish a robust foundation for societal cohesion in the New Sudan. When individuals are guided by reason and acknowledge the significance of peace, self-preservation, and respect for others, they lay the groundwork for a thriving community. Such a society is resilient and equipped to navigate challenges with a spirit of collaboration and a shared purpose.

Essentially, the Law of Nature reflects the universal truths that transcend cultural and temporal boundaries. By embracing these principles, societies can cultivate environments where positive relationships flourish, conflicts are minimized, and collective well-being is prioritized, ultimately contributing to a more just and harmonious world.

2. The Law of Divine Command

This goes beyond rational governance, suggesting that moral actions are aligned with a higher divine authority. Throughout history, in many cultures and societies, the influence of divine command has been significant, often leading to the establishment of moral codes that resonate with the beliefs and teachings of various religious traditions. These moral codes shape community values and govern social interactions, thereby informing what is deemed right or wrong within that society. For example, in cultures where religious frameworks are integral to daily life, divine commandments may dictate everything from interpersonal conduct to broader societal issues, fostering a sense of accountability to a higher power that transcends human-made laws.

In the specific context of Sudan, the interplay between divine command and moral conduct has been abused and used by the elites for political pursuits. In South Sudan, our political parties must use the country's diverse ethnicities and religious beliefs to contribute to a rich tapestry of values that are often influenced by spiritual teachings. This is because, in many South Sudanese communities, adherence to divine command is regarded as essential for maintaining social harmony and ethical integrity. This belief system not only informs personal behavior but also shapes the collective identity of the community, reinforcing bonds and communal ties through shared moral principles.

Moreover, the Law of Divine Command can serve as a stabilizing force during times of moral crisis or societal upheaval. In such moments, communities often turn to their spiritual foundations for guidance, seeking to align their actions with the divine will to navigate ethical dilemmas. This reliance can strengthen communal resilience and foster a shared sense of purpose as individuals and groups endeavor to adhere to a moral compass that is believed to be divinely ordained.

In essence, the Law of Divine Command provides a compelling lens through which to understand moral behavior, particularly in societies like South Sudan, where spirituality is traditionally interwoven with daily life. It highlights the importance of connecting ethical conduct with a sense of divine accountability, promoting a vision of morality that transcends human limitations and aspires to a higher standard of integrity and justice. By recognizing the profound influence of divine command, we can appreciate the foundational role it plays in shaping not only individual character but also the collective ethos of the community of nations.

3. The Law of Civil Society

This law underlines the importance of formalized governance structures that articulate and enforce moral behavior. It emphasizes that coherent governance must reflect the will of the people and uphold justice and accountability. In this regard, it plays a crucial role in shaping the framework of governance and social order within a community. At its core, this law emphasizes the necessity of formalized governance structures that not only articulate the rules and norms of behavior but also ensure their enforcement. This implies that a society must have clear mechanisms through which moral and ethical standards are defined and upheld, contributing to the collective well-being of its members.

One of the fundamental principles of the Law of Civil Society is that effective governance must genuinely reflect the will of the people it serves. This necessitates participatory frameworks that allow individuals to have a voice in decision-making processes. When governance structures are built on the foundation of inclusivity and representation, they are more likely to command trust and legitimacy among the populace. The active involvement of citizens in governance not only fosters a sense of ownership but also ensures that policies and laws are aligned with the values and aspirations of the community.

Furthermore, upholding justice is critical within this law. Justice refers not only to the fair treatment of individuals but also to the equitable distribution of resources and opportunities. A society governed by principles of justice underpinned by political morality[34] is one where individuals feel secure and valued, knowing that their rights

---

34   Dr. Cirino Hiteng of the SPLM first introduced me to the term "political morality" at a workshop on participatory governance organized in 1999 by the Horn of Africa Center for Democracy and Development (HACDAD), one of the SPLM think tanks established in Nairobi, Kenya, in 1997

are protected and that there are mechanisms to address grievances. This component is essential for fostering social cohesion and reducing conflict, as it contributes to a shared sense of purpose and belonging.

The Law of Civil Society also highlights accountability as a vital aspect. Governance structures must establish clear lines of responsibility, where leaders and institutions are held accountable for their actions and decisions. This accountability can be achieved through various means, including independent judicial systems, transparency in governance, and mechanisms for citizen feedback. When leaders know they are answerable to the people, it promotes integrity and discourages corruption, enhancing public trust in governance.

By aligning their practices with the above-stated moral principles, leaders can foster a political environment conducive to trust and collaboration. Ultimately, the SPLM's adherence to the principle of "We Say What We Practice and Practice What We Say" serves as a guiding ethos, reinforcing the importance of integrity in political leadership and societal governance in Sudan and South Sudan. This commitment to moral coherence is what can help heal divisions, build trust among communities, and pave the way for a more cohesive and prosperous society.

The moral principles in the then-Sudan do, in our view, include political agreements/promises between Northern and Southern political parties. In this context, Dr. John developed this idea, particularly in light of a long history of political agreements being dishonored, a point well-articulated by Abel Alier in his 1990 book, *Southern Sudan: Too Many Agreements Dishonored*. A journey backward through the political history of Sudan (2005, 1994, 1983, 1965, 1955/1956, 1947, 1924, 652, and so on) indicates that the country had been trapped in a vicious circle of political immorality.

The relationship between voluntary actions and the laws that govern political societies forms the bedrock of what we consider political morality. This principle is encapsulated in the idea, "We say what we practice and practice what we say." It implies that one's actions must align with one's words; if a person claims to uphold certain values but fails to enact them in practice, they deviate from the essential tenets of political morality. This inconsistency undermines trust and credibility, suggesting a disconnect between stated intentions and actual behavior. To illustrate this concept of political morality more concretely, we can draw parallels from the political landscape of Sudan, where adherence—or lack thereof—to public commitments has significant implications.

In this context, it becomes crucial for political entities to implement robust mechanisms for transparency and accountability. By fostering a culture of civic engagement, grassroots movements can play a vital role in pressuring leaders to uphold their promises and commitments. This active participation of citizens not only holds leaders accountable but also serves to rebuild the essential trust that is often eroded in political discourse. When the electorate engages critically and consistently, it challenges leaders to remain true to their obligations, thereby reinforcing the notion that political morality is not merely an abstract concept but a lived reality that demands continuous validation and struggle.

This ongoing struggle reflects not only a failure of political leadership but also a broader societal challenge—an urgent call to break free from cycles of disillusionment and build a future grounded in authentic political morality and accountability. We support this statement through three examples in addition to those given by Abel Alier (1990). Ali, Elbadawi, and EI-Batahani (2005, 198) articulate the first example as follows:

> *"Between the Juba Conference and the declaration of independence by the Sudanese Parliament in January 1956, the Torit massacre and the subsequent reprisal had substantially damaged the relationship between North and South. In addition, limited progress in the safeguards of 1947 did not inspire confidence. Against this background, southern representatives in the parliament demanded a pledge be made to establish a federal system of government in the future in return for their agreement to the declaration of independence. They received the consent of their northern colleagues to this proposal."*

The above quotation summarizes it all. Northern colleagues of Southern Sudanese honored neither their agreement on the safeguards agreed upon at the Juba Conference in 1947, the first formal contact between North and South, nor their pledge to establish a federal system of government. Such behavior has come to epitomize Sudanese political culture, and the South has disproportionately endured most of its consequences.

The Khartoum Agreement of 1997 is the second example of the incompatibility of Northern Sudanese political culture and political morality. The agreement was between the Southern Sudan Independence Movement (SSIM) and the *Inkaz* GoS. One of the key elements of this agreement was that a referendum on self-determination for Southern Sudan would be conducted at the end of five years. The fate of this agreement was not to be different from the previous agreements between North and South of Sudan. Riek Machar Teny, the primary signatory to the Khartoum Agreement and leader of the August 28, 1991, failed coup against John Garang de Mabior, returned to the SPLM in January 2002 with some of his followers.

They were welcomed back to their movement with sincerity and treated with dignity and respect. This is also a testimony to Dr. John's courage, for many people in the SPLM/A did not want Riek Machar back in the movement after the destruction of human lives and property his SSIM had inflicted on the people of Southern Sudan.

The third example is the dispute between the SPLM and the National Congress Party (NCP) over the ministerial portfolios of the economic sector. As part of the CPA, the two political parties reached an understanding on a partnership for governing Sudan during the first half of the interim period preceding the midterm multiparty general elections. The ministerial portfolios of the GoNU were categorized into three clusters: sovereignty, economic, and social/service. The SPLM was allotted 28 percent, while the NCP was given 52 percent of the total number of ministries. Moreover, there was an agreement on the procedures for selection in each cluster, with alternating selection rounds in which each partner chose a single ministry at each round.

For instance, if the SPLM were the first to make a choice, then the next turn would be for the NCP to choose from the remaining ministries in the cluster. This procedure was followed with respect to two clusters: sovereignty and social/service. It was, however, not respected in the economic cluster, as the NCP was the first to select. Instead of choosing a single ministry, it opted for two: the Ministry of Energy and the Ministry of Finance and National Economy, a clear violation of the ground rules the two partners had agreed upon to govern their partnership.

In light of the preceding paragraph, the NCP had not disentangled itself from the vicious circle of the Sudanese political immorality. What was at stake then was the unity of the country, which required honesty and integrity. In this regard, the selfish behavior of some elements in the NCP had undermined the Sudanese desire to "**belong to a** community **where you understood what others said, where you could move freely, where you had emotional as well as economic, social and political bonds**" (Berlin 1960, 9).

At that point, the chances of making Sudan's unity attractive, as Dr. John Garang de Mabior envisaged, started to dwindle thanks to the political greed of these elements in the NCP. Such behavior is contrary to what Dr. John stood for: "**a strong and widespread national identity**" that "**can dampen support for secession and violence against the state**" (Nicholas Sambanis 2005, 307).

Moreover, in our view, the initial conditions for conflict in Sudan were created by a weak and narrow-based national identity, which is endogenous and not caused by exogenous factors, such as the colonial administration's Southern Policy, as Ali Abdel Gadir Ali and others (2005) argued. This weak and narrow-based national identity is inherent in political greed, which breeds grievances, a sense of marginalization, and, consequently, violent conflict. Sambanis (2005, 329) articulates:

> *"Indeed, we often see more political greed and economic grievance than the other way around. If political institutions can reduce grievances and if economic variables can influence the stability of political institutions, then economic variables will indirectly affect "grievance" factors in the Collier-Hoeffler model. And if state failure or government illegitimacy turns domestic politics into near-anarchy world, then what Collier and Hoeffler call "greed" is really synonymous to the pursuit of survival. Civil war may be a response to either greed or grievance, but most often, it is the result of both."*

We argue that sufficient safeguards were in place to prevent the onset of a third civil war in Sudan in response to either greed or grievance being perpetuated by the NCP. The SPLM leadership, as stated in Chapter Two, acted wisely in resolving the dispute over the Ministry of Energy and Mining portfolio. Salva Kiir did not respond to disorganized anger within the SPLM leadership, and in that way, he avoided the resumption of violent conflict. He strategically opted to wait for the D-day of the referendum on self-determination, rather than risking it through disorganized anger. It was time to listen to the voice of reason by retreating, as Socrates advised, instead of "foolish endurance," as the Athenian General Laches advocated.

Moreover, ordinary Southern Sudanese saw the SPLA as the key guarantor of the CPA, which in itself was a reinforcing factor for stability and sustained peace. In our view, a robust SPLA also served as a deterrent for those who might have considered overthrowing the GoNU via a military coup. The SPLA particularly discouraged the Northern-based government's propensity to dishonor agreements.

This dynamic illustrates the profound effectiveness of the one-country-two-systems model embedded in the CPA, highlighting the interdependence between political integrity and the credibility of governance structures. Ultimately, the commitment to "we say what we practice and practice what we say" becomes a vital thread that weaves together the aspirations of the Southern Sudanese people with the realities of their political landscape, fostering a solid foundation for peace and unity.

The moral foundation of the New Sudan (i.e., South Sudan) has not yet been laid out. This is evidenced by pervasive corruption that has beset the new country. Understanding our direction is crucial, but we must recognize that moral values, as discussed in the preceding paragraphs, are the foundation for achieving our goals. Theft and violence against public resources are unequivocally condemned across all societies.

Public policy objectives remain perpetually out of reach in environments tainted by such deep-seated immorality. President Salva Kiir Mayardit powerfully articulated this truth in his letter dated June 1, 2012, stating, "**We fought for freedom, justice, and equality. Many of our friends died to achieve these objectives. Yet, once we attained power, we forgot what we fought for and began to enrich ourselves at the expense of our people.**" [35]

This poignant statement was addressed to seventy-five current and former senior officials, including me. It resonates deeply with me, as I have lost friends, cousins, and three brothers in the quest for these noble aims. Yet, shockingly, only two individuals—Mrs. Awut Deng Acuil and I have acknowledged receipt of President Kiir's letter. The majority responded by retreating into silence, failing to engage with its critical message publicly.

That glaring disconnect highlights an urgent truth: ethical governance is not merely an ideal but a necessity for realizing our collective aspirations. To move beyond lip service and empty promises, we must confront the corrosive influence of corruption head-on. We cannot afford to forget the sacrifices made for our freedom and justice. The time has come to recommit ourselves to these values and create an environment where accountability and integrity are not just expected but demanded. Only then can we revitalize our vision for a prosperous South Sudan and honor those who fought for a better future.

---

[35] This citation is from page 2 of a letter from President Salva Kiir Mayardit, dated June 1, 2012, without a reference number, which is reported to have been sent to seventy-five current and former South Sudanese officials

The Institutional Foundation of the State

The second pillar of a viable state is the establishment of strong institutions.[36] Viable states require institutions that function effectively and can uphold the rule of law, implement policies equitably, and maintain order within their borders. These institutions must be built on transparency and accountability, allowing citizens to engage with their government and hold it accountable for its actions. Strong institutions are not only crucial for coherent governance but also for fostering the formation of social capital among the populace.[37] When citizens believe in the efficacy and fairness of their institutions, they are more likely to participate actively in the democratic process and contribute to social cohesion and political stability.

Moreover, the quotation at the beginning of this chapter demonstrates beyond doubt what we would call John Garang's doctrine, which is institutionalism. That is, institutionalism as a doctrine is reflected in the theory and practice of governance by the SPLM/A during 1983 - 2005. Institutionalism is used here as advanced by J. G. March and J. P. Olsen (1984) to mean "[a]n approach to politics which holds that behaviour is fundamentally molded by the institutions it is embedded in." A good example of an institution in which an individual's behavior is molded is the family, where social values and norms are typically nurtured, shaped, guarded, and internalized.

The family, as an institution, is the foundation of social capital in any community or society, which sustains such a community through networks of civic engagement embedded in its value system.

---

36   John R. Commons defines institution as "the working rules of collective action in restraint, liberation and expansion of individual action."

37   Robert D. Putnam (1995) refers to social capital as "connections among individuals-social networks and the norms of reciprocity and trustworthiness that arise from them."

Organizations also strive, just like a family, to create their own value systems (or core institutional values) within which their members operate and behave.

Similarly, Dr. John wanted, by providing guidelines to the negotiation committee, to ensure its members conduct their work within the institutional boundaries of the SSLM and its military arm (ANAF). The SPLM/A later used the same methodology at various peace negotiation forums. As one of the participants at the critical phase (2000-2004) of the peace process, we can state unambiguously that institutionalism enabled the SPLM/A negotiation team to achieve what their predecessors could not attain in the long and difficult North-South search for a lasting peace.

The 1972 Addis Ababa Accord provided important insights for developing negotiation strategies and conclusions aimed at securing significant political power for the South, safeguarded by the SPLA (Sudan People's Liberation Army). For instance, the Protocol on Security Arrangement (which constituted sufficient conditions for secession of the South's secession) is one of the pillars of the CPA that clearly articulates Dr. John's doctrine of institutionalism.

The SPLM/A teams involved in the peace process validated this institutionalism through excellent discipline within the various committees/groups negotiating with the NCP. The work (game plans, tactics, strategies, and so forth) of these teams was sustained through technical backstopping by the SPLM Technical Committee of Intellectuals (TCI), assisted by a strong network of the SPLM Diaspora. Students of institutional economics would agree that the military tradition of discipline inherent in the chain of command influenced the doctrine of institutionalism within the SPLM/A then and now. Economics in the form of division of labor (clear demarcation of roles/functions in a given organization/unit, small or large) also influences it.

Discipline in the context of institutionalism is one of the fundamental characteristics that make the military a high quality institution in a given country. This discipline is enforced through what Dr. John Garang used to remind us of as the chain of command. Any communication within the military institution outside the chain of command is essentially a recipe for indiscipline and possibly mutiny. I came to value this principle of discipline in the military in 1999 when the Economic Society of New Sudan (ESNS) held its first annual conference in Yambio, Western Equatoria.

I presented a paper at the conference titled "Liberation Economics." The conference marked the beginning of our intellectual inquiry into the leading issues of the development of the liberated areas. The theme of the paper was that *talimatization* and *senioritization* of whatever we do in the SPLM/A were the main constraints on the economic development of the liberated areas.[38] Dr. John inaugurated the conference and participated in some of the deliberations.

He later discussed the paper with me, and he pointed out that the two terms I had used in the paper were essentially two faces of the same coin, which is discipline. He rightly elaborated that there is no well-functioning system on Earth where juniors give orders to their seniors. This would simply mean anarchy.

In short, *talimatization* (giving orders) and *seniorization* (giving hierarchy or rank priority over knowledge and/or experience in the conduct of business within the SPLM) should not have been the

---

38   I have coined *talimatization* from an Arabic word *talimat* that means orders and *senioritization* from the English word *seniority*. It is common in the SPLM to hear some leaders who are not able to argue their point of view to resort to such terms. This is order, I am senior to you, and so forth. This culture has now, in the absence of visionary leadership, led to sclerotic management in the SPLM bureaucracy.

constraints if they were institutionalized, that is, carried out within a clearly defined chain-of-command system.

Dr. John then reminded me of books I had sent him following his visit to Washington, D.C., in June 1989 for his perusal as references in the conduct of the war of liberation. These books included *The Art of War* by Sun Tzu. He then read a paragraph from this book on the theory of managing soldiers. Here, the passage from Sun Tzu that Dr. John encouraged me to internalize articulates the concept of discipline underpinning the chain of command. "**If words of command are not clear and distinct, if orders are not thoroughly understood, the general is to blame. But if his orders ARE clear, and the soldiers nevertheless disobey, then it is the fault of their officers.**" [39]

I checked in 2013 to find out how many of our gallant SPLA commanders have internalized this principle. Lieutenant General Oyay Deng Ajak, who vividly cited it with clarity, reassured me that the best of our commanders have internalized it. The mission of the SPLA has undoubtedly changed from waging a war of liberation to the conventional role of the military, the defense of the national sovereignty of South Sudan. But for the shift in roles to be understood by the rank and file of the SPLA, our top generals must provide unambiguous words of command about the new role, protecting the sovereignty of the new country that they have sacrificed so much for to achieve its liberation. An institution that does not know its mission and associated functions cannot fulfill this role.

In addition, the military, as a national institution, must reflect all the elements that constitute a nation-state. Events in North Africa (the Arab Spring) have demonstrated beyond doubt how the institution of the military can save the country from self-destruction by performing

---

39   Sun Tzu, The Art of War

its legitimate role. The SPLA is no longer a military arm of the SPLM. It is the real People's Liberation Army (PLA) of South Sudan, and it must be so in spirit, motivation, outlook, character, aspirations, and orientation. The chain of command is not only confined to the institution of the military.

It is in any system/organization (even in the family) where authority is exercised. For instance, social norms and values are not nurtured in a vacuum, but within a family and/or community with a clearly defined hierarchy. That is, the directives of the head of an organization must be unambiguous to ensure that all elements and individuals within it understand them. This would then enhance the overall effectiveness and efficiency of the organization in achieving its stated objectives and targets. Chester Irvine Barnard (1938), in his work on the functions of the executive, recommends seven basic rules for a communication system of an organization:

The channels of communication should be definite.
- Everyone should know the channels of communication.
- Everyone should have access to the formal channels of communication.
- Lines of communication should be as short and direct as possible.
- Persons serving as communication centers should be competent.
- The line of communication should not be interrupted while the organization is functioning.
- Every communication should be authenticated.

Barnard's seven rules are consistent with the passage quoted earlier from Sun Tzu's theory of managing soldiers. Those of the SPLM/A would recall the communication system of a "message to all units" that Dr. John used during the war of liberation. To the best of our knowledge, Commander Salva Kiir Mayardit used this system for the last time in communicating the sad news of the untimely death of Dr. John Garang.[40]

The SPLM/A endured the tragedy with a remarkable sense of purpose and determination to accomplish the mission, as the fallen hero and founding father of the movement had conceptualized. This endurance is, in our view, a function of institutionalism. However, some voices within the SPLM do now think that stringent adherence to institutionalism discourages creativity and innovation, especially in a situation of weak, incoherent, and confused leadership.[41] This is particularly true in an environment with no systematic internal discourse on the critical public policy issues.

Creativity and innovation have always been among the key drivers of renewal and vitality within the SPLM/A, especially in overcoming the consequences of a significant crisis, such as the unfortunate incident of August 28, 1991. Therefore, a party (or organization) cannot ignore creativity and innovation, as exemplified by the SPLM, which was founded on the principles of public service and personal sacrifice

---

40   Commander Majak d'Agoot drafted the message while the late Dr. Samson Kwaje and I drafted the press release. We were bound by duty to act swiftly that early Monday morning of August 1, 2005, to inform our gallant forces, the nation, and the world about the tragedy even though it was quite hard for us to believe that Dr. John had left us so soon.

41   Foreign advisers drafting letters for the President to sign in the absence of his aides. Vice President Riek publicly contradicted the President's figure of $4 billion allegedly stolen and rightly corrected the misleading figures of the oil deal with Khartoum. Speaker Wani disabled the National Legislative Assembly (NLA) to perform its legitimate role, and Secretary General P'agan gave away our oil assets (the two pipelines, central processing facilities, Khartoum Refinery, Petrodar Tower in Khartoum, Marine Terminals in Port Sudan, and so forth) with impunity.

in pursuit of the ideals of liberty, dignity, and justice. More importantly, these characteristics are at the heart of Dr. John's doctrine of institutionalism, as some of us know.

Factional fighting and inappropriate responses to disorganized anger within the SPLM leadership do explain the failure to pursue Dr. John's vision. ***The SPLM Strategic Framework for War-to-Pace Transition*** was shelved. This strategic framework prioritizes institutional transformation in which institutions of the guerrilla movement are transformed into resilient institutions for effective governance. Associated with institutional reform/transformation were human capital development and participatory governance. With Salva Kiir bogged down in managing disorganized anger, the consequence was weak institutions underpinned by inadequate human capital development, limited participatory governance, and the absence of institutional transformation.

As Chapter Two explains, visionary leadership is crucial as it inspires and mobilizes communities toward a common goal, setting a clear direction for institutional growth and integrity. Without leaders who can articulate a compelling vision, institutions risk stagnation and disconnection from the needs of the populace. Furthermore, human capital development is essential; investing in education and skills training not only empowers individuals but also fosters a knowledgeable workforce capable of driving innovation and reform within institutions. Effective participatory governance ensures that citizens have a voice in decision-making, leading to more inclusive and accountable institutions.

When people feel heard and represented, they are more likely to invest their efforts in supporting the institutions that represent them. Lastly, institutional transformation is vital for adapting to changing circumstances and emerging challenges. Weak institutions often cling to outdated practices and structures, making them ineffective in responding to societal needs. Emphasizing vision, skills, citizen engagement, and adaptability is essential for building robust institutions that foster progress and social cohesion. Strengthening these areas will undoubtedly lead to more resilient institutions that promote equity, justice, and prosperity for all, thereby avoiding disappointment.

This shift is evident in the growing public and leadership concerns regarding our failure to uphold our commitments under the Revitalized Agreement for the Resolution of Conflict in the Republic of South Sudan (R-ARCSS). It reflects a disturbing trend of evading accountability for our own shortcomings, whether stemming from a lack of action or indecisiveness, echoing the very political malaise that plagued the ruling elites of old Sudan.

For instance, the partnership established between the SPLM and six other political parties to form the Revitalized Transitional Government of National Unity (RTGoNU) was grounded in a mutual understanding that required all parties to relinquish certain aspects of their individual identities in pursuit of sustained peace. This arrangement aimed to restore peace, undertake comprehensive reforms in the security sector and the economy, and adopt a permanent constitution.

Significantly, it is widely acknowledged that the SPLM assumed the role of the senior partner in this "unholy partnership/alliance" of seven political parties characterized by its inherent imbalance. With this position comes a moral obligation to cultivate and uphold the partnership/alliance diligently. Despite these dynamics, it is essential to recognize that the ordinary South Sudanese people placed their trust in the SPLM and its commitments. This trust should have galvanized the SPLM and its various factions (i.e., IO and FDs) to fully reunite as stipulated in the Arusha Reunification Agreement of 2015. This would have enabled the SPLM to develop strategies and tactics that accurately reflect its identity and moral authority in the genuine implementation of the R-ARCSS.

The Legal Foundation of the State

Lastly, the rule of law is the third essential pillar supporting the viability of a state, particularly significant for South Sudan as it struggles to formulate its permanent constitution. This principle ensures that laws are applied consistently and fairly, without discrimination or favoritism, fostering an environment of justice. In a nation striving to define its identity and coherent governance, the rule of law safeguards individual rights and freedoms, providing a crucial framework for society to operate harmoniously. It is especially vital for South Sudan, where establishing trust in legal processes can encourage social stability and cohesion among diverse communities.

Moreover, the rule of law creates a predictable environment that not only allows businesses to thrive but also instills a sense of security in citizens regarding their personal and communal lives. For South Sudan, affirming the rule of law is critical; for a state to truly be viable, it must enforce laws that reflect the moral values of its society and nurture institutions that can execute these laws impartially and effectively. These pillars create sustainable peace, economic growth, and poverty eradication. This, in turn, allows the nation to coexist with its neighbors and flourish while remaining committed to its own internal stability and mutual respect among different ethnic and cultural groups, ultimately guiding South Sudan toward a more unified and peaceful future.

However, the absence of a permanent constitution is compounded by the presence of a parallel administration in the form of the United Nations Mission in South Sudan (UNMISS) with 17,000 troops and more than 3,000 civilians. Such a huge presence serves as a warning that South Sudan is governed as a quasi-trusteeship of the United Nations. The citizens of South Sudan have had, in effect, a dual government. Surprisingly, the people of South Sudan do not know the size of the budget of UNMISS, or how that budget is allocated to meet various activities and necessary operations.

Moreover, in a serious blow to South Sudan's treasury, UNMISS enjoys huge tax exemptions, which are depriving the government of millions of dollars of annual revenue. Since the publication of the first edition, the cumulative treasury loss from these exemptions is very likely to be in the billions of U.S. dollars. The possible uses of those tax proceeds are many, and their careful deployment could have made enormous contributions toward achieving sustainable peace, economic growth, and poverty eradication.

Seen in this light, there is an emerging concern among the "policy community" that UNMISS may actually be an obstacle on the path to a coherent South Sudanese state. This concern is informed by the fact that the presence of UNMISS did not prevent factional quarrels within the ruling party—the Sudan People's Liberation Movement (SPLM)—from exploding into a devastating violent conflict on 15 December 2013 and then again on 8 July 2016. Moreover, Nasir's events of March 2025 solidify the questioning of the usefulness of UNMISS in South Sudan.

B. Progress Made Toward the Establishment of the New Sudan

The independence of South Sudan is not just a milestone in the region's history; it is a profound testament to the influence of Garang's art of creative reasoning, which has sparked a series of transformative events. The SPLM has raised the expectations of South Sudanese that they will enjoy tranquility, sustained peace, prosperity, and happiness once they have crossed the river to the promised land. However, the new state did not have a coherent governance. That is, we crossed the river on 9 July 2011 to a land of abundant resources and people, but without a state exhibiting the three fundamentals/pillars of a state.

We discussed the three pillars of a viable state earlier in this chapter. The SPLM was envisaged to create these fundamental attributes during the Interim period from January 2005 to 9 July 2011. It didn't, and in less than twelve months in the promised land of liberty, freedom, human dignity, prosperity, and happiness, the new country was declared a failed state.[42] That was not surprising to some of us, for we saw some signs of a failing state coming, as Noam Chomsky (2006, 38) articulates:

> *"Among the most salient properties of failed states is that they do not protect their citizens from violence-and perhaps even destruction-or that decision makers regard such concerns as lower in priority than the short-term power and wealth of the state's dominant sectors. Another characteristic of failed states is that they are "outlaw states," whose leaderships dismiss international law and treaties with contempt. Such instruments may be binding on others but not on the outlaw state."*

Dr. John's idea of "disappointment is a function of expectations" was quickly realized. A *Los Angeles Times* reporter, Robyn Dixon, vividly illustrates this in an article, "South Sudan's Dreams Slipping Away Already," published on March 22, 2012:

---

42   According to the Failed States Index (FSI), Sudan and South Sudan ranked third and fourth, respectively, on the list of failed states in 2012. Somalia tops the list, followed by the Democratic Republic of Congo (DRC).

*"**Long marginalized by the Sudanese government in Khartoum, the Southern part of the country was one of the most destitute, least developed places on Earth, with just a few miles of paved road. But last year's peaceful secession sparked a surge of hope among South Sudanese. With their own flag, their own government, their own oil, they would build a decent country. Instead, the government has taken the well-worn path of many other rebels-turned-leaders. Corruption and nepotism** are pervasive, **public services are negligible, and on a recent visit to Juba there was more evidence of demolition than of reconstruction ... In January, the government suspended oil production, which accounts for 98% of its revenue, in a dispute with Sudan over transit fees for shipping crude through the North by pipeline. The joy of independence is a distant memory. Austerity is the new refrain."*

It was not meant to be this way because Dr. John knew the well-worn path of many rebels-turned-leaders before him. He firmly believed the SPLM/A owed a profound debt to our people, and it is now time to fulfill that obligation with unwavering commitment and decisive action. Dr. John's vision was never to replicate the failures of past rebel leaders but to embody Nelson Mandela's exemplary leadership.

He wanted to follow the Nelson Mandela model. [43] Dr. John

---

43   About eighty senior SPLM/SPLA members led by Salva Kiir Mayardit and Dr. Riek Machar were sent in March-April 2005 for a two-week attachment to the various government institutions in South Africa. This group spent the first three days of the attachment at the South African presidency being walked through what I consider to be an important policy document, "Ready

strongly believed it was payback time for our people by the SPLM/A, which is elucidated by the following passage:

> *"The next period will be payback time by the SPLM to the Sudanese people who fought and sacrificed for the last 21 years. The major problems and programs that will require extensive attention by the SPLM-based GOSS and the State Governments of the Nuba Mountains, Southern Blue Nile and Abyei during the Interim Period and beyond fall in the areas of physical infrastructure, good governance, financial infrastructure and viable markets, development and provision of social services and basic necessities: health, education, water, food security, employment opportunities, building the SPLA as an army that will safeguard the agreement, building the SPLM in both North and South to lead the political transformation of Sudan, and above all, dignity rather than elitism."* [44]

The next period became dominated by factional fighting within the SPLM, and no extensive attention was given to payback time as articulated by the above passage. Hence, the newly born state fell into a fragility trap. We discuss in the next section the idea of the fragility trap as one of the current challenges facing the realization of the vision of New Sudan in the form of an independent South Sudan.

---

to Govern: ANC Policy Guidelines for a Democratic South Africa." Members of the SPLM/A team were then attached to the respective ministries and institutions after this exposure. I was in the team that was attached to the Ministry of Finance and the Reserves Bank of South Africa.

44   From Dr. John Garang de Mabior's Address at the Signing Ceremony of the Comprehensive Peace Agreement (CPA) in Nairobi, Kenya on January 9, 2005.

C. Current Challenges Facing the Realization of the Vision of New Sudan

Understanding the concept of the fragility trap is a significant challenge currently facing analysts and policymakers in South Sudan. The second associated challenge is what a fragile state, such as South Sudan, can do to exit the vicious cycle of fragility. In this regard, our scheme of thought in an attempt to discuss these two challenges is organized as follows:

a. The first thing/step South Sudan can take to exit fragility is to understand and internalize the concept of fragility sufficiently.
b. The second step is to embark on building resilient institutions and coherent governance to promote security and development; and
c. The third step is to seek help from the international development community in general, and the IMF in particular.

Understanding Fragility[45]

To enhance our understanding of fragility, we would categorize the key characteristics of a fragile state into two categories. The first category is what we would like to call "**drivers of conflict-induced fragility**." A report of the Organization of Economic Cooperation and Development (OECD) has identified four drivers of conflict in a fragile state[46]. Three of these drivers – **injustice, inequality, and ethnic tensions** – are more relevant to our discussion here. The second category constitutes what the same OECD report identifies as dimensions of fragility:

---

[45] Most of this section is taken from: What Can Countries Do to Exit Fragility Trap? My **Opening remarks at a meeting of the Advisory Group for Sub-Saharan Africa (AGSA) of the IMF, April 20 -21, 2015, Washington, DC (USA).** I was a member of AGSA during the period 2013 – 2018.

[46] States of Fragility 2015: Meeting Post-2015 Ambitions, OECD Publishing, Paris, France

a. Violence dimension;
b. Justice for all dimension;
c. Institutions dimension;
d. Economic foundations dimension; and
e. Capacity to adapt to shocks and natural disasters dimension.

We would call OECD's dimensions as symptoms/indicators of fragility, which are manifested in violent conflict on the one hand, and weaknesses in the system of justice, institutions, economic foundations, and capacity on the other.

But what is fragility? The IMF defines fragile states as "states in which the government is unable to reliably deliver basic public services to the population – face severe and entrenched obstacles to economic and human development." The IMF further explains that: "While the definition of fragility and country circumstances differ, fragile states generally have a combination of weak and non-inclusive institutions, poor governance, and constraints in pursuing a common national interest.[47]"

The first category would be understood if we conceptualize the drivers of conflict-induced fragility as a triangle of fragility (ToF), which is depicted in Figure One on the following page.

Ethnic-based injustice is likely to create unequal opportunities (inequality) between the various ethnic groups (nationalities/tribes) comprising a given country. That is, when one ethnic group dominates access to resources and wealth creation opportunities, the excluded groups would resist by all means available to them, the resultant injustice and associated inequality. In this regard, these drivers, in turn,

---

47   Quoted from *Building Resilience in Fragile States in Sub-Saharan Africa*, chapter 2 of *Regional Economic Outlook for Sub-Saharan Africa*, African Department, International Monetary Fund, October 2014.

Figure One: Triangle of Fragility (ToF)

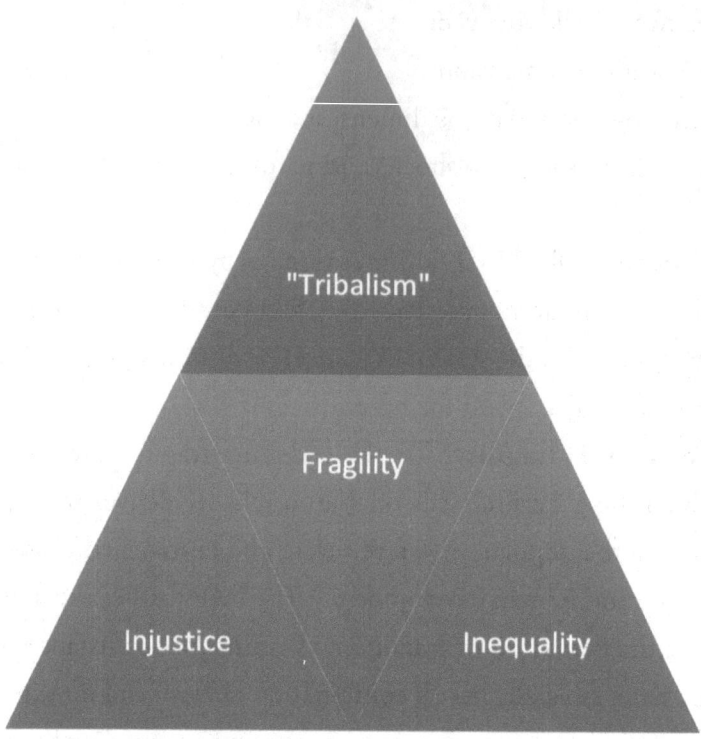

deepen the fragility of the state, creating a vicious circle of fragility that is difficult to break, especially where there is a knowledge gap on how the drivers and dimensions of fragility interact and reinforce each other.

In the case of South Sudan, for instance, we would argue that the new country was born with the three drivers of conflict-induced fragility very much entrenched. Moreover, there was no clear strategy to address the underlying causes of fragility. The elite have shown a marked disposition to act predatory toward the nation's income and wealth, thereby deepening the nation's fragility. The underlying political and economic conditions became too fluid and too risky to encourage savings and long-term investment, with communities and individuals focusing on quick returns instead.

The symptoms of fragility became clear in less than three years after independence on July 9, 2011. That is, a violent conflict erupted on December 15, 2013. But, for twenty (20) years, the country has been in the hands of the groups that are now in violent conflict with one another, as well as dividing the country along ethnic lines. During the last two decades, nothing tangible has been done to improve devastated social and economic infrastructures; to settle communal disputes over land and access to resources; to resettle and integrate returning populations; and/or to take even rudimentary steps toward the consolidation of a state at the service of its population.

Moreover, for twenty years, the leaders now in violent conflict stood back and let international partners[48] do all the work of providing few basic services that are now available, while devoting essentially all of its time and energy to angling for a portion of the oil revenue stream.[49]

The case of a fragile state, such as South Sudan would be understood in the context of a fragility trap. The World Bank articulates five critical phases of the vicious cycle of fragility, which is a product of the two categories. The Bank states that, "If countries experience repeated cycles of poor governance, low investment, new stresses and violent relapses, they can remain stuck in a fragility trap[50]." In Figure 2 below, we present a modified version of the vicious cycle of fragility. It is our sincere hope that all the stakeholders in the viability of fragile African states would try to internalize the phases of the fragility

---

48   Close to 80% of health is provided by the NGOs and education shares in similar neglect

49   Evidenced by the letter of President Kiir to 75 current and former senior officials accusing them of having stolen $4.5 billion.

50   The Way Out of Fragility Trap, a presentation made at the World Bank South Sudan Country Team Retreat, May 28 – 30, 2014 at Windsor Resort, Nairobi, Kenya.

Figure Two: Fragility Trap as Conceptualized by the World Bank

trap, so as to help these countries to exit from fragility. We would use South Sudan to walk the reader through the various phases/cycles of the fragility trap.

The first phase (**brown circle**) is when a country out of conflict (or newly independent country, such as South Sudan) misses an opportunity to reform institutions of resistance to those of a nation-state. It would be recalled that the Sudan People's Liberation Movement (SPLM) issued its blueprint in August 2004, the **SPLM Strategic Framework for War-to-Peace Transition**, which called for a comprehensive reform. President Kiir (then first deputy SPLM chairman) was in charge of transforming the Sudan People's Liberation Army (SPLA) from a guerrilla army into a professional army of a state.

Former Vice President Igga (then head of the SPLM political commission) was responsible for transforming the SPLM into a political party ready to govern in a multi-party democracy environment. Dr. Riek Machar (then second deputy SPLM chairman) was tasked with transforming the Civil Authority of New Sudan (CANS) into a robust civil service of Southern Sudan and eventually of an independent South Sudan.

The SPLM strategic framework was shelved after the tragic death of Dr. John Garang de Mabior, Chairman/founder of the SPLM and First Vice President of Sudan (9 – 30 July 2005). This failure to reform institutions and structures of resistance, in turn, led South Sudan to the second phase (**blue circle**) of low investment in key areas or the five dimensions of fragility. There was, for instance, a low or lack of investment in critical areas, such as basic services, social capital, human capital, physical capital, infrastructure, and so forth.

Our estimates indicate that the Government of Southern Sudan (GoSS) and the Government of the Republic of South Sudan (GRSS) received an estimated total of $20.0 billion in oil revenues from 2005 to June 2014. Furthermore, World Bank records reveal that GoSS/GRSS claimed to have spent $1.3 billion on roads during this period, yet it is common knowledge that there is only one highway measuring 192 km (the Nimule – Juba Road). However, this highway was funded by the United States Agency for International Development (USAID). That money ($1.3 billion) could have constructed 1,300 km of paved roads.

Low investment in the key areas that we have just mentioned, in turn, led to generalized discontent and new stresses, constituting the third phase (**yellow circle**) of the fragility trap. The stresses were manifested in political recklessness and misguided actions by a number of warlords and militias (e.g., George Athor Deng, David Yau Yau,

Gabriel Taginyang, Peter Gadet, Bapiny, Oluny, Peter Abdurrahman Sulu, etc.). The SPLM also demonstrated political recklessness. In our view, the two press conferences of December 6 and 8, 2013, laid the basis for the eruption of the senseless war that ensued, in which all the factions of the SPLM are losers.

The fourth phase (**red circle**) is the eruption of violent conflict, as it happened on December 15, 2013. The fifth phase (**green circle**) is the ARCSS and R-ARCSS aimed at ending the violent confrontation. The two agreements have failed to address the problem. And we are back to the first phase (or **brown circle**) of missed opportunities to address the root causes of the crisis of governance.

The ARCSS was witnessed and guaranteed by the then Ethiopian Prime Minister, Hailemariam Dessalegn, who was also the Chairman of the IGAD Assembly at the time. The key paragraph in that agreement is, in our view, the following:

> *"Agree that a transitional government of national unity will offer the best chance for the people of South Sudan to take the country forward; and that such a government shall oversee government functions during a transitional period, implement critical reforms, as negotiated through the peace process, oversee a permanent constitution process, and guide the country to new election; and thus direct our respective representatives to the IGAD-led peace process to negotiate the terms of a transitional government of national unity."*

A transitional government of national unity (TGoNU) as conceptualized in the above-cited passage was not envisaged that South Sudan would remain for a long time in the vicious cycle of fragility.[51] In fact, TGoNU was a misnomer, for it should have been the transitional government of the SPLM Unity (TGoSU). This is because the "IGAD-led peace process to negotiate the terms of a transitional government" was dominated by the three factions of the ruling party – the Sudan People's Liberation Movement.

Once fragile states understand the concept of fragility, they will be in a better position to embark on the process of building resilient institutions and effective governance for security and development.

Building Resilient Institutions

We have seen in the preceding section two categories – drivers and symptoms/dimensions - of fragility as shown in two figures. In the rest of this section, we would like to provide some "tips" for South Sudan to seek, as a fragile state, institutional designs sensitive to its social, economic, political, and cultural characteristics. The underlying objective of "**building resilient institutions**" is the establishment of a coherent governance that would, in turn, eliminate injustice, inequality, and tribalism on the one hand, and provide equal access to resources and opportunities for wealth creation on the other.

We believe that fragile South Sudan can emerge from fragility if it is assisted in internalizing three key concepts—**governance, capacity, and institutions**—at the early stages of building resilient institutions.[52]

---

51 This framework agreement has never been translated into a peace accord and the violent conflict continues!

52 The designs of post-conflict recovery and reconstruction programs are most likely to be driven by the donor community than by the countries themselves. Donors have initiated a new assessment tool known as the Joint Assessment Mission (JAM), which is usually jointly led by the World Bank and UNDP on behalf of the UN system. JAM sets priorities that are quantified and presented to the donor

Stated differently, the desired result out of environments of fragility is to achieve a coherent governance, which requires effective capacities and quality institutions to produce it. This entails that the point of departure for the process of building resilient institutions and effective governance is the situation analysis of the prevailing types of governance, capacities, and institutions. Such an analysis should cover all the actors at the national, sub-national/regional, and local levels. It should also determine the most appropriate roadmap, consisting of the following likely stages:

- <u>Stage One</u>: Where are we now, i.e., current situation, which is already illustrated by Figures One and Two in the preceding section;
- <u>Stage Two</u>: Where do we want to be, which basically means the vision and mission statements of a fragile state planning to exit from fragility;
- <u>Stage Three</u>: How to get there (i.e., roadmap), which concerns the strategy and action plans of a fragile state; and
- <u>Stage Four:</u> How to stay there once you have reached your final destination – concerns issues of sustainability (i.e. the five dimensions/indicators of fragility) once the country has exited from fragility.

Building Coherent Governance

In our view, a common understanding of the term governance among all the stakeholders is a *sine qua non* for reforming institutions of coherent governance. There is an emerging body of empirical work

---

community for funding at a donor conference. For instance, the World Bank in case of Sudan resisted issues of institutional reform and capacity building and it was only after the Sudanese insisted after which they were added to the list of clusters constituting the JAM.

on governance that would assist fragile states in internalizing this concept. Information and Communication Technology (ICT) has now made information easily accessible to analysts. For instance, policy analysts in South Sudan could benefit from an empirical body of research on governance, which is accessible at the World Bank website. Daniel Kaufmann, Aart Kraay, and Massimo Mastruzzi (KKM) give a comprehensive definition of governance:[53]

> *"[T]he traditions and institutions by which authority in a country is exercised. This includes (1) the process by which governments are selected, monitored and replaced, (2) the capacity of the government to effectively formulate and implement sound policies, and (3) the respect of citizens and the state for the institutions that govern economic and social interactions among them." (2003:3)*

The KKM's definition tells us that traditions and institutions by which authority is exercised must be inclusive for countries to exit from fragility or avoid it altogether. That is, they must include traditions and institutions of all the stakeholders (e.g., ethnicities/tribes), to ensure better governance at all levels relative to the one that contributed to the violent conflict in the first place. An important point to note here is that institutions are a critical component of governance, but not synonymous with it. That is, governance is an outcome (i.e., output in an economic sense), while institutions and capacity are inputs (factors of production) necessary for its production.

Coherent governance should be viewed as a function of quality institutions and strong capacity. Additionally, this definition will help

---

53   See htt://www.worldbank.org/wbi/governance/Kaufmann.

organize this section around the key dimensions of governance with the necessary capacities and institutions.

1. Indices of Governance

Countries emerging from fragility would undoubtedly like to know the attributes of good governance. They could do this by conducting a situation analysis. A situation analysis of the prevailing types of governance in those countries that have successfully exited from fragility would benefit, in our view, from the work of KKM cited in the preceding paragraphs. A comparative analysis of governance would guide these countries in prioritizing steps to be taken in the restoration/establishment of effective governance. The sequencing of actions to be taken would, in turn, avoid overloading the institutional reform/building process to achieve good/effective governance.

Policy analysts do not, therefore, need to reinvent the wheel when they can be guided by empirical research. For instance, KKM had constructed the overall index of governance consisting of the following six indices that a fragile state must strive to achieve:

a. Voice and accountability;
b. Political stability and absence of violence;
c. Government effectiveness;
d. Regulatory quality;
e. Rule of law; and
f. Control of corruption.

A brief look at the first index of governance would illustrate comprehending the other five indices. Understanding these indices would also help identify capacities and institutions for establishing good governance by answering the capacity for what and which institutions questions. Policy analysts should not be bogged down with numeric values of the indices, but rather with the qualitative dimensions of governance, to appropriately guide them in identifying and designing capacities and institutions as critical inputs for the "production" of coherent governance.

2. Voice and Accountability Index

This is a composite index, which is constructed through the following four indicators:

i) The Political Process

It has to be inclusive through a system of equity in access that is transparent and easily understood by ordinary people. This is a process through which all citizens (stakeholders/actors) participate in government selection (appointment and removal) without resorting to violent or unconstitutional methods.[54] For post-conflict countries, the process would seek to incorporate all the systems of various actors (ethnicities/nationalities/tribes, etc.) that competed against each other through violent means to advance their visions and agendas. An inclusive political process provides equity in access to resources (political, economic, social, legal, etc.) for all its inhabitants irrespective of gender, ethnicity/tribe, region, religion, or political affiliation. In this regard, an inclusive political process would move the country from a triangle of fragility (ToF) to a triangle of Resilience (ToR) characterized by justice, equality in opportunities, and peaceful coexistence among all the nationalities comprising the nation state (see Figure Three).

---

54 A clear system of checks and balances between the conventional three branches of government – legislature, executive, and judiciary – is a critical component of the political process.

Figure Three: Triangle of Stability (ToR)

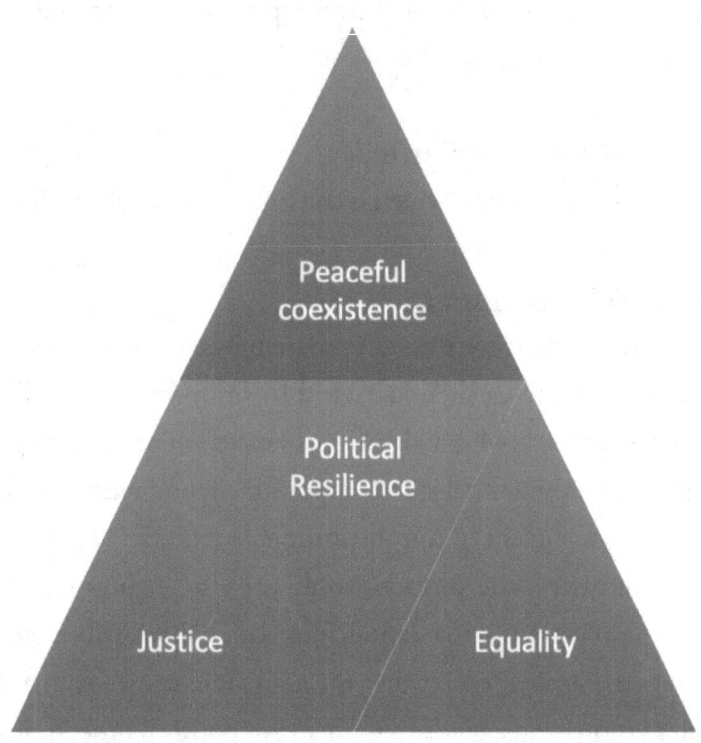

This implies that a fragile state must establish a government of national unity, inclusive of all the political parties, at the early stages of the process of exiting from fragility.

ii) Civil Liberties

KKM provide a checklist of 13 questions used by Freedom House in assessing the state of civil liberties in 193 countries. Civil liberties are defined as "freedom to develop views, institutions, and personal autonomy apart from the state." [55] **A fragile state must answer 13 questions in the affirmative (i.e., put in place mechanisms**

---

55 A definition provided by Freedom House in KKM (2003:73).

to ensure civil liberties are exercised without interference) if it were to leave the fragility trap forever.

iii) <u>Political Rights</u>

These are "those freedoms that enable people to participate freely in the political process" (KKM 2003:73). **A fragile state should strive to include these rights in the constitution and/or any legal framework governing the rules of political behavior.**

iv) <u>Independence of Media</u>

To what extent is the freedom of the press protected by law? **It is in the best interest of a fragile state to guarantee the freedom of the press within the overall framework of democratic governance**.

3. Capacity-Building/Strengthening for Coherent Governance

Developing a deeper understanding of capacity has led us to quickly survey its various definitions. This, in turn, provided us with a working definition, which is based on a combination of the UNDP and the World Bank definitions. UNDP defines capacity as "the ability of individuals and organizations or organizational units to perform functions effectively, efficiently and sustainably" (UNDP, 1997:11). An alternative definition provided by the World Bank, defines capacity as "the ability to access and use knowledge to perform a task" (World Bank, 2002).

A combination of the above two definitions enabled us to formulate a working definition, where we define capacity as **the ability of individuals or organizations to acquire and use knowledge and skills to perform a specific task effectively, efficiently, and sustainably**. In deriving this working definition, we have added three key notions: **acquire, skills, and specific**, which would in turn facilitate critical examination of two groups of factors underlying the main features of capacity, **ability,** and **performance**. "Acquire and skills" center on inputs that lead to ability (i.e., determinants of ability).

The ability to acquire knowledge, which implies learning, is important in the understanding of this feature of capacity. In this regard, learning is a process of acquiring an asset, which is knowledge. One of the important points of this definition is that we cannot appoint persons with limited technical knowledge and experience and expect them to perform well. A point that has not been fully internalized by many leaders involved with post-conflict reconstruction and development.

Moreover, to "acquire" knowledge is more critical than to "access" it. A learner can access information but not knowledge; for knowledge is earned (i.e., learnt or acquired). Similarly, a person may have access to knowledge, but without necessarily learning much to enable her/him to undertake a given task that requires a certain level of know-how in order to ensure effectiveness and efficiency. Although interrelated and sometimes used in place of the other, skills and knowledge are quite different.

For this discussion, skill is viewed as the "**art of doing**" things instead of the "**know-how to do**" things, which is knowledge. Two individuals may have the same knowledge but different skills. Learning in this sense can then be viewed as a process of acquiring an asset, which is knowledge.

The ability to acquire knowledge at the individual level is a function of economic, social, and mental well-being on the one hand, and the learning environment on the other. In this sense, capacity largely depends on a combination of endogenous and exogenous factors. These factors would undoubtedly be different at the meso and macro levels (e.g., organizational unit or entity/state) of analysis. For instance, social and mental well-being for a state emerging out of conflict would be described as trust and norms.

The lack of trust (i.e., a high degree of mistrust) is one of the contributing factors to most conflicts. Hence, trust would be among the key inputs in the ability of an emerging state (government) out of conflict to effectively perform (addressing symptoms/dimensions of fragility) the basic functions of policymaking, implementation, service delivery, and aid management and coordination.

A second characteristic of capacity is performance and results as articulated by Lee Kuan Yew the founding father of Singapore as follows: "the acid test of any legal system is not the greatness or the grandeur of its ideal concepts, but whether, in fact, it is able to produce order and justice." [56] This is of particular interest, especially as it relates to efficiency, effectiveness, and sustainability, as well as the quality of performance (i.e., delivery). The quest for quality is the ultimate objective in the performance of any task by an individual, organization and/or state. But in order to ensure quality performance, a task to be performed must be clearly defined.

In fragility setting, ensuring order and justice would be two of the primary tasks to be performed by the state and its organs. The effectiveness of the exit strategy from fragility would be judged, among other things, on how the overriding objectives of establishing justice and equal access to resources have been addressed.

As captured in the discussions thus far on the concept of capacity, there are multiple levels and numerous dimensions of capacity. Literature review on capacity development pinpoints three levels of capacity – system/state, entity, and individual (UNDP, 1997; Mizrhai, 2003); and more than 50 dimensions/areas of capacity (VanSant, 2000). For the sake of clarity, we would not use the terms level and

---

56   From Lee Kuan Yew: Lessons for leaders from Asia's 'Grand Master', by Graham Allison, Special to CNN Updated 1817 GMT (0217 HKT) March 28, 2015

dimension interchangeably. The level refers to a point at which capacity is being assessed (i.e., whose capacity question), while dimension is about the type/category of capacity (i.e., capacity for what?)

4. Dimensions of Capacity-Building/Strengthening: "Capacity for what?"

The multi-dimensional and multi-level aspects of capacity-building would undoubtedly burden those seeking to identify the most appropriate capacities for managing the exit from fragility (or war-to-peace transition for post-conflict environment). Hence, the point of departure for such search is to reduce the categories/dimensions of capacity to a manageable size by asking the question – "capacity for what?" This critical question of "capacity for what" in the context of post-conflict situations would seem to have been answered by Ian Bannon[57] in stressing four "different, but inter-related dimensions" of capacity. Such a narrow focus would, in turn, enable countries emerging out of conflict to address the problem of absorptive capacities.

The absorptive capacity[58] problem would then center on the following five key dimensions – four of which have been identified by Bannon:

i. <u>Decision-making capacity</u> refers to the ability to make decisions. Poor decision-making systems are often associated with

---

57 I was a consultant with the World Bank Institute (WBI) at that time when Ian Bannon responded on June 18, 2003, to an e-mail message from Markus Kostner (with a copy to me) about a proposed study on institutional reform and capacity development in post-conflict countries, which I was working on. Bannon identifies four dimensions of capacity as policy reform capacity, implementation capacity, service delivery capacity, and aid management capacity.

58 Absorptive capacity is being used in a broader sense to include the five dimensions of the capacity for what question in the context of an exit strategy for fragile states.

the centralization of decision-making, institutional weakness, and capacity deficits, which can, in turn, be a major constraining factor on absorptive capacity during the transition period. This is a critical area, especially in Africa, where traditional African decision-making systems/processes are based on consensus – elders can sit under a tree and debate a single issue the whole day until all those present have spoken. Such a system of decision-making would undoubtedly, in our view, contribute toward the general problem of absorptive capacity within the overall framework of post-conflict recovery and reconstruction. **Hence, capacity-building for timely and effective decision-making must be one of the priorities for a fragile state to exit from fragility**.

ii. <u>Policy formulation capacity</u>: which, in the context of a fragile environment, refers to the ability of a fragile state leadership to put in place a set of rules, policies, and strategies for good governance. These rules, policies, and strategies would, in turn, create or foster an enabling environment for all stakeholders to undertake economic activities at the macro, meso, and micro levels of a newly established governance system resulting from a peace agreement. **In this regard, capacity-building for effective policy formulation (e.g., macroeconomic policy framework) is imperative for a fragile state**.

iii. <u>Implementation capacity</u>: the ability to translate policies into actions -- implement formulated policies, strategies, and associated programs/projects within given resource constraints, including time, human, and financial resources. It would also include capacity for monitoring and evaluating programs being implemented, capacity for budgeting and financial management, and capacity for procuring goods and services.

In the case of South Sudan, the SPLM leadership was aware of this potential constraint, so it decided earlier on (2003) to outsource the public financial management (PFM) task to KPMG. **Capacity-building for the efficient and timely implementation of government policies and programs is one of the urgent actions required for a fragile state to embark on**.

iv. Service delivery capacity: the ability of a fragile state to provide basic public services, e.g., security and administration of justice, including human rights protection, education, health, water, and physical infrastructure, is one of the imperatives for a successful exit from fragility. **Hence, building capacities for effective service delivery is a must do for a fragile state wishing to exit from fragility.**

v. Accountability capacity: The ability to efficiently utilize public resources, including development assistance, and effectively coordinate donors' support is one of the key preconditions for a country to exit fragility. **This is also one of the priority areas of capacity-building with respect to fighting corruption, auditing, and public financial management, including procurement of goods and services**.

5. Building Resilient Institutions for Effective Governance

We have stated earlier that institutions are critical factors for producing effective governance. In this regard, a critical determination in building resilient institutions for effective governance is deciding "which formal institutions" would enable fragile states to exit from fragility. These institutions would generally be required to formulate appropriate policies, implement programs, deliver basic services, and manage public resources efficiently, including external aid. Reminiscent of "capacity," there are numerous definitions of institutions. However, for the purpose of this discussion, only five definitions would suffice. These are:

i. "Working rules of collective action in restraint, liberation, and expansion of individual action," John R. Commons (1959:73).[59]

ii. "Rules and conventions of society that facilitate coordination among people regarding their behavior."[60] Vernon Ruttan and Yujiro Hayami (1984).

iii. "The rules of the game in a society or, more formally, are the humanly devised constraints that shape human interaction" Douglas C. North (1990).

iv. "Social phenomena which restrict and pattern interactions in society like laws, regulations, rules, norms, established practices and routines" Klaus Nielsen and Björn Johnson (1998: xvi).

v. "Rules, enforcement mechanisms, and organizations" The World Bank (2002:6).

The term rules is a common denominator among all five definitions of institutions that we have presented above. Nonetheless, the definitions of institutions given by Commons and Ruttan et al are preferable due to the broader considerations of institutional tenets. The other definitions emphasize the constraint/control aspect of institutions and, in this sense, make them as if they are static. Commons stresses three tenets – restraint, liberation, and expansion – or aspects of the 'working rules of collective action,' hence, the dynamic feature

---

59   From 1990 edition

60   Quoted from Daniel Bromley (1989:22).

of institutions is inherent in this definition. It is also imperative to distinguish between institutions and organizations, as they are often used interchangeably.

If institutions are the rules of the game, then organizations can be defined or viewed as formal groups of players subject to a common subset of these rules. This interpretation notwithstanding, there are, however, occasions in which the divergence between organizations and institutions is not easily distinguishable. For example, the World Bank Group is widely considered to be an organization and at the same time, also an institution.

As an institution, the Bank has its own 'working rules of collective action' stipulated in the articles establishing it as an International Bank for Reconstruction and Development (IBRD). These articles guide (restrain, liberate, and expand) the Bank's operations, policies, and strategies. On the other hand, the Bank functions like an organization, governed by rules stipulated in the articles (i.e., working rules of collective action formulated by the founders) establishing the Bank.

Literature suggests that the central role of institutions in economic performance and growth is now widely acknowledged, due largely to the recent empirical evidence, which indicates institutions as one of the key determinants of economic development (North, 1990; Rodrik et al, 2002). According to Douglas North, institutions may be created (e.g., written constitutions) or may simply evolve over time (e.g., common law). The challenge then is on utilize existing empirical evidence in the proper design of resilient institutions that would produce effective governance for sustained escape from the fragility trap.

The importance of establishing a robust analytical framework cannot be overstated when addressing the challenge of identifying which institutions are most capable of facilitating the exit strategy from fragility. Such a framework serves as a critical tool that guides decision-makers in discerning the institutional actors that possess the requisite capacity, legitimacy, and commitment to advance peace-building and state-building efforts effectively. Without this analytical rigor, efforts to stabilize fragile contexts risk becoming fragmented, inefficient, or misdirected.

In this context, the strategic insights offered by Dr. John's path-goal theory assume a position of paramount importance. This approach to leadership and institutional development underscores the necessity of aligning organizational goals with clear, attainable objectives that motivate and empower institutional actors. Specifically, Dr. John's strategy emphasizes the creation of pathways that enable institutions to navigate complex political and social landscapes toward the achievement of defined aims. It is through this lens that the operationalization of the exit strategy gains coherence and direction.

Ultimately, the overarching goal remains the realization of the vision of New Sudan as a viable and sovereign South Sudanese state. This state must not only achieve internal peace but also cultivate harmonious relations with its neighbors. The successful implementation of the exit strategy hinges upon the capacity of selected institutions to embody this vision, translating it into tangible outcomes. Thus, the combination of a rigorous analytical framework and the application of Dr. John's path-goal strategy provides a compelling blueprint for overcoming the challenges inherent in fragile state contexts and advancing sustainable peace and development.

Furthermore, and in the context of fragile states, the main components of John Commons' definition provide four broad categories that could be used in building resilient institutions for exiting from fragility:

  i. A new constitution that considers legitimate grievances and aspirations of all the stakeholders/ethnicities/nationalities/

tribes. The working rules of collective action would be embedded in such a constitution. The constitution is a critical framework for building resilient institutions for coherent governance that would, in turn, ensure justice, equal access to resources and opportunities for wealth creation, and peaceful coexistence in a post-fragility environment. **Here, resilient institutions would be the three conventional branches of government - legislature, executive, and judiciary**.

ii. Restraint (e.g. though shall not…type of constraints/commands) entails that all the citizens/nationalities/tribes or members of a given organization are aware of the prevailing rule of law (or what we would prefer to call administration of justice), so that nobody takes the law into her/his own hands. It also calls for the observance of prescribed social values, ethics, and moral norms. **Here, law enforcement agencies and security sector organizations derive their existence /legitimacy from this tenet and must be established with this tenet inherent in their behavior**. For instance, these institutions must refrain from taking sides in competitive political party politics.

iii. Liberation in this context means liberty and freedom of whatever one does, though within the 'working rules of collective action' or the rule of law. This tenet provides legal foundation and institutional frameworks for establishing social, political, and economic organizations/agencies. Or what Lee Kuan Yew calls: "the ultimate test of the value of a political system is whether it helps that society establish conditions which improve the standard of living for the majority of its people, plus enabling the maximum of personal freedoms compatible with the freedoms of others in society." [61] **Here, a robust judiciary, effective civil society, vibrant private sector, strong press, and active research and academic institutions would act as guarantors for liberty and freedom that lay the basis for effective governance.**

iv. Expansion is the third tenet, which provides the dynamic aspect of the institution in that it allows change (i.e., technical and organizational change) to occur in order to obtain growth and development. Agencies and organizations that focus on innovation and social change would derive their strategic visions from the expansion aspect of the 'working rules of collective action.' The working rules of collective action allow expansion to occur in space and over time. **Here, the role of the universities and research centers, critical thinking and innovation, is the driving force of this tenet.**

6. Reforming Institutions for Coherent Governance

In the previous section, we highlighted the idea of building resilient institutions. However, the idea of New Sudan was underpinned by the strategic approach of reforming the institutions of the guerrilla movement into those of democratic governance. In this regard, the ***SPLM Strategic Framework for War-to-Peace Transition*** was intended to start with the reforming of its institutions before building new ones. As we have stated earlier, this blueprint policy document was shelved after the premature departure of Dr. John from our world, only 21 days after assuming the position of the President of Southern Sudan.

The core technical team, once tasked with addressing the question

---

61   From Lee Kuan Yew: Lessons for leaders from Asia's 'Grand Master', by Graham Allison, Special to CNN Updated 1817 GMT (0217 HKT) March 28, 2015

of institutional reform, was rendered dysfunctional, and the process was stagnant for two decades. Today, however, a profound opportunity emerges to decisively reinvigorate the reform of the guerrilla movement's institutions. On 22 May 2025, the Chairman of the SPLM, Cde. Salva Kiir Mayardit, entrusted the liberation struggle to the "Seeds of Nation," the dynamic young generation of SPLM leaders. He appointed Dr. Benjamin Bol Mel Kuol as First Deputy Chairman, with the hope that he will revisit the reform process. It is imperative that all stakeholders within the SPLM recognize this moment as a critical juncture to advance meaningful and lasting transformation.

The new leadership of the SPLM will have to embark on a deeper understanding of institutions and associated capacities. In this regard, Klaus Nielsen and Björn Johnson's (1998) work is relevant. It argues that institution is a core concept for understanding the types of institutional change envisaged during the war-to-peace transition. The call, then, is a realization of the fact that institutions created and/or evolved during the conflict were, in most cases, for the overall objective of applying 'working rules of collective action in restraint, liberation, and expansion of individual action' in the pursuit of the war efforts.

Countries emerging out of fragility should therefore seek to reform or build resilient institutions with a view of making them democratically accountable institutions, which are tasked with the implementation of the exit strategy. Thus, institutional building/transformation is, with the advent of stability, required to ensure:

i. A functioning state at the macro-level, which would in turn provide an overall governance system through an enabling institutional environment for other levels (meso and micro) of governance to operate. This implies the adoption of a new constitution with a clear definition of intergovernmental relations, basic principles of human rights and civil liberties, property rights, and promotion of private initiative or entrepreneurial spirit, the rule of law, social values, and norms. In this regard, there is an urgent need to first clearly establish the separation of powers between the three branches – legislature, executive, and judiciary – of government, and secondly, put effective institutions of these branches in place. **By way of illustration, institutions of the economic sector, e.g. central bank and ministries of finance, petroleum, agriculture, trade, transport and so forth will have to be given priority in making them efficient and effective in the mobilization, management, and allocation of scarce public resources to meet the fundamental objectives of: a) sustained peace; b) economic growth; and c) poverty eradication for a country seeking to exit from fragility**.

ii. A robust system at the meso-level of corporate and communal governance within a set of principles, obligations, duties, social responsibility, and rules consistent with the overall policy thrust and the constitution. The constitution is a social contract between the state, respective communities, and /or civil society.

iii. Stable household governance at the micro-level, within which core and basic values of morality, ethics, and norms of civility and patriotism are learnt, internalized, obeyed, and respected. Here, the role of the household in combating corruption is imperative through emphasis on integrity, human dignity, and self-respect.

We want to conclude this section by summarizing what a fragile state like South Sudan can do to exit from fragility. The summary is presented in a policy matrix format.

Economic performance	- Promote growth that supports high levels of employment and rising wages - Reduce youth unemployment through Youth Empowerment Scheme (YES) - Create conditions for improving livelihoods of majority of people - Strive for competitive agriculture sector	- Ensure equal access to resources & opportunities for wealth creation - Establish a system of affirmative action for minorities who feel marginalized	- Establish Public Financial Management (PFM) systems, including institutions for revenue collection, budgeting, procurement, etc. - Financial sector reform, including rebuilding of central bank	- Create conditions for a functioning market economy, with emphasis on the market forces of demand & supply determining not only the price regime, but also what is to be produced - Formulate economic policies that will accelerate the exit from fragility, but must be monitored and evaluated through robust economic indicators, such as inflation, interest rate, economic growth, etc.	- Strengthen capacity of central bank to successfully manage monetary & exchange rate policy frameworks - Develop analytical capacities of the economic sector institutions - Strengthen capacities for decision making; policy formulation & execution; service delivery & accountability
Fiscal space & budget institutions	- Efficient allocation of resources (Political economy factors)	- Equity in the allocation of public resources within the framework of annual public budgets - Involve citizens in the budget process through public hearing sessions on the budget organized by the relevant committees of the legislature	- Establish institutions of fiscal federalism to ensure equitable sharing of resources between the various levels of government - Establish a national revenue authority - Develop budget management institutions, including internal audit units in all government organizations - Strengthen the office of the auditor general - Empower anti-corruption units	- Ensure fiscal policies that encourage economic growth and development of the private sector - Promote the flow of foreign direct investment (FDI) as a critical source of sustainable development	- Strengthen capacities for revenue collection - Strengthen capacities of budget institutions - Develop capacities for debt management - Develop capacities for procurement
Social outcomes	- Create an enabling environment for the restoration of social capital - Promote the desire for maximum personal freedoms compatible and consistent with the freedom of others in the society	- Effective, efficient, & equitable delivery & distribution of basic social services	- Put in place a robust institutional framework for ensuring sustained improvement in the indicators of poverty, literacy, infant mortality, etc. - Establish efficient health & education institutions - Research the introduction of conditional cash transfers	- Ensure free mobility of people, goods & services - Put in place a robust system of social security	- Strengthen capacities of the social sector institutions

Source: constructed by the author in 2014

Table 1: A Policy Matrix of Analytical Framework for Building Resilience in Fragile States in Sub-Saharan Africa

IMF's Dimensions of Progress in Exiting from Fragility	OECD's Dimensions of Fragility				
	Violence Dimension	Justice for all Dimension	Institutions dimension	Economic foundations dimension	Capacity Dimension
Conflict reduction & political stability dimension	- Security sector reform - Promote peaceful coexistence (e.g. promote positive images of other cultures) - Nurture culture of peace, tolerance, & pluralism based on diversity	- Ensure order & justice for all - Put in place inclusive political systems	- Establish effective law enforcement agencies, including judiciary - Professional national army, inclusive of all the nationalities/"tribes" in the country - Establish broad-based political parties - Establish accountable structures for effective governance	- Ensure macroeconomic stability - Put measures in place to diversify the economy, including development of the private sector - Formulate and implement a development strategy that aims at sustained peace, economic growth, & poverty reduction - For resource-rich countries, establish a system for direct wealth dividend (DWD) as by way of reducing inequality within the overall objective of poverty eradication	- Strengthen economic policy management capacities - Enhance tradition and institutional capacities by which authority is exercised in the country - Develop appropriate capacities for the management of conflict
Institutional improvements	- Promote institutions for peace and conflict management - Establish inclusive institutions that embrace the positive aspects of all the ethnicities/"tribes" of the country	- Establish anti-corruption systems - Promote freedom of the press and association	- Put in place legal & institutional frameworks for effective governance - Reform policies that perversely distort the incentives	- Put in place legal & institutional frameworks for the economy, e.g. rules governing the behavior of economic agents, investment laws, property rights, etc.	- Build institutional capacities for managing shocks and natural disasters - Implement policies that target specific market failures

Chapter Five

Political Developments Since 2013

"Here we offer a stark assessment of the lost decade for South Sudan. More importantly, we present an urgent agenda for making sure that South Sudan's Second Decade is better than its first. Political stability cannot tolerate an entire squandered generation. This special publication is neither the usual Ebony policy brief nor policy note – it is a reflection on the first ten years of independence and a forward looking to the second decade of South Sudan becoming a sovereign African state." [62]

Beyond the creation of a new nation, Dr. John Garang's vision played a crucial role in instigating political change across the old Sudan. His strategic vision has, as a result, led to the emergence of two distinct nation-states—South Sudan and Sudan—at least for the

---

62   From *The Lost Decade: A Sudden Urgency in South Sudan.* A Special Publication on the 10th Anniversary of South Sudan Independence, by the Ebony Center, July 2021. Juba, South Sudan.

time being. We contend that the formation of the new nation of South Sudan would not have materialized within our lifetime without the robust conceptual framework proposed by Dr. John Garang aimed at addressing the multifaceted Sudanese dilemma.

This assertion will be explicated in greater detail as the discussion progresses. Furthermore, we wish to underscore the critical role that creative and visionary leadership plays in shaping a collective destiny and mobilizing them toward a common purpose. Dr. John Garang adeptly employed a path-goal approach that ultimately contributed to resolving the protracted Sudanese conflict, underpinned by the identity crisis. This shows how strategic foresight can drive positive change in a divided society.

Since 2013, the political landscapes of Sudan and South Sudan have been marked by significant turmoil and conflict, which have profoundly influenced the stability and governance of both nations. The legacy of John Garang, whose vision contributed to the eventual independence of South Sudan, continues to resonate amidst ongoing struggles for power and peace.

In Sudan, the longstanding regime of Omar Al-Bashir, which was characterized by strict Islamic governance and widespread human rights abuses, came to an end in April 2019 following mass protests and internal dissent. The political vacuum left by Al-Bashir's ousting precipitated a fragile transitional period. However, the balance of power between the Sudanese Armed Forces (SAF) and the Rapid Support Forces (RSF), a paramilitary group with roots in the Janjaweed militias, has been a source of persistent instability. The rivalry between these two factions escalated into open conflict in 2023, undermining efforts to establish a cohesive civilian-led government and casting uncertainty over Sudan's political future. This conflict has resulted in widespread violence and displacement, exacerbating humanitarian challenges.

Meanwhile, South Sudan, which gained independence in 2011, has grappled with its own internal conflicts, particularly between the government led by President Salva Kiir Mayardit and the opposition forces under Dr. Riek Machar, leader of the Sudan People's Liberation Movement-in-Opposition (SPLM-IO). The peace agreement signed in 2018, which aimed to end years of civil war, was a hopeful step toward reconciliation. Nevertheless, the renewal of hostilities in late 2021 marked a setback for the fragile peace process.

Deep-seated ethnic divisions, competition for political control, and disputes over resource management have driven the conflict between the government and the SPLM-IO. These clashes have caused significant civilian suffering and impeded South Sudan's efforts toward nation-building and economic development. Addressing insecurity in South Sudan is imperative for overcoming the broader crisis of governance. Strengthening institutions, combating corruption, ensuring sound economic management, and fostering a cohesive national identity are not merely policy goals; they are essential steps toward creating a safe and stable environment where all South Sudanese can thrive.

Only by linking insecurity to these critical issues can we begin to forge a future that upholds the people's aspirations and delivers on the promises of genuine peace and good governance. As Dr. John articulated, the time for action on payback is now—our collective future depends on it. Both nations continue to face considerable challenges as they navigate complex political transitions.

The interplay of military power struggles in Sudan and the unresolved tensions in South Sudan underscore the enduring impact of historical grievances and the difficulties inherent in establishing lasting peace and inclusive governance. The international community remains engaged in diplomatic efforts to support these countries in overcoming their divisions and achieving stability. However, lasting peace is fully in the hands of the leaders of the two Sudans.

In the rest of this chapter, we elaborate on political developments in Sudan and South Sudan.

For Sudan, the year 2024 stands as a pivotal juncture in the country's history, significantly impacted by the escalated conflicts of the previous year between the Sudan Armed Forces (SAF) and Rapid Support Forces (RSF). The SAF-RSF strife, culminating with the RSF taking control of Wad Medani, the capital of Aljazeera State, on 5 January 2024, had triggered the mobilization of the civil population in the form of Armed Popular Resistance (APR) under the ethos "**one people, one army**." In our view, this new development in the conflict has set the stage for many potential scenarios. Five scenarios and their implications for Sudan and, consequently, South Sudan should be of concern to us as policy analysts.

Those scenarios were formulated and debated in early 2024 within the Development Policy Forum Digital Platform (DPF-DP), which the Juba-based Ebony Center for Strategic Studies manages. The scenarios were:
- **Scenario 1: A United Front Leads to Resolution and Stability;**
- **Scenario 2: Escalating Ethnic Conflict and Regional Instability;**
- **Scenario 3: Stalemate and International Border Mediation;**
- **Scenario 4: RSF Consolidates Power, Causing Interstate Conflict;**
- **Scenario 5: Fragmentation and the Rise of Warlordism (or Somalization, Libyaization, Yemenization, etc.).**

We debated that the likely outcome of each of the above scenarios would, undoubtedly, have implications on the stability of the two Sudanese states and the region. Ten implications were identified as:

1. **Geopolitical Alignments**: Analyze potential alliances in the conflict. We thought that Egypt, Eritrea, and Iran have made their **strategic interest** very clear in supporting the Sudan Armed Forces (SAF) due to their national and geopolitical interests. Ethiopia, the United Arab Emirates (UAE), Kenya, Rwanda, Uganda, and Israel were likely to make their **strategic interest** clear in backing the Rapid Support Forces (RSF) as a counterbalance (witnessed by the tour of Gen. Hemedti to these countries). The dispute between Egypt and Ethiopia is over the Grand Ethiopian Renaissance Dam (GERD). Iran has a dispute with the UAE over Yemen (Houthis).

2. **Strategic Ambiguity by Global Powers**: Policy analysts should critically examine the implications of the strategic ambiguity taken by China, Russia, Turkey, and Saudi Arabia, how their neutral yet calculated stance could influence the conflict's trajectory and regional alliances, and how South Sudan can place itself in this group. Juba is well-positioned to lead a genuine mediation that focuses on a viable Sudanese state at peace within itself and with its neighbors.

3. **Regional Destabilization**: There is an urgent need to explore how conflict in Sudan could spill over into neighboring countries, potentially escalating into a wider regional conflict involving the Red Sea countries, Gulf States, and the Horn of Africa, hindering trade routes and strategic maritime passages. The Clinton Administration envisaged such a scenario and tried to come up with the Greater Horn of Africa (GHA) comprising more than 10 countries. This approach saw Sudan

as the most strategic country for the stability of the whole continent, and hence its membership in the GHA was critical, and this was the point at which the USG's support to the SPLM/A started. Eritrea, Ethiopia, Uganda, and DR Congo became the frontline countries to make a regime change in Khartoum under the NIF, which turned into the NCP. The program fell apart when Eritrea and Ethiopia fought each other, and Uganda and Rwanda invaded the DR Congo!

4. **Intergovernmental Authority on Development (IGAD) Engagement**: IGAD must overcome internal divisions among its member states to effectively mitigate the conflict. It needs to assert unified leadership to restore credibility in peace efforts. Juba can reclaim mediation leadership by proactively engaging both SAF and RSF, demonstrating a clear commitment, and setting firm negotiation terms to drive progress forward.

5. **Economic Implications**: Policy analysts must discuss the potential impact on regional economies, particularly focusing on disruptions to oil and trade flows in the Red Sea, which could have significant implications for global trade dynamics. For Juba, this is a real threat for the RTGoNU could face enormous difficulties if the pipelines were to be destroyed and therefore leading to a complete shutdown of oil production in all our operating blocks. This could happen even if the Red Sea is not affected. The Economic Cluster must embark on serious thinking and innovative approaches to the transportation of our oil to the regional and international markets. We have wasted two years, since the eruption of conflict in Khartoum not encouraging our research institutions to do the thinking and provide a menu of policy options.

6. **Humanitarian Crisis Expansion**: Forecast the possible escalation of existing humanitarian crises in the region, including refugee flows and food security issues, if the conflict in Sudan evolves into a regional confrontation.

7. **Military Build-up and Arms Race:** Assess the risk of a regional arms race and increased military expenditures as countries may ramp up defense capabilities in anticipation of potential engagement or as a deterrent strategy. Besides Dr. Majak D'Agoot, we have many DPFers with the necessary analytical skills on security and military matters. We understand the SSPDF and NSS have done some analytics, so let's hope that we are ready for any eventual scenario here. Issues of Hofara el-Nahas, Mile 14, Abyei, and Panthou (the so called Higelige) must be reviewed critically and scenarios provided. There is no hiding. Our compatriots in the opposition and who have not signed the R-ARCSS (i.e. Pa'gan, Thomas, Malong, Oyai, Simon, etc.) as well as the unarmed groups, such as the PCCA must assist with the analytics.

8. **UN Security Council Dynamics**: Investigate how the conflict in Sudan could affect deliberations within the UN Security Council, as members may be divided, with some supporting intervention to prevent regional spillover and others opposing involvement.

9. **Counterterrorism Initiatives**: Examine the consequences for counterterrorism efforts in the region, which may be disrupted or leveraged by various actors seeking to gain an advantage in the conflict or protect their interests.

10. **Maritime Security Concerns**: Assess the potential threats to maritime security due to increased militarization around the Red Sea and Gulf of Aden, as countries involved may seek to

protect their shipping lanes and economic interests, leading to a heightened risk of confrontations at sea. This might not seem to be of immediate concern to South Sudan, but this is not true - this affects the Greater Horn of Africa, of which we are an integral part.

Let's turn to South Sudan, where the vision of New Sudan was expected to set the new country on the path to achieving sustainable peace, economic growth, and poverty eradication. A brief highlight of these developments from July 2013 to June 2025 is appropriate. Here are some of the significant events:
1. Cabinet. Reshuffle of July 2013 and subsequent violent conflict on 15 December 2013,
2. SPLM Arusha Reunification Agreement of 2015,
3. Agreement on the Resolution of Conflict in the Republic of South Sudan (ARCSS) of August 2015 and its collapse on 8 July 2016,
4. The National Dialogue (ND) during the period 2017 – 2019,
5. Revitalized Agreement on the Resolution of Conflict in the Republic of South Sudan (R-ARCSS) of September 2018, and
6. The passing of the torch on 22 May 2025 to a new generation of SPLM leaders.

The Cabinet Reshuffle of July 2013 and the Subsequent Violent Conflict of December 2013

In July 2013, President Salva Kiir Mayardit undertook a significant cabinet reshuffle intended to embark on institutional reform, establish coherent governance, and address emerging political challenges. However, this reshuffle precipitated heightened tensions underpinned by disorganized anger within the ruling Sudan People's Liberation

Movement (SPLM). The culmination of these tensions was witnessed in the outbreak of violent conflict on 15 December 2013, which plunged the young nation into a devastating civil war.

The conflict in South Sudan has inflicted profound and far-reaching damage, not only shattering the fragile hopes for sustainable peace but also severely jeopardizing the nation's prospects for economic development and social cohesion. This turmoil has plunged the country into a persistent fragility trap, perpetuating cycles of instability that hinder progress and undermine governance. While some analysts contend that South Sudan emerged as a fragile state from its inception—a notion extensively examined in chapter 4 of this volume—the reality remains that ongoing conflict exacerbates existing vulnerabilities, thwarting efforts to build resilient institutions and foster inclusive growth.

Policymakers and stakeholders must draw lessons from Dr. John's ideas, recognize the critical urgency of this situation, and commit to comprehensive strategies that address the root causes of instability. Only through concerted and sustained action can South Sudan break free from this destructive cycle and embark upon a path toward lasting peace and prosperity.

The SPLM Arusha Reunification Agreement of 2015

The Arusha Reunification Agreement was signed in early 2015 in an effort to restore unity within the SPLM. This accord sought to reconcile the divergent factions that had emerged in the aftermath of the civil conflict. The agreement represented a hopeful step toward healing the political rifts and reviving the collective vision for South Sudan's future, underpinned by the art of creative reasoning. Despite its promise, the implementation of the agreement faced numerous obstacles, impeding its full realization.

It must be pointed out here that the Arusha Agreement represents a paramount effort toward reunification and political reconciliation in South Sudan, aiming to foster peace and cooperation among all factions. Despite Dr. Riek Machar's decision to refrain from rejoining the Sudan People's Liberation Movement (SPLM) and his choice to maintain leadership of the SPLM-in-Opposition (SPLM-IO), the spirit of Arusha underscores the necessity for continued dialogue and mutual understanding. It is imperative that all parties, including Dr. Machar, embrace the principles of the agreement to bridge divides and build a stable and inclusive governance framework. Only through steadfast commitment to the Arusha Agreement's ideals can lasting peace and national unity be realized in South Sudan.

The Agreement on the Resolution of Conflict in the Republic of South Sudan (ARCSS) and Its Collapse

The Agreement on the Resolution of the Conflict in the Republic of South Sudan (ARCSS), signed in August 2015, represented a pivotal milestone in the nation's tumultuous history. This accord was designed as a comprehensive peace framework to end the protracted hostilities that had ravaged the country. Central to its vision was establishing a transitional government, which sought to foster reconciliation and equitable power-sharing among the principal factions engaged in conflict. The agreement symbolized a collective aspiration for stability and a hopeful pathway toward national unity.

Regrettably, the promise embodied in the ARCSS was short-lived. On 8 July 2016, the accord effectively collapsed as renewed violence and deep-seated mistrust among the rival factions resurfaced with renewed intensity. This breakdown signified a failure to uphold the commitments outlined in the agreement and exacerbated the already fragile security situation. The collapse served to entrench instability further, undermining efforts aimed at peacebuilding and delaying the nation's progress toward a sustainable resolution to its internal strife.

The ramifications of the ARCSS's failure have been profound, influencing the country's political landscape and humanitarian conditions. The resurgence of conflict has impeded socio-economic development and perpetuated widespread suffering among the civilian population. Moreover, the erosion of trust between parties has complicated subsequent efforts, making the prospect of enduring peace increasingly elusive. It remains imperative that future initiatives learn from these setbacks to craft more resilient and inclusive frameworks capable of addressing the underlying causes of discord.

The National Dialogue (ND)

The National Dialogue of South Sudan, convened between 2017 and 2019. This was a ***national conversation*** that occurred over more than three years of bottom-up civic engagement. It was the first time, after the long process of liberation struggle, that the leaders of South Sudan consulted people at the grassroots level to discover what had gone wrong after seven years along the path of independence. The dialogue was marked by its broad participation, reflecting a commitment to inclusivity and collective problem-solving strategies.

The people of South Sudan have spoken with clarity and determination through the National Dialogue (ND) process, identifying four critical issues at the heart of the nation's challenges: governance, security, the economy, and the absence of social cohesion. These issues are not isolated; instead, they intertwine as the root causes of the crises in leadership and governance that have plagued the country. It is imperative that these concerns form the foundation for crafting a permanent constitution, ensuring a future of stability and prosperity.

Foremost among these is the matter of governance. Coherent

governance is the cornerstone upon which a just and functional society is built. Without transparent, accountable, and inclusive governance structures, the ambitions of the people remain unfulfilled, and the machinery of the state falters. Establishing a coherent governance framework, ideally within a federal system, promises to distribute power equitably, prevent the concentration of authority, and foster participatory decision-making. Such a system will not only enhance legitimacy but also promote the rule of law and respect for human rights.

Equally pressing is the issue of security. The persistent insecurity undermines all efforts toward development and peace. Citizens must be assured of their safety and protection from violence, which requires robust and reformed security institutions that are professional, impartial, and accountable. Addressing security concerns will create the conditions necessary for social and economic activities to flourish, thereby breaking the cycle of conflict and instability that has hindered the nation's progress.

The economic challenges confronting South Sudan are formidable and demand urgent attention. A stable and diversified economy is essential to alleviate poverty, generate employment, and provide public services. Strategic economic reforms and prudent management of resources will empower the country to harness its potential and reduce dependency on external aid.

Moreover, the absence of social cohesion exacerbates these economic difficulties, as divisions and mistrust among communities weaken collective efforts toward development. Fostering social cohesion is thus fundamental to healing societal fractures and nurturing a unified national identity, which is indispensable for sustainable peace and growth.

The National Dialogue has illuminated the path forward by

pinpointing these four critical issues. Addressing governance, security, economic stability, and social cohesion in a comprehensive and integrated manner will lay the groundwork for a resilient and prosperous South Sudan. Despite these commendable efforts, the outcomes of the National Dialogue yielded mixed reactions among the political actors, especially those in the SPLM-IO. While it succeeded in promoting a greater understanding of the underlying issues, significant challenges emerged in implementing its resolutions and recommendations.

The failure to effectively enact the resolutions and recommendations of the National Dialogue Conference undermined the dialogue's potential to produce lasting peace and stability, thereby highlighting the persistent difficulties in translating dialogue into tangible political progress. Policymakers and the general public alike must, therefore, embrace these imperatives with resolve and unity to ensure that the aspirations of the people are fulfilled through a permanent and effective constitutional order.

The Revitalized Agreement on the Resolution of Conflict in the Republic of South Sudan (R-ARCSS)

The Revitalized Agreement on the Resolution of the Conflict in the Republic of South Sudan (R-ARCSS), signed in September 2018, was intended to usher in a new era of peace and stability for the war-torn nation. However, the agreement's structural design reveals fundamental weaknesses that severely undermine its efficacy. Central to these flaws is the establishment of a collegial presidency composed of a president and five vice presidents, a framework that inherently breeds complexity and political instability. This multiplicity of vice presidents has not only diluted executive authority but also created competing centers of power within the government, thereby impeding unified decision-making and coherent governance.

Moreover, the R-ARCSS's failure to reconcile political leadership with military command has exacerbated tensions. Notably, Dr. Riek Machar, while serving as the First Vice President of the Republic of South Sudan, concurrently maintained his role as Commander-in-Chief of the SPLM-IO armed faction. This dual position epitomizes the paradox at the heart of the agreement: political leaders were permitted to retain control over independent armed forces. Such an arrangement inherently undermines the state's monopoly on legitimate use of force, fostering a precarious environment where political disputes risk escalating into armed conflict.

The presence of multiple vice presidents, some commanding their own militias, has thus perpetuated a fragmented power structure. Instead of consolidating peace, the agreement inadvertently institutionalized rivalries and loyalties to armed factions within the government apparatus. This fragmentation has led to repeated delays in implementing key provisions of the agreement, with extensions granted as temporary remedies rather than solutions. The instability embedded in the R-ARCSS framework has therefore impeded the establishment of a stable, unified government capable of steering South Sudan toward sustainable peace, economic growth, and poverty eradication.

Hence, while the R-ARCSS represents a commendable effort to resolve the longstanding conflict, its inherent structural weaknesses—most notably the multiplicity of vice presidents with autonomous armed forces—have critically compromised its success. For South Sudan to achieve enduring peace, future agreements must prioritize the unification of political and military authority under a singular, accountable leadership, thereby eliminating the competing power bases that continue to threaten the nation's stability.

The Passing of the Torch on 22 May 2025 to a New Generation of SPLM Leaders

Since South Sudan gained independence from Sudan in July 2011, the political dynamics in the two Sudans have been heavily influenced by Garang's thoughts on unity of purpose, peace, liberty, democracy, and social justice. Garang envisioned a multiethnic and inclusive Sudan that advocated for the rights of marginalized groups. This idea began to shape political discourse in South Sudan when various factions rallied around a united front against marginalization and inequality.

However, Garang's aspirations have faced significant challenges. This is articulated by the Ebony Center in its assessment of the first decade of independence, as follows:

> *"The exhilaration of independence is always sweet. It is also bitter. Now the hard work must begin. The sudden absence of a demon to blame for the difficulties of daily life can be disorienting. During the struggle, a unified purpose tends to blur important differences that, once freedom emerges, seem suddenly worth reconciling. The fight against a common enemy soon becomes an assortment of disagreements among former allies and comrades in arms. When there are abundant opportunities for promising livelihoods, reconciliation is relatively smooth. A large pie offers promising portions for everyone. When there is nothing but oil, the zero-sum tournament becomes bitter indeed. Iraq offers insights in this regard. Unfortunately, so does South Sudan."* [63]

---

63 From **"The Lost Decade: A Sudden Urgency in South Sudan."** A Special Publication on the 10th Anniversary of South Sudan Independence, by the Ebony Center, July 2021. Juba, South Sudan.

President Salva Kiir Mayardit has come to the same conclusion expressed in the above passage by the Ebony Center: "**Now, the hard work must begin**." Indeed, on 22 May 2025, a significant generational transition occurred within the SPLM leadership. This event symbolized a hopeful turning point, as emerging leaders assumed responsibility for guiding South Sudan toward renewed peace and development. The passing of the torch was anticipated to invigorate the political landscape with fresh perspectives and renewed commitment to the nation's founding vision.

The appointment of Dr. Benjamin Bol Mel, Mary Apayi, and Simon Kun Pouch as first, second, and third deputies of the Chairman of the Sudan People's Liberation Movement (SPLM) marks a momentous milestone in South Sudan's political evolution. This leadership transition is not merely a routine change of personnel but a profound generational shift, signaling a decisive break from the era of four decades (i.e., 42 years) dominated by the founding revolutionary guards. It heralds the dawn of a new chapter characterized by rejuvenated vision and dynamism.

Salva Kiir's decision to initiate a leadership transition at this pivotal juncture—two decades after the passing away of Dr. John Garang—stands as a testament to his unwavering dedication to the future prosperity of the nation. This deliberate and courageous move embodies a profound respect for Dr. Garang's vision while embracing the necessity of renewal and progress. By entrusting leadership to the next generation, exemplified by figures like Dr. Benjamin Bol Mel, Kiir signals a commitment to expertise, innovation, and forward-thinking governance.

This transition is not merely a change of personnel; it is the passing of the torch to the "Seeds of the Nation," ensuring that the ideals and aspirations of the SPLM remain vibrant and alive. The people and supporters of the SPLM are called to recognize and embrace this transformative moment as a crucial step toward sustainable national development and unity.

Mary Apayi stands as a trailblazer among the first cohort of women from Greater Equatoria to enlist in the SPLA, steadily ascending through the ranks to attain the distinguished rank of general. Her appointment as second deputy not only exemplifies her exceptional leadership and dedication but also embodies the SPLM's unwavering commitment to inclusivity and gender parity. Through her pioneering journey, Mary Apayi amplifies the voices of diverse leadership, reinforcing the party's resolve to broaden participation and empower women within its highest echelons.

Simon Kun Pouch's elevation to third deputy further consolidates this transformative leadership framework for gender, ethnic, and regional balance. His fresh perspective and dedication to public service embody the aspirations of a new generation of leadership eager to contribute constructively to South Sudan's peace and prosperity.

Collectively, these appointments embody a resolute break from the vestiges of former leadership—Dr. James Wani Igga, Gen. Daniel Awet Akot, and Gen. Kuol Manyang Juuk—whose foundational stewardship now yields to a new generation entrusted with the sacred charge of advancing the national vision. This decisive transition heralds a future imbued with unwavering dedication and transformative ambition, steadfastly aligned with Dr. John Garang's enduring dream of unity, prosperity, sustainable peace, economic growth, and poverty eradication.

The move toward transition holds immense significance for the SPLM and South Sudan at large. It injects renewed energy and optimism into the political landscape, fostering an environment conducive to innovative policies, coherent and inclusive governance.

By entrusting leadership to individuals with fresh perspectives, the SPLM reaffirms its commitment to *Garangism*.

Furthermore, replacing entrenched leadership with emerging, dynamic figures within the SPLM marks a pivotal moment in South Sudan's history. This decisive transformation not only revitalizes the party's legitimacy but also demonstrates an unwavering commitment to addressing the evolving socio-political realities faced by the nation. Such renewal is indispensable for fostering genuine national unity and signaling to both the South Sudanese people and international partners that the SPLM is resolutely advancing towards sustainable peace. Moreover, this change will catalyze accelerated progress in economic development underpinned by the eradication of poverty as envisioned by Dr. John Garang.

It is imperative that all stakeholders recognize and support this vital evolution as the foundation upon which South Sudan's prosperous and peaceful future will be built. This is because the appointments of Dr. Benjamin Bol Mel, Mary Apayi, and Simon Kun Pouch as the SPLM Chairman deputies represent a pivotal renewal moment. We believe that this generational handover is a testament to the party's foresight and dedication to South Sudan's founding ideals, underpinned by *Garangism*. It is a hopeful sign that the country's future will be guided by leaders who embody both continuity and innovation, ensuring a resilient and prosperous path forward.

Chapter Six

A Review of the Application of 'Garangnomics' Since 2013

> *"South Sudan was expected, in the light of rich natural resources and international political capital, to experience high rates of economic growth or at least to take steps toward a steady state of its economy. However, it did not, for the country was already in a fragility trap."* [64]

Since 2013, the aspirations embodied in Garang's vision for South Sudan have regrettably remained unfulfilled, according to those of us who consider ourselves to be students of John Garang. Despite the country's abundant natural resources and the considerable international political capital it commands, South Sudan has failed to embark upon a trajectory of combating poverty and a sense of marginalization all over the country. This failure can be chiefly attributed to the

---

[64] From *Identifying Binding Constraints on Growth in the Context of Fragility: The Case of South Sudan.* By Lual A. Deng, Abdurohman Ali Hussien, Augustino Ting Mayai. A research project funded by the African Economic Research Consortium, 2014.

nation's entrapment within a fragility trap, a condition wherein the very structures necessary for economic advancement are undermined by persistent instability and institutional weakness.

As discussed in the preceding chapter, the fragility trap impedes the establishment of a steady economic state, thereby stalling progress and thwarting developmental initiatives. This would not have happened if Dr. John Garang's students and associates had been given the opportunity to implement the SPLM blueprints for post-conflict reconstruction. We would unambiguously state that **disorganized anger** within the SPLM undermined our quest for sustainable peace, economic growth, and poverty eradication.

The promise of South Sudan's abundant natural resources and the goodwill garnered through diplomatic avenues remain tragically unrealized. Entrenched fragility and weak institutions have stymied the anticipated dividends of prosperity and stability. *Garangnomics* demands that we confront these systemic vulnerabilities with unwavering resolve. Without the establishment of resilient governance structures, Dr. John Garang's noble aspirations—to eradicate poverty and heal the wounds of marginalization—will remain elusive dreams.

It is incumbent upon policymakers and development stakeholders to recognize that economic wealth alone is insufficient; only through steadfast institution-building can the foundations for sustainable development be laid. The path forward is clear: embrace *Garangnomics* not as a mere vision, but as an urgent mandate to transform South Sudan's destiny. Failure to act decisively condemns the nation to continued instability and unfulfilled potential.

This conclusion of not acting decisively will be appreciated by focusing the discussion in the rest of this chapter on the following two key sections:

1. A Brief Highlight of the theoretical underpinnings of Garang's ideas on development; and
2. The ongoing struggle against poverty and marginalization.

Theoretical Underpinnings of Garang's Ideas on Development [65]
We must review the theoretical underpinnings of Dr. John Garang's ideas on development as a prerequisite for understanding his quest to combat poverty and a sense of marginalization in South Sudan. It must be stated here that the triple objectives of the post-conflict development strategy were sustainable peace, economic growth, and poverty eradication. They were framed based on *Garangnomics*. However, the theoretical underpinnings were not sufficiently understood and internalized by the SPLM cadre assigned to govern Southern Sudan during the Interim Period.

Hence, we are morally obliged to explain the economic mechanics of violence and economic growth so that all stakeholders can understand this elusive concept of *Garangnomics*.

Conflict-induced fragility and growth theories are exciting for understanding *Garangnomics* in the context of South Sudan. As people who were associated with Dr. John, the most appropriate approach is to look at the growth literature and the economics of violence literature. The preferred approach would have been to look at the literature on conflict-induced fragility instead of the economics of violence. However, we do not yet have a theory *per se* of the economics of fragility. Therefore, our approximation of this theory is the economics of violence. The two theories (growth and violence) complement

---

65   Most of this section is informed by our research paper on *Identifying Binding Constraints on Growth in the Context of Fragility: The Case of South Sudan.* By Lual A. Deng, Abdurohman Ali Hussien, Augustino Ting Mayai. A research project funded by the African Economic Research Consortium, 2014.

each other in our search to identify the binding constraints on the application of Dr. John's ideas on development.

The economics of violence theory enables us to identify the necessary (or first-order) conditions of *Garangnomics*. This means demonstrating that **peace** is a prerequisite for combating poverty and addressing a sense of marginalization. We achieve this by explaining the behavior of economic agents in a highly uncertain environment created by violence. Households in rural areas are, for instance, competing over factors (i.e., land and labor) of production with both the government and armed opposition groups in South Sudan. The government and armed opposition groups are essentially competing over the monopoly of violence, which is informed by a production function of a monopolistic firm.

Economic growth theory unequivocally reveals that the economy must expand as an indispensable prerequisite to eradicating poverty and confronting the pervasive sense of marginalization experienced in South Sudan. Within the framework of *Garangnomics*, growth is not merely desirable but constitutes a fundamental and sufficient condition for sustainable development and social equity. It is imperative that all stakeholders prioritize robust economic advancement to fulfill these critical objectives and secure a prosperous future for the nation.

1. The Economics of Violence Literature

The literature review in this sub-section is anchored in microeconomics theory, which offers a robust framework for understanding the behavior of economic agents within contexts marked by violence and fragility. Microeconomics is particularly well-suited to analyze the decision-making processes of households and firms operating under macroeconomic policy constraints. This analytical lens provides policymakers with critical insights into how individuals and businesses respond to national policies amid conflict.

Consequently, leadership is imperative in public policy formulation, which attentively considers the opportunities, incentives, preferences, and scarcity constraints that shape the choices of the South Sudanese populace in such an environment. This nuanced understanding is essential for crafting effective and responsive policies that address the unique challenges faced in fragile settings. This is because visionary leadership constitutes a fundamental determinant of economic development, as extensively documented in growth literature.

It is, therefore, imperative to comprehend the behavior of leaders across various entities—be they countries, households, or firms—within conflict environments. The state of insecurity profoundly influences rational decision-making; leaders on opposing sides of conflict often harbor uncertainty regarding their prospects for forgiveness and protection should they relinquish power peacefully.

Absent a clear vision and adherence to political morality, such leaders tend to maintain their positions until an inevitable outcome is realized. Besouw et al. (2016) underscore the critical importance of understanding violence in this context, highlighting the intricate dynamics that govern leadership conduct amid conflict:

> *"Violence is key to understanding human interaction and societal development. A society that is unable to contain violence will be disrupted and cannot be expected to sustain high levels of welfare, as is painfully illustrated by the current situation in Afghanistan, Libya or, perhaps most conspicuously, parts of Sub-Saharan Africa. Countries like Congo, Somalia, and Sudan are almost continuously torn up by extortion and coercion under*

the threat of violence, factional strife, and intermittent periods of open violence. Such conditions may destroy lives and capital goods, and deter interaction, exchange, investment, trade, and the benefits of specialization that come with trade, leading to significant welfare losses." [66]

We can draw key implications for South Sudan analysts and policymakers from the above quotation, to include the following steps:
1. Prioritize violence containment and reduction to stabilize society and enable sustainable welfare improvements.
2. Address factional strife and coercion to prevent ongoing disruptions that destroy lives and capital.
3. Create conditions conducive to economic interaction, exchange, investment, and trade by reducing insecurity.
4. Recognize that persistent violence deters specialization and economic growth, so peacebuilding is essential for development.
5. Develop comprehensive strategies that integrate security, social cohesion, and economic policies to reverse welfare losses caused by violence.

Another helpful passage is from Charles Schultz's Nobel Prize Lecture on 8th December 1979:

"Most of the people in the world are poor, so if we knew the economics of being poor, we would know much of the economics that really matters. Most of the world's poor people earn their living from agriculture, so if we knew the economics of agriculture, we would know much of the

---

[66]　Besouw et al., 2016:139

economics of being poor." [67]

Understanding John Garang's ideas on economic growth is not just an academic exercise—it is an urgent necessity for anyone committed to lasting peace and prosperity. Why? Because Garang recognized that economic growth cannot be separated from the realities of insecurity and conflict that plague countries like South Sudan. With over 81% of the population affected by violent conflict, the stakes couldn't be higher.

Think about it: when people live in environments riddled with violence, their livelihoods are deeply insecure. Garang's insight, echoing Schultz's tradition, teaches us that if we truly grasp the economics of violence, we unlock the economics of insecurity itself. This is the economic dimension that "really matters."

Bromley (2014) sharpens this point by showing that civil conflict is not just about politics or power—it is about young people facing bleak prospects. When they can't find better livelihoods, predatory behaviors become an understandable response to desperation and idle time. Garang's framework compels us to see economic growth as a tool to change this dynamic.

For policymakers and development professionals, this means that fostering economic growth is not just about numbers on a balance sheet. It is about creating pathways to security and stability by addressing the root causes of conflict. We venture to state here that poverty and marginalization are among the root causes of conflict in South Sudan. Hence, ignoring Garang's ideas means missing a critical piece of the puzzle. In short, embracing Garang's vision guides us toward policies that promote sustainable development, peace, and human

---

67   Schultz, 1979:1

dignity. It is time to take these ideas seriously because economic growth without understanding its link to insecurity will never be truly transformative.

Such a situation also creates, according to Besouw et al. (2016:141), an opportunity for **"a group of individually optimizing violence specialists"** to recruit young males to advance their own agenda. This, in turn, reduces the size of the labor force that would have been engaged in productive economic activity necessary for the economy to growth. There is not yet a theory of economics of violence, though the work of Besouw et al. (2016) could be considered as the beginning of a formal theoretical framework. They have introduced an important concept of what they call "violence specialists" comprised of elite coalitions and warlords. They introduce their work as follows:

> *"We stress that the nature of violence considered in this paper, however, is of a higher level than the banditry-type of violence commonly considered in the literature on the economics of conflict and appropriation...and that ordinary producers cannot therefore decide to become specialists in violence. In addition, the capacity for large-scale violence is the domain of a small, but substantial group of violence specialists who do not necessarily work together, instead of a monolithic elite or elite group."* [68]

The above sentiment about the effect of violence has been echoed earlier by the *Economist* magazine on 14th April 2011 when commenting on the World Bank Annual Development Report. It stated: "**Yet the World Development Report suggests that the main constraint**

---

68   Besouw et al., 2016:140

on development these days may not be a poverty trap but a violence trap. Peaceful countries are managing to escape poverty—which is becoming concentrated in countries riven by civil war, ethnic conflict and organized crime. Violence and bad government prevent them from escaping the trap."

The economics of violence literature also helps us to explain how conflict (or war) affects what we call the secondary drivers of economic growth. A point articulated by Besouw and others and quoted earlier in the preceding paragraphs as follows: "**Such conditions may destroy lives and capital goods, and deter interaction, exchange, investment, trade, and the benefits of specialization that come with trade, leading to significant welfare losses**" (Besouw et al., 2016:139).

South Sudan emerged from a fundamentally fragile Sudanese state. It unequivocally exemplifies a natural state, characterized by a societal structure wherein a subset of the population, empowered to mobilize organized large-scale violence, constitutes an elite coalition that effectively controls both violence and coercive appropriation (Besouw et al., 2016:140).

Moreover, the ruling elite's behavior was underpinned by the inability to internalize the economics of peace within the newly independent state and with its neighbors. For instance, Alemayehu Geda and Steve Kayizzi-Mugerwa (2012) did advise the Sudanese and South Sudanese policy makers as follows:

> *"Notwithstanding the number of outstanding issues that need the immediate attention of the two governments, the agreement on future economic relations is undoubtedly the most pressing one. Specifically, the immediate task should be to negotiate on the issue of oil, debt, currency and related economic issues. The viability of the two*

economies is to a large degree conditional on a workable agreement on these issues and having a stable macroeconomic environment in both North and South Sudan. This stable macroeconomic environment relates to the issue of low inflation, stable exchange rate and prudent fiscal and external balance." [69]

The Government of the Republic of South Sudan (GRSS) ignored the above advice, evidenced by the shutdown of oil production just six months after independence from Sudan. Geda and Kayizzi-Mugerwa (2012) proposed an analytical framework for negotiating issues of oil, debt, and currency, which could have yielded a win-win outcome if the GRSS' experts had understood its theoretical underpinning. They did not, and the consequences of that failure are vividly captured by the inability to combat poverty and a sense of marginalization.

2. The Growth Literature

A retrospective examination of the evolution of economic thought reveals that the primary inquiry has consistently been the factors driving economic growth. This enduring quest for understanding and explanation can be traced back to the seminal work of Adam Smith, *"An Inquiry into the Nature and Causes of the Wealth of Nations,"* first published in 1776. To underscore this point, we reference a passage from the introduction of the *Wealth of Nations*, which eloquently encapsulates the foundational importance of this inquiry. Such a historical perspective not only highlights the continuity of scholarly pursuit but also reinforces the critical relevance of economic growth as a central theme in economic analysis:

---

69   Geda and Kayizzi-Mugerwa, 2012:3

> *"The annual labour of every nation is the fund which originally supplies it with all the necessaries and conveniences of life which it annually consumes ... bears a greater or smaller proportion to the number of those who are to consume it.... [B]ut this proportion must in every nation be regulated by two different circumstances: first, by the skill, dexterity, and judgment with which its labour is generally applied; and secondly, by the proportion between the number of those who are employed in useful labour, and that of those who are not so employed."* [70]

In light of the above passage, it is imperative to recognize the profound insights provided by Dr. John Garang regarding combating poverty and a sense of marginalization within the overall framework of economic development. His vision, which intricately links social cohesion and equitable resource distribution with sustainable growth, offers a nuanced framework that transcends conventional economic paradigms. Garang's emphasis on inclusive development underscores the necessity of integrating marginalized communities into the economic fabric of the nation, thereby fostering resilience and long-term prosperity.

Moreover, this perspective aligns with contemporary understandings that economic advancement is not solely predicated on material capital but equally reliant on social capital and institutional integrity. Consequently, embracing Garang's holistic approach facilitates formulating policies that promote economic vitality and social justice, ensuring that development benefits are broadly shared and enduring.

---

[70]   *An Inquiry into the Nature and Causes of the Wealth of Nations* first published in 1776, p.3.

Such a paradigm is indispensable for scholars and practitioners committed to advancing comprehensive and equitable economic progress underpinned by human capital. That is, we must effectively and efficiently utilize the annual labor of South Sudan as a fundamental strategy for combating poverty and a sense of marginalization.

Simon Kuznets articulates further the idea of human capital in the process of economic growth:

> *"If technology is to be employed efficiently and widely, and, indeed, if its own progress is to be stimulated by such use, institutional and ideological adjustments must be made to effect the proper use of innovations generated by the advancing stock of human knowledge."* (Kuznets, 1971:1)

Kuznets (1971) identified in his Nobel Memorial Lecture the following six characteristics of economic growth:

1. High rates of increase in per capita product and of population in developed countries;
2. High rates of increase in output per unit of all inputs;
3. High rate of structural transformation;
4. Changes in the structures of society and its ideology, e.g. urbanization and secularization;
5. Globalization or what Kuznets describes as "**propensity to reach out to the rest of the world**" (1971:2); and
6. Growing gap between developed and developing countries in "**that the economic performance in countries accounting for three-quarters of the world population still falls far short of the minimum levels feasible with the potential of modern technology**" (Kuznets, 1971:2).

Stephen Broadberry's empirical research, grounded in the rigorous analysis of quantitative data on GDP, population, and per capita GDP extending to medieval periods, robustly modifies and confirms the defining characteristics of modern economic growth. His findings, corroborated by esteemed economic historians such as Maddison, van Zanden, Malanima, and Alvarez-Nogal, represent a significant advancement in our understanding of economic history, underscoring the enduring relevance of longitudinal data in economic scholarship.:

> *"...we provide a summary statement of the revised characteristics of modern economic growth, arrived at inductively from the growing availability of quantitative evidence on the long run growth process over the last millennium and presented in the previous section."*
> (Broadberry, 2016:21)

The characteristics are:
1. Sustained growth of per capita product, with the ending of growth reversals;
2. Demographic transition;
3. Sustained structural transformation from agriculture to services and to industry;
4. Institutional change: fiscal centralization and parliamentary control;
5. Market integration; and
6. Great Divergence.

While the characteristics of economic growth outlined above are significant, they unfortunately do not inform us about how and why growth and performance vary between countries and over time. In other words, we require a growth theory that explains the proximate and fundamental causes of economic growth. Nonetheless, Petrakos and Arvanitidis (2008) point out that there is no unified growth theory.

It is worth emphasizing that a substantial volume of empirical research has a multi-theoretical basis due to the lack of a unifying theory on economic growth. This means that studies draw on several theoretical frameworks and examine factors highlighted by many paradigms. As a result, findings are often contradictory and far from conclusive (Petrakos and Arvanitidis, 2008:12).

We are, however, comforted by Daron Acemoglu in that:

"While there is disagreement among macroeconomists about how to approach short-run macroeconomic phenomena and what the boundaries of macroeconomics should be, there is broad agreement about the workhorse models of dynamic macroeconomic analysis. These include the Solow growth model, the neoclassical growth model, the overlapping-generations model and models of technological change and technology adoption. Since these are all models of economic growth, a thorough treatment of modern economic growth can also provide (and perhaps should provide) an introduction to this core material of modern macroeconomics." (Acemoglu, 2009: xi)

It is, therefore, evident that technological progress is a function of human knowledge (i.e., the skill, shrewdness, and judgment with which labor is used in producing goods and services). In this context, we consider the *Wealth of Nations* to be the first economic growth theory where labor was the primary driver of growth. Daron Acemoglu further defines technology as: "**advances in techniques of production, advances in knowledge, and the general efficiency of the organization of production**" (Acemoglu, 2009: 25).

The work of Daron Acemoglu (2009) is critical in understanding the theoretical underpinnings of *Garangnomics*. His work is extensive in that he uses theory and empirics to differentiate between proximate and fundamental causes of economic growth. In our view, this is a major contribution to understanding economic growth in a fragile and post-conflict setting, such as South Sudan. We have stated earlier that our interest in growth theory is because South Sudan's economy must grow in order to combat poverty and a sense of marginalization.

On proximate determinants of growth, Acemoglu (2009) identifies physical capital, human capital, and technology as the proximate causes of economic growth. We add to this list savings and investments, or more precisely, the savings ratio and capital-output ratio, which were the focus of earlier theoretical frameworks such as: a) the Harrod-Domar model of economic growth;[71] and b) the Lewis model of economic growth (i.e., of a dual economy with unlimited supply of labor).

The Harrod-Domar model is considered to be a classical Keynesian model of economic growth. The model simply states that the GDP growth rate is equal to the savings ratio divided by the capital-output ratio. In this sense, we could say that it is mainly concerned with a study of the conditions that influence the smooth and uninterrupted growth of national income in a country. Therefore, the central premise of this model is the process of capital accumulation. The assumption makes it evident that the model considers both the demand side (i.e.,

---

71   The model had been developed independently by Roy F. Harrod in 1939 and Evsey Domar in 1946.

investments) and the supply side (i.e., savings) of capital accumulation. For ease of exposition, we illustrate the Harrod-Domar model of economic growth using a virtual cycle in Figure 4 below.

The concepts of foreign and external borrowing are fundamentally rooted in the economic model addressing the challenges faced by developing countries due to insufficient domestic savings. Typically, these nations experience limited investment opportunities, primarily because their internal savings rates are inadequate to finance necessary developmental projects. To bridge this savings-investment gap, developing economies such as South Sudan may seek development assistance through foreign aid or engage in borrowing from developed countries and prominent international financial institutions (IFIs). These institutions include, but are not limited to, the World Bank, the International Monetary Fund (IMF), and the African Development Bank (AfDB).

By securing such external financial resources, these countries can augment their savings capacity, which, in turn, facilitates increased investment in critical sectors. Investments may encompass infrastructure development, acquisition of advanced equipment, machinery, and other essential capital goods. Consequently, this process not only promotes economic growth but also fosters sustainable development by enabling the accumulation of productive assets necessary for long-term prosperity.

Increased investments (Figure 4 opposite) lead to higher stock of capital, which would in turn be used in the production of what Kuznets calls "**increasingly diverse economic goods**" (Kuznets, 1971:1). Increases in GDP (i.e. diverse economic goods and services) would lead to higher levels of income, bearing in mind that savings in this model is a function of income. We are back to the point (i.e. circle) where we started this virtual cycle – increased savings as a consequence of higher national income would lead to increased investment to higher capital stock and the cycle continues.

Figure 4: Graphical Illustration of the Harrod-Domar Growth Model

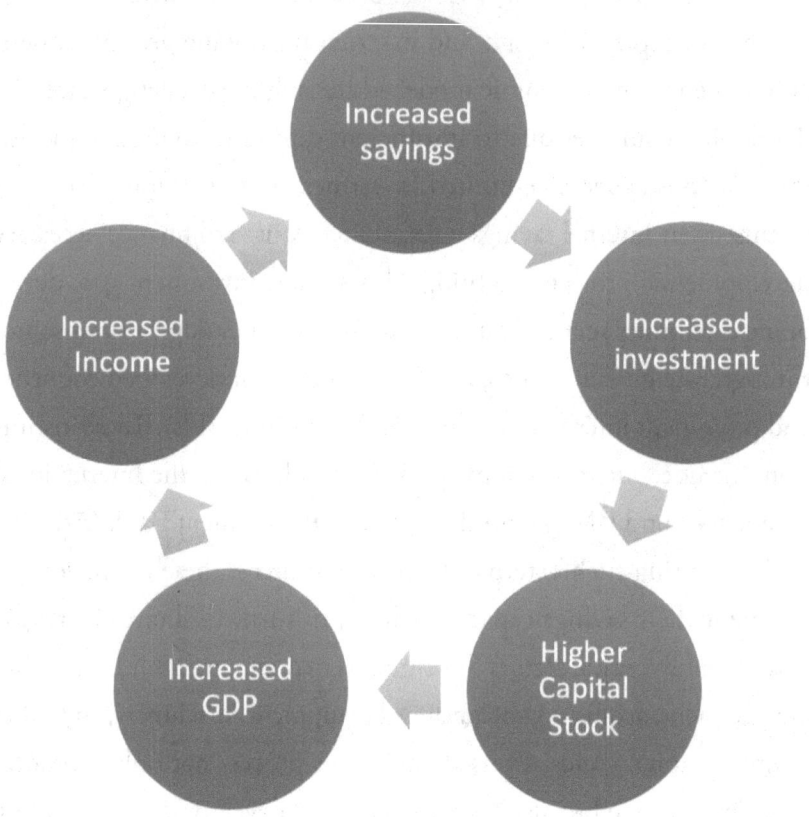

There is a general agreement among the four main theoretical frameworks underpinning our growth literature review that physical capital accumulation is one of the proximate determinants of economic growth. The four theoretical frameworks are: a) Harrod-Domar model of economic growth; b) Lewis model of economic growth (i.e., of a dual economy with unlimited supply of labor); c) Neoclassical growth model (especially Solow-Swan model); and d) New growth theory.

We have not included Walt Rostow's stages of economic growth among these frameworks, for our focus is not on stages of growth per se, but rather on determinants of growth.[72] However, the third stage of Rostow's model (i.e., takeoff) is relevant to our discussion here, especially when read together with Lewis and Harrod-Domar growth models.

The graphic illustration in Figure 4 above of the Harrod-Domar growth model is based on a large volume of empirical literature. For instance, Nkurunziza (2017) citing the work of Bosworth and Collins (2003) states "**that capital accumulation was the key to the successful growth experience of East Asian economies**" (Nkurunziza, 2017:16). He concludes "**African countries will need to substantially scale up their rates of capital accumulation to deliver high and sustainable rates of economic growth**" (Nkurunziza, 2017:16). This is because capital accumulation is affected, according to the growth literature, by low returns to economic activity and high cost of finance (Hausmann et al., 2005; Rodrik, 2013).

Moreover, Dani Rodrik (2013) explains using GDF that low returns to private investment and "**therefore inadequate demand for investment is due to: government failures, market failures, and problems in other markets.**"

We would be remiss if we did not mention the Lewis model at this point before proceeding to the fundamental causes of economic growth. W. Arthur Lewis is considered as one of the pioneers of development economics.[73] He was awarded the Nobel Prize in 1979 for

---

72   Walt W. Rostow in his book: *Stages of economic growth: A non-communist manifesto* published in 1960 identified five stages of economic growth: 1) Traditional society; 2) Pre-conditions for takeoff; 3) Takeoff; 4) Drive to maturity; and 5) Age of mass consumption.

73   Lewis, W. Arthur. 1954. *Economic development with unlimited supplies of labour*. The Manchester School. 22: 139–91.

his path-breaking work on capital accumulation in the dual economy characterized by two sectors–the traditional sector dominated by subsistence agriculture and a modern capitalist sector led by industry. There are six assumptions underpinning the Lewis growth model, which are:

1. A developing economy has a surplus of unproductive labor in the agricultural sector.
2. These workers are attracted to the growing manufacturing sector, where higher wages are offered.
3. The wages in the manufacturing sector are more or less fixed.
4. Entrepreneurs in the manufacturing sector make profits because they charge a price above the fixed wage rate.
5. These profits will be reinvested in the business as fixed capital.
6. An advanced manufacturing sector means an economy has moved from traditional to industrialized.

We present in Table 2 opposite the comparative features of the Lewis dual economy growth model in a tabular format:

Table 2: Characteristics of the Lewis Dual Economy Growth Model

Traditional sector (subsistence agriculture)	Capitalist sector (industrial sector)
1. Labour-intensive production process	1. Capital-intensive manufacturing process relying on the use of reproducible capital
2. Low average wages	2. Higher average wages
3. Low marginal and average productivity	3. Higher marginal and average productivity
4. Low dependency on capital	4. High demand for labour

We should point out that the dual economy growth model has other characteristics, such as formal versus informal sector, traded versus non-traded, and cash versus non-cash economy (Rodrik, 2016). The South Sudanese economy exhibits these characteristics of dualism, and hence the relevance of the Lewis dual economy growth model to *Garangnomics*. For instance, we can argue that the surplus labor in the traditional sector (i.e., the rural sector of South Sudan in which more than 80% of the population derives livelihood from) is being diverted toward the production of violence by both the government and armed opposition groups.

The foundational determinants of economic growth have been profoundly advanced through the new economic growth theory, as evidenced by seminal contributions from Kremendi and Mequire (1985), Lucas (1988), Grier and Tulock (1989), Romer (1990), Barro (1991), Acemoglu et al. (2005), Acemoglu (2009), and Rodrik (2018). It is essential to recognize that the neoclassical growth model emerged as a robust response to the limitations inherent in the Harrod-Domar growth framework. Central to this progression is the Solow-Swan model, which serves as the cornerstone of neoclassical growth theory by adopting a comprehensive long-term perspective.

The emphasis of the Solow-Swan model on the aggregate production function, particularly of the Cobb-Douglas form, provides a rigorous analytical foundation for understanding sustained economic expansion. Consequently, these theoretical advancements have significantly enriched the discourse on economic growth, offering vital insights for scholars and practitioners alike.

The growth accounting framework is another significant contribution of the Solow model (Acemoglu, 2009). It provides an essential framework for utilizing tools from both macroeconomics and microeconomics to understand the determinants of growth. Acemoglu underscores this contribution as follows:

> *"Another major contribution of Bob Solow to the study of economic growth was the observation that this production function, combined with competitive factor markets, also gives us a framework for accounting for the sources of economic growth. In particular, Solow (1957) developed what has become one of the most common tools in macroeconomics, the growth accounting framework."* (Acemoglu, 2009:87)

Furthermore, Smriti Chand[74] provides a good summary of the Solow-Swan economic growth model. The model "**postulates a**

---

74   Cited from *The Solow-Swan model of economic growth – Explained*: Article shared by Smriti Chand at http://www.yourarticlelibrary.com/macro-economics/growth-models/the-solow-swan-model-of-economic-growth-explained/31196

continuous production function linking output to the inputs of capital and labour, which leads to the steady state equilibrium of the economy." [75]

We would like to stress here that a **steady state equilibrium of an economy** refers to a condition where key economic variables such as capital stock, output, and population grow at constant rates, resulting in a stable economic structure over time. In this state, the economy's growth path is balanced so that the ratios of important factors like capital to labor remain constant, and there are no inherent forces causing the economy to move away from this position. Essentially, the steady state represents a long-run equilibrium where the economy grows sustainably without fluctuations in its growth rates or structural imbalances.

At this pivotal stage in the review of growth theory, it is imperative to underscore several pertinent points that may significantly deepen our understanding of the economics underlying the growth model as they relate to our discussions of the theoretical underpinnings of Dr. John Garang's ideas of development:

1. The output growth rate in the steady state is exogenous and independent of the savings rate and technical progress.
2. If the savings rate increases, it increases the output per worker by increasing the capital per worker, but the growth rate of output is not affected.
3. Another implication of the model is that growth in per capita income can either be achieved by increased savings or a reduced rate of population growth. This will hold if depreciation is allowed in the model.
4. Another prediction of the model is that in the absence of continuing improvements in technology, growth per worker must

---

75   Ibid.

ultimately cease. This prediction follows from the assumption of diminishing returns to capital.
5. This model predicts conditional convergence. All countries with similar characteristics, such as savings rate, population growth rate, technology, etc., that affect growth will converge to the same steady-state level. This means that poor countries with the same savings rate and level of technology as rich countries will reach the same steady-state growth rates in the long run.[76]

The new growth theory fundamentally advances the neoclassical framework, specifically the Solow model, by rigorously incorporating technological progress as an endogenous factor. Daron Acemoglu distinctly elucidates this critical development, underscoring its profound implications for contemporary economic analysis, which is relevant to our review of the application of *Garangnomics*:

> *"In all of our models, especially in those that endogenize physical capital, human capital and technology accumulation, individuals will respond to (profit) incentives. Economic institutions shape these incentives. Therefore, we will see that the way that humans themselves decide to organize their societies determines whether or not incentives to improve productivity and increase output will be forthcoming. Some ways of organizing societies encourage people to innovate, to take risks, to save for the future, to find better ways of doing things, to learn and educate themselves, to solve problems of collective action and to provide public goods." (Acemoglu, 2009:143)*

---

76   Ibid.

The passage from Acemoglu underscores the pivotal role of economic institutions in shaping incentives that drive productivity, innovation, and societal progress. For South Sudan, a nation striving to overcome the legacies of conflict and underdevelopment, this insight is profoundly instructive. Moreover, the passage articulates John Garang's idea that poverty is a function of marginalization. As students of John Garang, we can now state unambiguously that we have the theoretical backing to pursue the realization of his noble ideas.

Firstly, policymakers must recognize that the organization of societal institutions directly influences individuals' motivation to innovate, save, educate themselves, and contribute productively to the economy. In line with Dr. John Garang's vision, which emphasized empowerment, unity, and self-reliance, South Sudan's development strategy should prioritize the establishment of inclusive and robust economic institutions that foster equitable participation and collective action.

Secondly, economic policies should be designed to create an environment that rewards risk-taking and innovation while addressing collective action problems. This approach resonates with Garang's advocacy for social justice and the provision of public goods as foundational elements for sustainable peace, economic growth, and poverty eradication. By ensuring transparent governance, property rights protection, and equitable access to resources, South Sudan can stimulate productive incentives essential for growth. Moreover, these economic policies were premised on the idea of combating poverty and a sense of marginalization in South Sudan, which we have conceptualized as *Garangnomics*.

Thirdly, human capital development must be central to policy formulation. Encouraging education and skill acquisition aligns with the passage's emphasis on learning and productivity improvement. This commitment reflects Garang's call for investment in the people of South Sudan, enabling them to participate actively and benefit from economic advancement.

Finally, recognizing that institutions are human constructs subject to change, South Sudanese leaders and analysts should actively engage in shaping institutions that reflect the country's unique cultural, social, and historical context. This dynamic process is critical to fostering an economic environment conducive to sustained growth and social cohesion. In this regard, integrating Acemoglu's institutional economics with Dr. John Garang's developmental philosophy offers a comprehensive framework. It could guide South Sudan toward building institutions that incentivize innovation, education, and collective responsibility—foundations indispensable for the nation's prosperous future.

Let us now turn to the fundamental causes of growth. above passage Daron Acemoglu (2009) highlights these causes as follows:

> *"At the risk of oversimplifying complex phenomena, we can think of the following list of potential fundamental causes: (i) luck (or multiple equilibria) that leads to divergent paths among societies with identical opportunities, preferences and market structures; (ii) geographic differences that affect the environment in which individuals live and that influence the productivity of agriculture, the availability of natural resources, certain constraints on individual behavior, or even individual attitudes; (iii) institutional differences that affect the laws and regulations under which individuals and firms function and thus shape the incentives they have for accumulation, investment and trade; and (iv) cultural differences that determine individuals' values, preferences and beliefs."*
> *(Acemoglu, 2009: 23)*

We identify five proximate determinants of economic growth: savings, investment, physical capital, human capital, and technology. Complementing these are four fundamental causes: luck, culture, geography, and institutions. To facilitate a comprehensive understanding of their interplay, we propose a policy matrix framework (Table 3) wherein the rows correspond to the proximate determinants and the columns to the fundamental causes.

This structured analytical tool is indispensable for policymakers, economists, and development professionals committed to formulating effective strategies aimed at eradicating poverty and addressing the pervasive sense of marginalization in South Sudan. Appreciating these complex interactions is essential for the design and implementation of targeted interventions that promote sustainable and inclusive growth.

Table 3: A framework for Understanding Intersections Between Proximate and Fundamental Causes of Growth

Proximate Determinants of Economic Growth	Fundamental Causes of Economic Growth			
	Luck (Leadership)	Culture	Geography	Institutions
Savings	Visionary leadership ensures: Conducive environment for domestic savings Mobilization of development assistance and effective utilization of foreign aid Efficient borrowing from both domestic and external sources	Influences society's savings rates	Lends natural resources, which directly contribute to growth in nation's wealth	Effective institutions, just like leadership ensure: Conducive environment for domestic savings Mobilization of development assistance and effective utilization of foreign aid Efficient borrowing from both domestic and external sources

Investment	Visionary leadership ensures: Adherence to the rule of law, which would in turn encourage Foreign Direct Investment (FDI) Private property rights Functioning markets underpinned by free movement of goods and services, including capital	Cultural differences that determine individuals' values, preferences and beliefs for undertaking investment activities	Geographical conditions determine the type and priority areas for investment	Inclusive political and economic institutions that ensure effective and efficient allocation of resources to priority areas of public investment, which in turn leads to: a) high returns to economic activity; b) low cost of financing
Physical Capital	Visionary leadership ensures investment: Capital goods Public goods, e.g. roads and bridges, railway, schools Power-generation, telecommunications	Influences society's willingness to accumulate physical capital	Geographical conditions determine the nature and magnitude of capital accumulation, which would in turn determine the pace of economic growth	Inclusive political and economic institutions that ensure effective and efficient capital accumulation for sustainable economic growth
Human Capital	Visionary leadership ensures investment: Education Health Research and Development (R&D)	Influences society's willingness to accumulate human capital	Geographical conditions determine the type of educational system that in turn enables the society or country to pursue economic growth strategies consistent with the geography the society finds itself in	Inclusive political and economic institutions that ensure effective and efficient human capital accumulation for sustainable economic growth

| Technology | Visionary leadership ensures: Creative destruction of old technology through innovation and adoption of new advanced technologies | Cultural differences that determine individuals' values, preferences and beliefs for the type of technological change and technology adoption | Geographical conditions determine the type of technological change and technology adoption that in turn enables the society or country to pursue economic growth strategies consistent with the geography the society finds itself in | Inclusive political and economic institutions that ensure effective and efficient systems that encourage advances in techniques of production, advances in knowledge, and the general efficiency of the organization of production |

Source: Constructed by the author

The second column identifies luck as one of the fundamental determinants of economic outcomes. However, Acemoglu et al. (2016) have refined this perspective by substituting "luck" with "ignorance" in their seminal work, *Why Nations Fail*. Their analysis is grounded in three robust paradigms—namely, institutional economics, development economics, and economic history—which they employ to rigorously evaluate the empirical validity of the four principal causes of growth. Concurrently, Jones and Olken (2005) approach the concept of luck through the lens of leadership, posing the critical question: Do leaders matter?

Their comprehensive investigation into leadership's influence on post-World War II economic growth offers compelling empirical evidence that not only confirms but firmly establishes leadership as a critical determinant of economic trajectories. By systematically analyzing diverse contexts and outcomes, this study reveals how leadership decisions and styles directly shape growth patterns, thereby providing deeper insights into the mechanisms driving economic development. This robust correlation advances our understanding of growth dynamics and underscores the indispensable role of effective leadership in fostering sustained economic progress:

> *"We find robust evidence that leaders matter for growth. The results suggest that the effects of individual leaders are strongest in autocratic settings where there are fewer constraints on a leader's power. Leaders also appear to affect policy outcomes, particularly monetary policy. The results suggest that individual leaders can play crucial roles in shaping the growth of nations."* (Jones and Olken, 2005:835)

Brady and Spence (2009) support the above empirical evidence through their appraisal of the Report of the Growth Commission.[77] They state that:

> *"In a careful empirical study, Jones and Olken (2005) look across all post–Second World War economies and find 57 cases in which the country's leader suddenly dies or resigns, for example, thus allowing them to use the natural experiment change in leadership for exogenous reasons to solve the endogeneity problem. That is, the unexpected death of a leader gives us a chance to measure the leader's effect on growth. Of course, the change can be positive or*

---

[77] Commission on Growth and Development. 2008. The Growth Report: Strategies for Sustained Growth and Inclusive Development. Washington, DC: International Bank for Reconstruction and Development and the World Bank.

negative. They found that the change of national leaders is related to economic growth. The effects were strongest (both positive and negative) in autocratic settings where one or a few leaders have centralized authority." (Brady and Spence, 2009:4)

Besley et al. (2011) motivated by the work of Jones and Olken (2005) examined data on about 1,000 political leaders during the period 1875-2004. They found that **"heterogeneity among leaders' educational attainment is important with growth being higher by having leaders who are more highly educated"** (Besley et al., 2011:205).

We agree with the above findings in that a visionary leader, as discussed in Chapter Two of the book, is critical at the initial stages of a new country, such as South Sudan. This is because a visionary leader is required to lay the foundation for inclusive political and economic institutions, which would, in turn, formulate and execute growth-promoting policies. Therefore, leadership is, in our view, the primary driver of economic growth than institutions. Moreover, there is limited academic research on leadership and economic growth; a point which influences us to make long quotations from the empirical literature as by way of contextualizing our statement. Here is, for instance, a long passage from Brady and Spence:

"...our approach has been to separate the development process into different periods and to analyze leaders' roles at the various stages. The obvious first stage is where the leadership chooses an economic model or strategy, a general overall approach to development and growth, and then builds coalitions, institutions, or both, capable

of sustaining a politics that allows the plan time to bring dividends in terms of growth. The second stage is in some sense not delimited in time because it concerns how leaders adjust strategies and choices to changing circumstances—economic and political. These adjustments can be responses to shocks or unanticipated external events, but they also occur in response to the endogenous evolution of characteristics of the economy in the course of growth. These latter challenges can and do range from rising income inequality, a rising middle class, competitive pressures from the global economy, rising incomes and wages causing shifting comparative advantage, and institutions not adapted to the evolving characteristics and state of development economy." (Brady and Spence, 2009:5)

The second fundamental cause of growth is culture, which Acemoglu articulates as follows:

"By culture, we refer to beliefs, values and preferences that influence individual economic behaviour. Differences in religious beliefs across societies are among the clearest examples of cultural differences that may affect economic behavior. Differences in preferences, for example, regarding how important wealth is relative to other status-generating activities and how patient individuals should be, might be as important as or even more important than luck, geography and institutions in affecting economic performance. Broadly speaking, culture can affect economic outcomes through two major channels.

First, it can affect the willingness of individuals to tradeoff different activities or consumption today versus consumption tomorrow. Via this channel, culture will influence societies' occupational choices, market structure, saving rates and their willingness to accumulate physical and human capital. Second, culture may also affect the degree of cooperation among individuals, and cooperation and trust are often important foundations for productive activities in societies." (Acemoglu, 2009:131-132)

The above passage is underpinned, in our view, by the work of Weber (1930), Banfield (1958), Kuznets (1971), and Putnam et al (1993). In describing the contribution of Max Weber, Acemglou summarizes it as follows:

"Weber argued that English piety, in particular, Protestantism, was an important driver of capitalists development. Protestantism led to a set of beliefs that emphasized hard work, thrift, saving. It also interpreted economic success as consistent with, even as signaling, being chosen by God. Weber contrasted these characteristics of Protestantism with those of other religions, such as Catholicism and other religions, which he argued did not promote capitalism." (Acemoglu, 2009:146)

Geography is the third fundamental cause of growth. We again turn to Acemoglu for his insights on this:

"By geography, we refer to all factors that are imposed on individuals as part of the physical, geographic and

ecological environment in which they live. Geography can affect economic growth through a variety of proximate causes. Geographic factors that can influence the growth process include soil quality, which can affect agricultural productivity; natural resources, which directly contribute to the wealth of a nation and may facilitate industrialization by providing certain key resources, such as coal and iron ore during critical times; climate, which may affect productivity and attitudes directly; topography, which can affect the costs of transportation and communication; and disease environment, which can affect individual health, productivity and incentives to accumulate physical and human capital." (Acemoglu, 2009:131)

Alfred Marshall was the first to identify geography in his seminal book, *Principles of Economics* (1890), as an important element in economic growth.[78] Others supported this view through empirical work (Myrdal, 1968; Diamond, 1997; Sachs, 2000; 2001; Bloom and Sachs, 1998).

Institutions constitute the fourth fundamental determinant of economic growth. There is a large body of empirical work on the role of institutions and their effect on economic outcomes. This literature is well articulated by Acemoglu (2009), and Rodrik (2016). We categorize this literature into three categories. The first group is on the market, and those who emphasize it as an important institution include Polanyi (2001), Bates (1981), and Foundation for Economic Education (2016). The Foundation for Economic Education gives the working meanings of market and private property:

---

78   See Marshall, Alfred.1890. Principles of Economics. Prometheus Books.

"The free market means the freedom of everybody to dispose of his property, to exchange it for other property or for money, or to employ it for further production, on whatever terms he finds acceptable. This freedom is of course a corollary of private property. Private property necessarily implies the right of use for consumption or for further production, and the right of free disposal or exchange." 79

The second group is on property rights and includes the work of **Skaperdas (1992), Tornell and Velasco (1992)**. The third group focuses on the importance of policies within a given institutional framework and includes: Perotti (1993), Saint-Paul and Verdier (1993).

We conclude the review of the growth literature with two proposals. The first is to treat leadership as the primary driver (or first-order condition) instead of being one of the four fundamental causes of economic growth. The second is to conceptualize savings and investments as secondary drivers (or second-order conditions) of economic growth. Stated differently, factors behind cross-country differences with respect to economic growth could be summarized from our review of the growth literature into three categories composed of nine factors/conditions.

The first category is what we would like to call drivers of economic growth, which consists of three drivers: leadership as a primary driver and secondary drivers, comprised of savings and investments. The second category consists of three (i.e., culture, geography, and institutions) of the four fundamental causes of economic growth. The third category comprises the proximate causes of economic growth (physical capital, human capital, and technology).

---

79   Quoted from https://fee.org/articles/the-five-institutions-of-the-market-economy/.

The Struggle Against Poverty and Marginalization

Since gaining independence in 2011, South Sudan has faced a paradoxical reality that starkly contrasts with Garang's aspirations. Despite the country's abundant oil revenues, which should have provided a solid foundation for development, extreme poverty remains widespread. This dissonance is a testament to the lost decade and a half, during which the promise of prosperity has largely eluded the population. The persistence of poverty amidst substantial financial inflows exposes critical weaknesses in the nation's developmental trajectory.

A primary factor undermining progress has been the protracted civil conflict that erupted in 2013, just two years after independence. This internal strife severely disrupted economic growth, eroded social cohesion, and devastated infrastructure. The conflict diverted resources away from development projects toward military expenditures, deepening the hardships faced by ordinary citizens. Consequently, the fragile gains made in the early years of independence were reversed, plunging many into deeper deprivation.

Moreover, South Sudan's low levels of human capital, characterized by limited educational attainment and inadequate healthcare, have constrained the ability of its people to partake in and benefit from economic opportunities. The lack of essential infrastructure further impedes access to markets, services, and employment, perpetuating cycles of poverty and exclusion. These structural deficiencies highlight the gap between Garang's vision and the lived realities of South Sudanese citizens.

At the heart of these challenges lies weak and incoherent governance, which has been the most formidable barrier to realizing Garang's ideals. Governance failures have manifested in widespread corruption, lack of accountability, and ineffective public institutions. South Sudan's ranking as 179th out of 180 countries in the Corruption

Perception Index starkly illustrates the scale of this problem. Such pervasive corruption erodes public trust and siphons resources away from essential development initiatives.

The extensive growth literature unequivocally identifies human capital as one of the three fundamental drivers of economic development, alongside physical capital and technological advancement. Central to John Garang's economic philosophy is the assertion that poverty fundamentally results from marginalization, which undermines human potential and societal progress. Consequently, the cornerstone of *Garangnomics* is the deliberate and sustained formation of human capital, achieved through strategic investments in education and health.

It is absolutely critical that we establish an unequivocal and shared understanding of human capital. Only through this unified perspective can we accurately evaluate South Sudan's standing on the global stage and drive informed, strategic decisions that will shape its future.

The initial step involves distinguishing between human development and human capital. The United Nations Development Programme (UNDP) evaluates the former through the Human Development Index (HDI), defining human development as "**the expansion of individuals' freedoms to lead long, healthy, and creative lives; to pursue objectives they have legitimate reasons to value; and to participate actively in shaping development in an equitable and sustainable manner within a shared global context**[80]." This definition shows that human development is the outcome of a sustained investment in human capital formation.

Conversely, human capital is assessed via the Human Capital Index (HCI), established by the World Bank to **"quantify the contribution**

---

80   https://hdr.undp.org/data-center/human-development-index#/indicies/HDI

of health and education to the productivity of the next generation of workers. Countries are using it to assess how much income they forego because of human capital gaps, and how much faster they can turn these losses into gains if they act now." [81] In this regard, we could broadly treat human capital as an input in the production of human development. It is **the stock of knowledge, skills, and other personal characteristics embodied in people that help them to be productive**.

Hence, the Human Capital Index (HCI), as defined by the World Bank, constitutes an indispensable framework that policymakers and development professionals must urgently prioritize in assessing their economic growth. This metric enables countries to estimate the income lost due to deficiencies in human capital and to determine the potential acceleration of economic gains achievable through timely interventions. It rests firmly upon three critical pillars that collectively determine the future prosperity of nations. In addition, the three pillars are necessary in the struggle against poverty and marginalization.

First, survival, which rigorously measures the proportion of children who survive beyond the vulnerable age of five years, is non-negotiable for societal progress. Second, education, encompassing both the quantity—expected years of schooling by age eighteen—and the quality—harmonized test scores—forms the foundation of human capability and innovation. Third, health, evaluated through adult survival rates and the eradication of childhood stunting, ensures a robust and productive population. Poor households and marginalized communities are more likely than others to have low survival rates, high illiteracy and mortality rates.

---

81   https://www.worldbank.org/en/publication/human-capital/brief/the-human-capital-project-frequently-asked-questions#

Garangnomics can, in the light of the HCI, be understood as an urgent call for investment in human capital. This is because combating poverty and a sense of marginalization aligns closely with the idea of these pillars as fundamental imperatives. Just as the pillars demand immediate and unwavering commitment to secure sustainable development underpinned by human well-being, *Garangnomics* emphasizes holistic, long-term strategies focusing on inclusive economic growth, being environmentally responsible, and being socially equitable. In this context, *Garangnomics* would integrate such pillars as core principles in the pursuit of sustainable peace, economic growth, and poverty eradication.

South Sudan must, therefore, intensify its commitment to allocating adequate resources to the social sector to effectively combat poverty and the pervasive sense of exclusion. Such investments are not merely expenditures but essential catalysts for inclusive growth and national development, thereby addressing the root causes of marginalization and fostering a more equitable society.

Moreover, South Sudan stands at a critical crossroads in human capital development (see Table 4 below). Ranked among the least literate countries globally, this stark reality demands our immediate attention and action. Literacy is more than just reading and writing; it is the foundation for economic growth, health improvements, and social stability. Ignoring this challenge means condemning generations to poverty and missed opportunities. The data doesn't lie—South Sudan's future hinges on urgent investment in education and skill-building. We cannot afford to wait any longer. It's time to place South Sudan prominently on the map of human capital development and transform its potential into real progress. The moment to act is now!

Table 4: Some Indicators of Human Capital Development for the Ten Least Literate Countries in the World

Country	HCI	Literacy rate (%)	Annual Public Spending on Education (% of total public spending)	Annual Public Spending on Health as (%) of GDP	Nominal GDP per capita ($)	% of Rural Population
Chad	0.30	22.3	16.7	5.4	703	76.0
Guinea	0.39	32.0	10.2	4.0	1,543	62.3
South Sudan	0.31	34.5	6.582	0.8	417	83.0
Niger	0.29	35.1	12.0	6.2	631	83.1
Mali	0.32	35.4	4.4	4.3	913	54.7
Central African Republic	0.30	37.4	10.7	9.4	539	56.9
Burkina Faso	0.38	41.2	22.0	6.7	888	68.1
Benin	0.40	42.4	17.7	2.6	1,449	50.5
Afghanistan	0.40	43.0	10.9	15.5	413	73.4
Sierra Leone	0.36	43.2	12.7	8.8	415	56.2
Group Average	0.35	36.7	12.4	6.8	791.1	66.4

Source: Constructed by the author from various sources of data

Notably, nine out of the ten countries with the lowest literacy rates globally are in Africa (Table 4). Here, literacy is defined as the ability to read and write, distinct from the overall level of formal education attained. South Sudan ranks as the third lowest in the Human Capital

---

82   It is 13.4% in the FY2023/2024 budget, but this increase is due mainly to raised salaries of the universities.

Index (HCI) among 173 countries, following Niger and Chad, with the Central African Republic occupying the lowest two positions. Significantly, South Sudan allocates less than 10 percent of its total public expenditure to education and under one percent of its Gross Domestic Product to health. These figures underscore significant challenges in human capital development and resource allocation in these countries, warranting targeted policy interventions.

South Sudan, alongside Niger, exhibits one of the highest proportions of rural populations—approximately 83%—among the ten countries with the lowest literacy rates worldwide. This demographic characteristic underscores a critical challenge for human capital development, particularly in rural areas where educational and developmental interventions are most urgently needed. These regions' persistently low literacy levels exacerbate socio-economic vulnerabilities and hinder sustainable development efforts.

As a member of the East African Community (EAC), which comprises seven member states, it is essential to contextualize South Sudan's Human Capital Index (HCI) relative to its regional counterparts. The African continent averages an HCI of 0.40, with Kenya achieving a notably higher value of 0.55, ranking 93rd globally out of 173 countries. In contrast, South Sudan's HCI stands at a markedly lower 0.31, placing it 171st worldwide. This disparity, coupled with the global average HCI of 0.57, highlights the considerable developmental gap that South Sudan faces. These indicators call for targeted policy interventions aimed at enhancing educational outcomes and human capital formation to facilitate economic growth and integration within the EAC framework.

The Human Capital Index (HCI) rankings reveal that Singapore leads globally with a score of 0.88, followed by Hong Kong (0.81), Japan (0.80), South Korea (0.80), Canada (0.80), Finland (0.80),

Macao (0.80), Sweden (0.80), Ireland (0.79), and the Netherlands (0.79). These figures necessitate a thorough examination of underlying factors that may account for the superior HCI performance observed within these ten countries.

Three pertinent variables warrant detailed consideration: (a) general government expenditure on education as a proportion of gross domestic product (GDP); (b) general government expenditure on education as a percentage of total government spending; and (c) general government expenditure on health expressed as a percentage of GDP. It is critical to note that general government expenditure encompasses current, capital, and transfer payments across all sectors, including education, health, and social services.

Furthermore, this expenditure metric incorporates funding derived from international transfers to national, state, and local government entities. Such comprehensive fiscal data provides a robust foundation for analyzing the relationship between government investment in human capital domains and the resultant HCI outcomes.

In 2021, Singapore allocated 2.81 percent of its GDP to general government spending on education, positioning it 28th among 36 countries analyzed. This figure is notably below the average of 4.52 percent. Namibia and Sierra Leone lead in this category, allocating 9.64 percent and 9.09 percent, respectively, while Bermuda ranks last with 1.9 percent. Such disparities underscore the variability in educational investment across nations.

However, when examining government spending on education as a proportion of total general expenditure, Namibia again ranks highest at 24.7 percent among 63 countries, with the global average at 14.56 percent. Singapore's ranking of 38th, with 13.28 percent, further illustrates its relatively modest prioritization of education within its overall budget.

Turning to health expenditure, the average general government spending on health as a percentage of GDP in 2020 was 7.04 percent across 179 countries. Notably, Monaco, despite ranking seventh globally in the Human Capital Index (HCI), reported a low health expenditure of 1.67 percent, suggesting that high health spending is not necessarily a prerequisite for elevated human capital scores. This observation indicates that neither educational nor health expenditure alone sufficiently accounts for Singapore's leading HCI of 0.88.

A more salient factor appears to be literacy rates. Analysis of the top ten countries with the highest HCI reveals consistently high adult literacy, ranging from 94 percent, as seen in Hong Kong, to a complete 100 percent in Finland. This positive correlation suggests that literacy—the fundamental ability to read and write—plays a critical role in human capital development. Consequently, literacy emerges as a primary explanatory variable underpinning the superior human capital outcomes observed in these nations.

A comparative analysis of the East African Community (EAC) reveals that, with the exception of South Sudan, member states consistently exhibit literacy rates exceeding the developing countries' average of 65 percent. South Sudan distinctly ranks lowest within the EAC across four pivotal indicators: Human Capital Index (HCI), literacy rate, public expenditure on education as a proportion of total government spending, and public health expenditure relative to GDP (refer to Table 5 below). Additionally, South Sudan allocates approximately twice the EAC average of general government spending to military expenditures as a percentage of total public spending.

It is imperative to contextualize these findings within South Sudan's nascent status, currently in its second decade of independence. Unlike its EAC counterparts, many of which are in their sixth decade post-independence, South Sudan's developmental trajectory is comparatively premature. These disparities underscore the necessity for South Sudanese policymakers to strategically target convergence with regional averages by the conclusion of the second decade of sovereignty, thereby fostering sustainable human capital development and optimized allocation of public resources.

Table 5: Human Capital and Related Indicators for the East African Economic Community

Country	HCI	Literacy Rate (%)	Public Spending on Education (% of GDP)	Public Spending on Health (% of GDP)	% of total spending on education	% of total spending on the military
Burundi	0.39	85.5	4.9	6.5	20.6	7.2
DR Congo	0.54	77.2	2.7	4.1	18.4	7.5
Kenya	0.55	78.0	4.8	4.3	25.0	4.1
Rwanda	0.38	71.3	4.8	7.3	12.7	4.5
South Sudan	0.31	34.5	3.0	0.8	6.583	17.2
Tanzania	0.39	80.4	3.3	3.8	14.3	5.8
Uganda	0.38	73.8	2.7	4.0	8.5	10.1
Regional Average	0.42	71.5	4.9	4.4	15.1	8.1

Source: Constructed by the author from various sources of data

The data presented in Tables 4 and 5 incontrovertibly justify the urgent need to develop a binding and strategic narrative for investing in the human capital of South Sudan's workforce. At the culmination of the second decade of independence, such investment is not merely desirable but essential for enhancing productivity and sustainable

---

83   It is 13.4% in the FY2023/2024 budget, but this increase is due mainly to significant rise in the salaries of the academic staff of the public universities.

economic growth. This imperative must align with two critical and interrelated principles that the Sudan People's Liberation Movement/Army (SPLM/A) championed during the liberation struggle.

First, the conceptualization of agriculture as the primary engine of economic growth and sustainable livelihoods must be embraced without reservation. This paradigm centralizes farming households as the fulcrum of development, thereby necessitating their acquisition of literacy skills. Literacy is not a peripheral asset; it is the gateway to knowledge, enabling farming households to engage in lifelong learning and capitalize on sustainable livelihood opportunities. More importantly, literacy facilitates the integration of these households into broader markets and the global economy, which is increasingly mediated by digital technologies such as the Internet, social media, and information and communications technology (ICT).

The capacity to read, write, and comprehend is foundational for empowering rural populations to access critical information, engage effectively with customers, and make informed decisions. This literacy extends beyond traditional text to encompass digital competencies, including the use of mobile financial services like M-Gurush, MoMo, and M-Pesa. Consequently, prioritizing literacy development in rural South Sudan, where over 83 percent of the population resides, is an indispensable strategy for the struggle against poverty and marginalization.

Second, the principle of "taking towns to the people" encapsulates the necessity of delivering essential services to rural communities. Among these services, rural electrification stands paramount. Universal access to electricity by 2030 is not an aspirational goal but an achievable target for South Sudan, given its abundant potential for solar, wind, hydro, and diesel energy generation. Electricity serves as the critical nexus enabling the expansion of social services (education and health), market access, local governance institutions, and civic engagement centers. These elements collectively foster trust, social cohesion, and effective governance.

Historical lessons from South Sudan's liberation war underscore the transformative power of human capital development. The late Dr. John Garang's exhortation to "hold pens in the right hands and guns in the left hands" exemplifies a visionary strategy that yielded remarkable outcomes. The achievements of the "lost boys," many of whom have attained doctoral degrees and leadership positions abroad, demonstrate the profound impact of investing in education even under adverse conditions.

Replicating this dual-focus strategy within the South Sudan People's Defense Forces (SSPDF) by initiating a comprehensive five-year literacy campaign targeting farming households is a pragmatic and necessary initiative. Such a campaign, supplemented by diaspora-supported distance learning programs, will significantly enhance human capital formation. The success of national symbols, such as the Bright Stars basketball team, further illustrates the tangible benefits of literacy and education.

Policymakers must urgently address a fundamental question: What is the quantum of human capital a South Sudanese child born today will possess upon reaching adulthood? South Sudan has the potential to achieve the global average value of HCI of **0.57** by the end of the second decade of its independence. This is, however, conditional on the urgent formulation and implementation of a 5-year literacy campaign program within the overall framework of making agriculture the engine of economic growth and sustainable livelihoods.

Revisiting and operationalizing Article 2.9 (1) of the Transitional Constitution of South Sudan (TCSS, 2011) as amended, which guarantees education as a right without discrimination, is imperative. It is both a moral and strategic obligation to ensure that South Sudan graduates from its status among the world's least literate nations by the end of the second decade of independence. The time for decisive action is now.

Despite commendable progress in various domains, the struggle against poverty and social marginalization endures. Poverty remains entrenched in many communities, manifesting in limited access to basic services, inadequate income levels, and vulnerability to external shocks. Marginalized groups, including ethnic minorities, women, and rural dwellers, often bear the brunt of these challenges. Social exclusion and systemic barriers hinder their full participation in economic and political processes, contravening the principles of inclusivity and equity central to Garang's vision.

Efforts to combat poverty have included targeted social protection programs, livelihood diversification initiatives, and community empowerment projects. While these interventions have alleviated hardship for some, their reach and impact must be expanded to comprehensively address the structural causes of poverty.

The intersectionality of poverty and marginalization demands an unequivocal and robust response that transcends isolated interventions. Poverty is not merely an economic condition but a multifaceted phenomenon entangled with social exclusion, cultural stigmatization, and political disenfranchisement. Addressing this complex reality necessitates integrated approaches that confront these dimensions simultaneously to dismantle the systemic barriers perpetuating inequality.

Integrated approaches must encompass economic empowerment, social inclusion, cultural recognition, and political participation. Economic strategies should include equitable access to quality education, sustainable employment opportunities, and social protection programs that provide a safety net for the most vulnerable. Social inclusion efforts must dismantle discriminatory practices and promote community engagement, ensuring marginalized groups gain full participation in societal life.

Cultural recognition is vital to affirm the identities and rights of marginalized populations, thereby fostering dignity and respect. This can be achieved through inclusive policies that protect cultural heritage and combat prejudice. Political participation must be enhanced by facilitating access to decision-making processes and legal frameworks that guarantee rights and representation, enabling marginalized voices to influence policies that affect their lives.

Achieving these integrated objectives requires unwavering commitment and coordinated action from governmental bodies, civil society organizations, and international partners. It is imperative that these stakeholders collaborate strategically to design and implement holistic programs. Only through such concerted efforts can the entrenched nexus of poverty and marginalization be effectively dismantled, paving the way for a just and equitable society.

The inability to realize the visionary goals set forth by John Garang underscores a multifaceted crisis rooted in internal conflict, structural inadequacies, and governance failures. These challenges have hindered the full application of *Garangnomics*, preventing the transformation of South Sudan into a stable and prosperous nation. It is imperative to acknowledge that such obstacles are not merely incidental but are deeply embedded within the political and social fabric of the country, necessitating comprehensive and sustained intervention.

Despite these setbacks, John Garang's enduring legacy remains a potent symbol of hope and unity for South Sudan. His vision continues to inspire aspirations for a more inclusive and equitable society. However, this legacy alone is insufficient to surmount the prevailing difficulties. It requires active engagement and collaboration among policymakers, scholars, and all stakeholders to devise and implement strategies that address the root causes of instability and underdevelopment.

In this context, the forthcoming leadership transition within the Sudan People's Liberation Movement (SPLM) on 22 May 2025 represents a critical juncture. The new generation of leaders bears the significant responsibility of reinvigorating the principles of *Garangnomics* while adapting them to contemporary realities. Their success will depend on their capacity to foster unity, promote good governance, and implement reforms that eradicate poverty and marginalization across all regions of South Sudan.

Ultimately, the realization of John Garang's vision demands more than rhetoric; it calls for decisive action and unwavering commitment from all sectors of South Sudanese society. Only through addressing the intricate and interrelated challenges can the nation hope to fulfill the promises made by its Founding Fathers. This endeavor is not merely a political imperative but a moral one, essential for securing a stable and prosperous future for all citizens.

Chapter Seven

Lessons Learned and Future Directions

"This document marks the end of the last phase of our armed struggle and the beginning of a new era of Peace through Development in our long quest for New Sudan of freedom, liberty, human rights, equality and social harmony among our people. When we took up arms 21 years ago, our aim was to establish a New Sudan in which all the Sudanese participate equally in its governance irrespective of race, ethnicity, gender, religion, socio-economic status or political affiliation. The armed struggle of two decades long has now created an enabling environment (policy, institutional and technical), in the form of the comprehensive peace agreement, for articulating the key elements of the Sudan People's Liberation Movement (SPLM) strategic framework for war-to-peace transition that would in turn create the necessary and sufficient conditions for achieving our vision of the New Sudan.

Indeed, the peace agreement provides us with both challenges and opportunities to translate the SPLM vision of New Sudan into practice. The peace agreement also provides a unique Sudanese model for resolving the problem of armed conflict in other parts of the country, such as the ones now raging in Darfur and Eastern Sudan." [84]

The above passage provides an important point of departure for examining lessons learned in applying Dr. John Garang's ideas and vision of the New Sudan in both Sudan and South Sudan, and future directions.

The initial implementation of Garang's ideas was marked by meticulously devised strategies aimed at achieving sustainable progress. These strategies, grounded in a deep understanding of prevailing conditions, sought to translate visionary concepts into practical realities. However, the early application of these strategies encountered significant challenges. Obstacles such as resource limitations, resistance to change, and unforeseen complexities hampered smooth execution. Nonetheless, these difficulties underscored the resilience and adaptability required to pursue such transformative goals.

In light of these experiences, it becomes evident that the initial hurdles were integral to refining and strengthening the approach. The lessons learned during this formative period laid a foundation for more effective future endeavors, thereby affirming the enduring relevance of Garang's vision.

The New Sudan concept represents a visionary framework aimed at redefining the political, economic, and social landscape of Sudan and subsequently South Sudan. We briefly examine the lessons learned

---

[84]   From a Foreword, by John Garang de Mabior, to *The SPLM Strategic Framework for Peace-to-War Transition*. Published by the SPLM Economic Commission in August 2004, New Site, Kapoeta County.

in applying this visionary framework to the political, economic, and social landscapes of the two Sudans and highlight future directions in economic management.

1. Lessons from the Political Dynamics of Garang's Ideas and Vision

The political landscape shaped by Garang's ideas and vision offers profound lessons on the nature of leadership, governance, and political strategy in complex environments. His approach to politics was not merely theoretical but deeply intertwined with practical engagement with existing political structures and the art of coalition-building. This narrative seeks to elucidate these dimensions, emphasizing the enduring relevance of Garang's political philosophy and strategic acumen.

John Garang envisioned a united Sudan on a new basis where equality and justice prevailed for all peoples, transcending ethnic, religious, and regional divisions. His ideas, as we have presented them in the preceding chapters, centered on comprehensive national reconciliation and the establishment of a democratic system that would guarantee human rights and people-oriented development.

Garang's visionary framework emphasized the importance of self-determination for marginalized communities. However, this quest for self-determination was to be guaranteed through their inclusion in the security sector, governance, and a national political system that creates access to economic opportunities. In this regard, Dr. John sought to end decades of conflict in the Sudan by promoting peace through political dialogue underpinned by an unwavering commitment to combat poverty and a sense of marginalization all over the country.

It was the failure to apply this visionary framework to transform Sudan into a viable Sudanese state erected on moral, institutional, and legal foundations that resulted in the birth of South Sudan as an independent state on 9th July 2011. Another lesson is the fall of Al-Bashir's regime in April 2019 and the subsequent conflict between the SAF and the RSF, which continues up to the moment this manuscript of the second edition was going for printing in June 2025.

Hence, we can unambiguously state that one of the key lessons from the political dynamics of Garang's ideas and vision is that the two Sudans, which emerged from the ruins of old Sudan, are not viable states. Why are they not viable states? Because of weak leadership, incoherent governance, and a dysfunctional political party system. They are not at peace within themselves, which is a necessary condition for the viability of a state, and this is primarily due to the nature of leadership, governance, and political strategy in place. This point would become clearer through a brief highlight of the following:

    a. Interaction with existing political structures, and

    b. Insights on coalition-building and governance.

1.1 Interaction with Existing Political Structures

Garang's political strategy was marked by a nuanced understanding of the importance of engaging with established political institutions. Rather than rejecting existing frameworks outright, he recognized the necessity of navigating these structures to advance his vision. This approach underscores a pragmatic realism that is often overlooked in political discourse.

For instance, Garang accepted the ten states of Southern Sudan that were created by the NCP-led government under Omer Al-Bashir. This was instead of three regions of Bahr el-Ghazal, Equatoria, and Upper Nile that were part of the New Sudan structures of governance. By accepting the existing structures, Garang was able to leverage institutional mechanisms to further his objectives. Furthermore, he accepted to operate within the Government of National Unity (GoNU) of Sudan, though it was established under a one-country-two systems arrangement of the CPA.

That interaction was not passive; it involved a dynamic process of negotiation, adaptation, and sometimes confrontation. His ability to work within the system while simultaneously challenging its limitations exemplifies a sophisticated political tactician. Moreover, Garang's engagement with political institutions reflected a vision that extended beyond immediate gains. He sought to reform and transform the political landscape from within, fostering a gradual evolution that respected the complexities of governance. This lesson is critical for contemporary leaders who must balance idealism with practical realities.

1.2 Insights on Coalition-Building and Governance

Garang's approach to coalition-building within the National Democratic Alliance (NDA) and other armed groups, such as those that were operating in Darfur, was inclusive and visionary. He endeavored to unite disparate groups around shared objectives, emphasizing common interests rather than differences. This approach facilitated the creation of a political unity that was resilient and capable of withstanding internal and external pressures.

The National Democratic Alliance (NDA) played a pivotal and strategic role in opposing Omar Al-Bashir's regime, serving as a cornerstone in the broader struggle for political transformation in Sudan. Central to this effort was John Garang's political philosophy, which emphasized the necessity of broad-based coalitions to achieve coherent governance and lasting change. Recognizing that Sudan's political landscape was deeply fragmented, Garang understood that no single group could single-handedly dismantle the entrenched power structures upheld by Al-Bashir's National Congress Party (NCP).

The NDA was formed as a coalition that brought together the Sudan People's Liberation Movement (SPLM) and various Northern Sudanese political parties united in their opposition to the NCP regime. This alliance was far more than a tactical convenience; it was a strategic imperative aimed at consolidating diverse opposition forces to present a united front against authoritarian rule.

Through the NDA, the opposition was able to coordinate efforts, share resources, and amplify their political voice, which was crucial in challenging the legitimacy and policies of Al-Bashir's government. The NDA's existence underscored the power of coalition-building in a divided political environment, enabling the SPLM/A to negotiate the CPA from a position of strength. In this regard, the NDA's role was instrumental in the success of the Comprehensive Peace Agreement (CPA), which marked a turning point in Sudanese politics.

The alliance demonstrated that collaboration across regional and ideological lines could lead to meaningful political progress. It ultimately paved the way for the CPA's achievements in addressing decades-long conflicts and set the stage for future governance reforms. Hence, the NDA was not just an opposition group; it was a transformative political force that embodied Garang's vision of inclusive and collaborative governance. Its strategic coalition-building was essential in confronting and eventually overcoming the Al-Bashir regime's dominance, making it a crucial instrument in Sudan's journey toward peace during the Interim Period (2005 – 2011).

The governance model envisioned by Garang was one that embraced diversity and fostered participatory decision-making. His coalition-building efforts were aimed at establishing a governance framework that was representative and accountable. This vision highlighted the importance of inclusivity in political processes, which remains a vital lesson for contemporary governance challenges. The evidence in support of this statement is his appointment in July 2005 of the care-taker governors of Southern Sudan ten states. They included Dr. Riek Machar, Dr. Lam Akol Ajawin, and Dr. Theoplus Ochang who had just returned to the SPLM after their defection in 1991 to Omer Al-Bashir's NCP government of Sudan.

Furthermore, Garang's coalition-building was not static; it was an evolving process that required continuous dialogue, compromise, and mutual respect. His leadership demonstrated that effective governance is contingent upon the ability to sustain alliances through trust and shared commitment.

To conclude this subsection section of the chapter, it is important to note that the political dynamics surrounding Garang's ideas and vision provide invaluable insights into the interplay between political structures, coalition-building, and governance. His pragmatic engagement with existing institutions and his visionary coalition-building strategies offer a compelling blueprint for political leadership. These lessons underscore the enduring importance of adaptability, inclusivity, and strategic negotiation in the pursuit of transformative governance.

2. Economic Management Perspectives

Economic management, especially Public Financial Management (PFM), forms another cornerstone of John Garang's vision. The visionary framework concerning the economy was the idea of making agriculture the engine of economic growth, fueled through oil revenues by investing in infrastructure and the agricultural value chain. This investment targeted an initial network of 10,000 km of roads, railways, and river transport. It was also envisaged to support agricultural infrastructure - credit, extension services, research centers, and storage facilities.

However, making agriculture the engine of the economy requires a robust framework for economic management underpinned by transparency and accountability in the utilization of public resources. It also requires a correct understanding, by all the stakeholders of development, of the following six phases of the agricultural value chain:

1. **Planning:** This phase involves making decisions about what crops to grow, how to grow them, and when to harvest them.
2. **Production:** This phase involves the actual growing of the crops.
3. **Harvesting:** This phase involves gathering the crops from the field.
4. **Storage:** This phase involves storing the crops until they are ready to be processed or sold.
5. **Processing:** This phase involves transforming the crops into food or other products.
6. **Marketing:** This phase involves selling the crops or processed products to consumers.

The foundation of a robust framework is Public Financial Management (PFM). Hence, before concluding the Comprehensive Peace Agreement (CPA) negotiations, it became abundantly clear that establishing a Public Financial Management (PFM) system was not merely an option but a pressing necessity. Dr. John recognized this urgency and promptly sought financial support from the Government of the Kingdom of the Netherlands in September 2003. This funding facilitated the creation of a Capacity Building Trust Fund (CBTF), managed by UNICEF on behalf of the Economic Commission of the SPLM.

The establishment of the CBTF mandated the recruitment of two credible international financial firms tasked with the dual objectives of creating a PFM system and a public procurement mechanism. Among these firms, KPMG was selected and commenced operations in early 2004. Renowned globally for its audit, tax management, and financial advisory expertise, KPMG is among the elite Big Four accounting firms, including Deloitte, Ernst & Young, and PricewaterhouseCoopers.

The London-based Crown Agent was in the process of being engaged to establish a public procurement authority, a crucial step in enhancing public financial management. Unfortunately, Dr. John Garang's untimely passing on July 30, 2005, hindered the realization of this important component, leaving a significant gap in the intended reforms.

However, the ambitious contract for the Interim Period was clear: KPMG was to build the soon-to-be Government of Southern Sudan (GoSS) capacity, adhering to annual performance assessments. In 2004, KPMG introduced a "free balance system," a financial mechanism crucial for effective fiscal management. This system delineated the portion of available funds within an account, distinguishing it from reserves earmarked for specific obligations.

On Christmas Day, December 25, 2003, I had the distinct honor of presenting the PFM system, alongside a representative from KPMG, to the SPLM Leadership Council in Nairobi. This pivotal meeting laid the foundation for a robust framework for economic management during the Interim Period and subsequently for an independent South Sudan. This momentous occasion occurred at the residence of Dr. John Garang de Mabior, Chairman of the SPLM. This presentation was made on behalf of Cde. Arthur Akuein Chol, then SPLM Secretary for Finance, who was unable to attend due to commitments in Australia.

The atmosphere in the room was charged with anticipation, as council members recognized the weight of the decisions they were about to make. It was here, during hours-long deliberations, that the SPLM Leadership Council reached a historic consensus regarding economic management, particularly focusing on Public Financial Management (PFM). This decision was not merely an administrative shift; it marked a profound commitment to transparency and governance accountability, principles envisioned to guide the nascent nation in its post-conflict recovery.

As the discussions unfolded, the importance of strategic economic governance became evident, underscoring the SPLM's dedication to fostering a resilient framework capable of supporting sustainable development. The decisions made that day reverberated through the corridors of power and established a foundation upon which future policies would be built. Indeed, the SPLM-LC's resolution represented not just an immediate response to economic challenges but a visionary step toward a stable and prosperous future for South Sudan.

The SPLM-LC was conscious that effective financial governance is paramount in the complex landscape of post-conflict recovery. Hence, KPMG's commitment to providing technical support and on-the-job training to the SPLM Secretariat of Finance represented a pivotal step in ensuring the sustainable management of financial resources, particularly oil revenues, anticipated once the Government of Southern Sudan (GoSS) was established. Implementing the "free balance system" showcased our innovative approach, embedding a robust control mechanism that prioritizes transparency and accountability. This system enhances financial oversight and builds the necessary institutional capacity to manage resources effectively, equitably, and efficiently.

However, in early 2006, the built-in control mechanism was disabled, leading to a troubling trend. Successive finance ministers since October 2005 have ignored the importance of enhancing financial oversight inherent in the "free balance" concept. The ramifications of this gross neglect have been stark, as evidenced by the dismal performance of our economy since 2005. This narrative serves as a cautionary tale, highlighting the critical importance of sound financial management and the dire consequences that arise from neglecting fundamental principles. Hence, we can conclude that poor economic management is the key driver of the dismal performance of our economy in the last two decades.

Poor economic management in South Sudan is compelling and critical to understanding the nation's struggles to achieve stability and progress since gaining independence in 2011. Despite abundant natural resources, including oil, South Sudan has faced persistent economic challenges, mainly from two sources: a) institutional weakness; and b) the 'resource curse.'

2.1 Institutional Weakness

As explored in the preceding chapters, the institutional weaknesses in South Sudan are a fundamental factor contributing to the nation's poor economic performance. Here, we use the Country Policy and Institutional Assessment (CPIA) index of the World Bank to give us an idea of the nature and magnitude of the weakness of our economic policy management. The index clearly shows the nature and magnitude of the poor management of our economy. A score of 6 gives the highest quality of policies and institutions of a country, while a score of 1 indicates poor quality (i.e., the lowest level) of policies and institutions. The overall CPIA score for South Sudan ranges from 2.1 in 2012, the highest so far, to a low of 1.7 in 2023 (see Table 6 below).

Moreover, in 2023, South Sudan's CPIA score of 1.7 compares poorly to that of the World Bank's International Development Association (IDA) eligible countries; Sub-Saharan Africa (SSA) 's score of 3.1. Low CPIA scores for South Sudan indicate an inappropriate mixture of lubricants for our economic machine. We further analyze the trend and performance of these indicators to illustrate the extent of institutional weakness in South Sudan.

Table 6: The Nature and Magnitude of Institutional Weakness in South Sudan As Measured by CPIA During the period 2017 – 2023

Cluster	CPIA Scores by Year							
	2017	2018	2019	2020	2021	2022	2023	Change in CPIA Scores from 2017 to 2023
Economic Management	1.0	1.0	1.0	1.2	1.5	1.5	1.7	0.7
Structural Policies	2.0	2.0	1.8	1.8	2.0	2.0	2.0	0.0
Policies for Social Inclusion and Equity	1.7	1.5	1.5	1.5	1.5	1.6	1.7	0.0
Public Sector Management and Institutions	1.4	1.4	1.4	1.4	1.4	1.4	1.3	-0.1
Overall CPIA	1.5	1.5	1.4	1.5	1.6	1.6	1.7	0.2

Source: Constructed by the author from Assessing Africa's Policies and Institutions, World Bank

Analysis of CPIA Trends in South Sudan (2017-2023)

Table 6 presents the CPIA scores for South Sudan across various clusters from 2017 to 2023. A detailed analysis of the trends reveals significant insights into the performance of each cluster and the overall CPIA score during this period.

Economic Management Cluster

This cluster comprises monetary & exchange rate, fiscal, and debt management policies. These elements constitute a macroeconomic policy framework, which is formulated and implemented by the Ministry of Finance and Planning and the Bank of South Sudan. In this context, economic policy outcomes are a consequence of the execution of the macroeconomic policy framework. The CPIA helps policymakers follow the trend and performance of macroeconomic policy over time.

- **Trend:** The CPIA score for economic management has shown a gradual improvement, increasing from **1.0** in 2017 to **1.7** in 2023.
- **Performance:** This represents a change of **0.7**, indicating a positive trend in economic management practices over the seven-year period. However, South Sudan is still far below the African average

Structural Policies Cluster

The cluster consists of the trade, financial sector, and business regulatory environment.

- **Trend:** The scores in this cluster have remained relatively stable, maintaining a score of **2.0** from 2018 to 2023, with a slight decline to **1.8** in 2019 and 2020.
- **Performance:** The overall change from 2017 to 2023 is **0.0**, indicating stagnation in the effectiveness of structural policies.

Policies for Social Inclusion and Equity Cluster

The cluster comprises: gender equality, equity of public resource use, building human resources, social protection and labor rating, and policies and institutions for environmental sustainability.

- **Trend:** Scores in this cluster fluctuated slightly but ultimately remained constant at **1.5** from 2018 to 2021, before increasing to **1.6** in 2022 and **1.7** in 2023.

- **Performance:** The overall change from 2017 to 2023 is **0.0**, suggesting limited progress in social inclusion and equity policies.

Public Sector Management and Institutions Cluster

The cluster comprises the following: property rights, quality of budgetary and financial management, efficiency of revenue mobilization, quality of public administration, and transparency, accountability, and corruption in the public sector.

- **Trend:** This cluster's CPIA score decreased from **1.4** in 2017 to **1.3** in 2023, reflecting a decline in public sector management effectiveness.
- **Performance:** The change of **-0.1** indicates a concerning trend in the public sector's management and institutions.

Overall CPIA Performance

The analysis of the CPIA scores from 2017 to 2023 reveals significant disparities in performance across various clusters. Notably, Economic Management has exhibited the most substantial improvement. In contrast, both Structural Policies and Public Sector Management necessitate immediate and focused intervention to enhance their efficacy. Addressing these areas is imperative for advancing the overall institutional effectiveness in South Sudan.

- **Trend: The overall CPIA score has shown a modest increase from 1.5 in 2017 to 1.7 in 2023, reflecting a positive trend across certain clusters, particularly in Economic Management.**
- **Performance: The overall change of 0.2 suggests that while some areas have improved, significant challenges remain, particularly in Structural Policies and Public Sector Management.**

In the context of the overall CPIA score, we present key lessons learned regarding economic management by thoroughly examining five critical institutional capacities: a) analytical capacity, b) decision-making capacity, c) policy formulation capacity, d) implementation capacity, and e) monitoring and evaluation (M&E) capacity.

To elaborate, the analytical capacity involves the ability to gather and interpret relevant data that informs economic decisions, while decision-making capacity pertains to the processes through which leaders make informed choices based on that data. Policy formulation capacity refers to the capability of the institutions to develop sound economic policies that address the unique challenges faced by the nation. Implementation capacity is crucial in translating these policies into actionable programs that can produce tangible results. Finally, monitoring and evaluation capacity ensures that there are frameworks in place to assess the effectiveness of these programs, providing insights for continuous improvement.

In essence, these five institutional capacities serve as the foundational pillars of effective economic management, and addressing their weaknesses is essential for enhancing South Sudan's overall economic stability and growth. It should be pointed out here that institutions are human constructs. They are managed by humans and are, therefore, subject to change according to a country's prevailing circumstances.

2.1.1 Analytical Capacity

This discourse pertains to the capacity for the collection and analysis of pertinent data that informs decision-making processes in the realm of public policy. Furthermore, it involves a thorough evaluation of intervening situations and the provision of strategic alternatives for leaders—whether they preside over groups, communities, or nations—faced with such challenges. Below, two instances of analytical capacity are presented: one from the Comprehensive Peace Agreement (CPA) process and the other from the post-independence period.

A. How the SPLM Utilized Its Analytical Capabilities During the CPA

The turning point of the CPA was the Machakos Protocol signed in July 2002. This was after a long, protracted negotiation process since 1989 between the NCP-led Government of Sudan and the SPLM/A. After 13 years of on-and-off negotiations, the breakthrough came when the SPLM leadership decided to utilize its Technical Committee of Intellectuals (TCI) to provide technical backstopping to the negotiating team under the leadership of Cdr. Salva Kiir Mayardit. The TCI, unlike all the other entities of the SPLM/A, had direct access to Dr. John because messages through the chain of command were sometimes slow or sabotaged.

The Norwegian Government established an Internet communication system for Dr. John to communicate with the TCI and diaspora community on issues of war and peace. When Gen. Lazaros Sumbeiywo, Chief Peace Mediator of the CPA, and his team presented the draft of the Machakos Protocol to the SPLM/A and GoS, the SPLM/A team called in the TCI. The TCI carried out a comprehensive analysis of the draft using the Venn Diagrams Analytical framework (see Figure 5 below) Dr. John developed to resolve the Sudanese crisis of state and identity.

The TCI concluded that the text of the draft was consistent with Dr. John Garang's conceptual framework. The TCI explained to the SPLM/A team that Model 2 is based on a one-country-two systems, which the Protocol proposes to govern Sudan during the Interim Period of six years. We explained that Dr. John's conceptual framework encompasses five models for solving the Sudanese problem. However, there are only two sustainable solutions, as he had envisioned in 1972.

These were Model 1 (transformed democratic new Sudan) and Model 5 (total independence of at least two Sudanese states). We also directly sent our analysis to Dr. John, who agreed with our conclusion

The people of Southern Sudan have expressed their desire for self-determination by selecting Model 5, with an overwhelming majority of 99 percent during an internationally monitored referendum held from January 9 to January 15, 2011. This substantial outcome was made possible through innovative and strategic reasoning that facilitated a clear path for the Southern Sudanese to participate in the voting process without encountering significant obstacles.

It is important to clarify that self-determination does not inherently imply separation; rather, it embodies the principle of allowing a populace to determine its own future and identity. A robust military presence, represented by the Sudan People's Liberation Army (SPLA), ensured the protection and support of this strategic endeavor throughout its course. Hence, the importance of analytical capacity in the quest for sustainable peace, economic growth, and poverty eradication.

B. Analytical Capacity in an Independent South Sudan

We have highlighted in the preceding paragraphs how the SPLM leadership effectively utilized its TCI in the articulation of the Machakos Protocol. We now turn to how challenging issues have been addressed in an independent South Sudan by the SPLM and GoSS. In this context, analytical capacity emphasizes the critical need to comprehend the influence of societal institutions on individuals' motivation to pursue education, foster innovation, save funds, and engage productively within the economy. A lack of understanding regarding the functioning of an economy can result in inadequacies in economic management. This concept can be effectively illustrated through a reference to the works of John Maynard Keynes:

"We have involved ourselves in a colossal muddle, having blundered in the control of a delicate machine, the working of which we do not understand. The result is that our possibilities of wealth may run to waste for a time—perhaps for a long time."

Indeed, the economy is a delicate machine that functions as a complex and sensitive system, necessitating the involvement of a highly skilled team of experts and policymakers for its effective management. This requirement inherently depends on the existence of strong analytical capabilities of the institutions of economic governance. A notable articulation of this can be found in the actions taken by the economic policy team of the Government of South Sudan (GoSS) in 2013. On the evening of November 11, 2013, the Bank of South Sudan (BoSS) released an official statement indicating that:

"As a critical component of macro-economic reform, which is aimed at ensuring price stability under a fixed exchange rate regime established by Section 53 (1)(2) of the Bank of South Sudan (BSS) Act 2011, the Bank of South Sudan (BSS) has decided to unify the official and parallel exchange rates."

This development indicates a 42.3% South Sudanese Pound (SSP) depreciation in relation to the United States dollar. As of November 12, 2013, the exchange rate stood at 4.5 SSP per 1.00 USD.

The market response in Juba, the capital of South Sudan, was markedly clear: there was a significant increase in the prices of essential commodities, including fuel, food items, and building materials, coupled with widespread hoarding behaviors. However, the primary

The Power of Creative Reasoning

Figure 5: John Garang's Venn Diagrams Analytical Framework for Resolving the Crisis of State and Identity in the Old Sudan

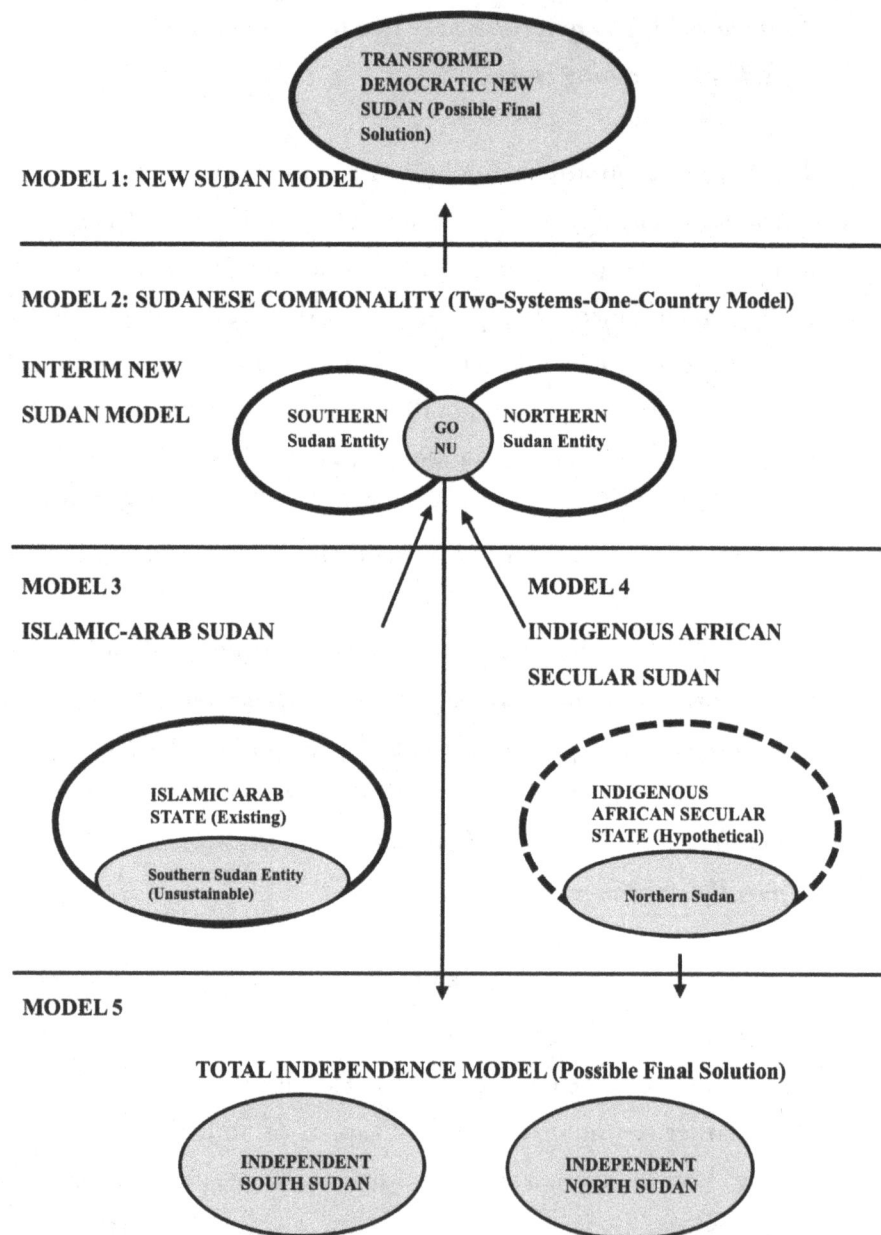

objective of the Bank of South Sudan (BoSS) was to unify the official and parallel (black) market exchange rates, aimed at reducing short-term exchange rate volatility and addressing rent-seeking behaviors while simultaneously stimulating economic activity. The implementation of this policy was, nevertheless, met with considerable challenges, resulting in public dissatisfaction due to fuel shortages and rising prices of consumer goods.

The political response to the consequential public outcry was swift. The National Legislative Assembly (NLA) intervened on Wednesday, 13 November 2013, and ordered the reversal of the devaluation decision. The BoSS leadership, in turn, did diffidently oblige. The Council of Ministers concurred on 22 November 2013 with the decision of the NLA. And the SPLM leadership established a Task Force under the National Secretariat to analyze and formulate a set of administrative and policy measures aimed, on the one hand, at calming the situation in the near term, and on the other, at undertaking poverty-sensitive economic reforms in the medium term.

The reactions observed in the market, public, and political spheres serve as compelling evidence of the insufficient analytical capacity of economic governance institutions. Hence, it is imperative that the economic policy management team, in the future, conducts a comprehensive analysis of such responses prior to endorsing the realignment policy. For instance, in Chapter Six, an analytical framework has been presented to elucidate the intersections between proximate and fundamental causes of economic growth. This framework exemplifies one of the analytical tools available to policy analysts.

Had our economic policy analysts of the Economic Cluster undertaken an appraisal of the objective conditions of the South Sudan economy, they would have found that our economy was largely owned and managed by foreigners, including kiosks, water tanks, retailing, and hairdressing. This manifested itself in the closure of most businesses, hoarding, and price hikes. The economic policy management team should have considered such a factor.

On the SPLM leadership side, Hon. Tulio Odongi Ayahu, Government Chief Whip, initiated the formation of the SPLM Economic Taskforce. Hon. Tulio Odongi Ayahu drew lessons of experience from Dr. John's style of leadership, for he was a TCI and peace negotiation team member during the CPA process. The Economic Taskforce operated under my leadership during the postmortem evaluation of the rejected realignment policy. Through a thorough analysis of the rationale behind the decision made by the Bank of South Sudan (BoSS), we arrived at a consensus regarding its theoretical foundations, as articulated in the following passage.:

> *"An exchange, as a price of one country's money in terms of another's is among the most important prices in an open economy. It influences the flow of goods, services, and capital in a country, and exerts strong pressure on the balance of payments, inflation and other macroeconomic variables. Therefore, the choice and management of an exchange rate regime is a critical aspect of economic management to safeguard competitiveness, macroeconomic stability, and growth."* [85]

However, the Taskforce stated that:

> *"We do not, however, agree with the manner in which*

---

85 FahrettinYagci (2001). *Choice of Exchange Rate Regimes for Developing Countries.* Africa Region Working Paper Series No. 16, The World Bank.

the leadership of BSS attempted to unify the exchange rates without full consideration to the timing of the announcement on the one hand, and putting in place appropriate measures to ensure price stability and growth of our economy on the other. There was evidently poor coordination within the economic team on the one hand, and the Presidency on the other. Moreover, the losers and winners of the unification of exchange rate policy should have been identified with a view of formulating operational packages for compensating the losers in the immediate aftermath of the coming into force of such a policy action." [86]

Furthermore, the Taskforce stated that "**the SPLM and its Government should take their moral obligations and responsibilities enshrined in the social contract they have entered into with the people of South Sudan**" to embark on the path to sustainable peace, economic growth, and poverty eradication.

The Taskforce then identified five essential prerequisites that must be fulfilled before any endeavor to realign the exchange rate. These prerequisites include: a) a stock of fuel (diesel and petrol) sufficient to last for a duration of 90 days; b) food reserves adequate for 90 days; c) building materials available for 90 days; d) pharmaceutical supplies that can sustain a 90-day period; and e) the rehabilitation of 1,135 kilometers of six primary roads that connect Juba with the production areas.

---

86   *Realignment of South Sudanese Pound – US Dollar Exchange Rate: What Are the Pre-requisites for the Success of Such a Policy?* Report Prepared for the Leadership of the Sudan People's Liberation Movement. By The SPLM National Economic Task Force, Juba, Republic of South Sudan, December 6, 2013.

A significant takeaway from the two examples highlighting analytical capacity is that although the leadership of the Sudan People's Liberation Movement (SPLM) has shown a commendable ability to mobilize a team for situation analysis during challenging circumstances, the institutions of economic governance within the Government of South Sudan (GoSS) have unequivocally demonstrated a lack of analytical capabilities. This disparity is particularly striking; the SPLM's proactive approach in responding to crises illustrates a certain degree of organizational resourcefulness and awareness, allowing them to effectively assess and navigate complex situations.

In contrast, the GoSS' institutions have struggled to develop the necessary analytical infrastructure and expertise, hindering their ability to formulate informed economic policies and responses to pressing issues. This lack of capacity not only limits the effectiveness of governance but also poses challenges to the overall stability and development of the nation.

2.1.2. Decision-Making Capacity

The evidence-based decision-making process serves as a critical component of effective problem-solving leadership. This type of leadership is characterized by its ability to assess a range of policy options, evaluate different scenarios, and understand the implications of these choices on the livelihoods of individuals and institutions functioning within a framework of coherent governance framework.

Effective leadership is essential for making quick decisions on various options presented by aides and advisers to address the complex challenges that communities encounter. For such decisions to be truly impactful, they must prioritize evidence-based practices. This involves not only relying on data and research to inform decisions but also actively seeking out diverse perspectives from a country's citizens. By incorporating these insights, leaders can ensure that their strategies are more reflective of the needs and realities of those they serve.

Additionally, streamlining decision-making processes is crucial. This means establishing clear protocols that facilitate timely responses while also fostering inclusivity. Engaging stakeholders at every level not only helps build trust but also enhances the legitimacy of the decisions made. In this way, leadership can become more adaptive and responsive, ultimately leading to more effective outcomes for the nation.

In the context of Africa, it is important to recognize that the decision-making process can often be time-consuming, primarily due to the emphasis on consensus-building among diverse stakeholders. This inclusive approach aims to ensure that all voices are heard and considered, fostering a sense of ownership and promoting long-term sustainability in governance.

In stark contrast to the optimal governance frameworks, the decision-making processes within the Government of South Sudan (GoSS) have demonstrated considerable dysfunctionality. This is particularly surprising given the previously noted strong analytical capabilities. Factors such as political instability, the absence of established communication channels, and a lack of decisiveness among decision-makers, have significantly hindered effective governance. As a result, this has led to decisions that inadequately address the urgent needs of the population.

In the fourteen years since its independence, South Sudan has experienced a significant turnover in its financial leadership, with eleven individuals holding the position of Minister of Finance. This turnover reflects underlying instability in the country's economic management and highlights the challenges of economic governance institutions. The situation indicates a complex environment for managing economic policy, particularly within a fragile economic context.

Some economic decision-makers may not have fully grasped the broader implications of their actions, resulting in an increased frequency of dismissals. A more concerning consequence is the reluctance of subsequent Ministers of Finance to make decisions independently, often waiting for clearance from the presidency before proceeding.

This situation is regrettable, as most economic decisions hinge on a thorough understanding of market dynamics and a detailed assessment of the potential outcomes of policies that foster sustainable peace, economic growth, poverty alleviation, poverty reduction, and eventually poverty eradication within South Sudan's economy. In this context, it is imperative that the President possesses complete confidence in any individual appointed as Minister of Finance for a duration of no less than 48 months. Consequently, we can assert with clarity that frequent changes in economic decision-makers represent one of the fundamental causes of weakened decision-making capacity in South Sudan.

2.1.3. Policy Formulation Capacity

This is an area where we could unambiguously state that there is a relatively strong capacity to formulate policies and associated strategies to implement them. The five protocols of the CPA are a good illustration of this statement. The Security Arrangement, Wealth-sharing, Power-sharing, Abyei, and the Two Areas of Nuba Mountain, and Southern Blue Nile Protocols were formulated to implement the Machakos Protocol of July 2002. The SPLM's various documents, such as the Manifesto, Peace Through Development, SPLM Strategic Framework for War-to-Peace Transition, and so forth, are also examples of a relatively strong capacity to formulate evidence-based policies.

Moreover, the formulation of GoSS' annual financial budgets is another example of the relative strength of the policy formulation capabilities within the executive and legislative branches of our government. Three examples are worth mentioning at this juncture: a) Report of the SPLM Economic Taskforce of November 2013; b) the Revised National Development Strategy (R-NDS) for the period 2021-2024; and c) the Public Financial Management Reforms Strategy (PFMRS) formulated in 2020.

A. Report of the SPLM Economic Taskforce

In examining the relative strength of policy formulation capabilities in South Sudan, it is imperative to recognize the pivotal role played by the SPLM Economic Taskforce. This Taskforce undertook an exhaustive postmortem analysis of the exchange rates policy, which was ultimately rejected by the Transitional National Legislature (TNL) in November 2013. The recommendations articulated in their report serve as a testament to a robust policy formulation capacity, underscoring a commitment to learning from past experiences and refining our approach to economic governance.

The ability to critically assess and learn from previous policy decisions is not merely an academic exercise; it is a fundamental component of effective governance that fosters stakeholder trust and confidence. By engaging in this reflective practice, the SPLM Economic Taskforce demonstrates its dedication to sound economic policy and its capacity to positively influence future legislative outcomes.

Thus, the strength of our policy formulation capabilities is not solely reflected in the recommendations made but also in the proactive stance taken to ensure that future policies are informed, responsible, and aligned with the nation's needs. This strategic approach enhances our credibility and positions South Sudan as a country committed to progressive and evidence-based policy development. It is essential for all stakeholders to recognize these strengths and support the ongoing efforts to fortify our policy formulation framework, which ultimately contributes to sustainable economic growth and stability.

Below are recommendations divided into periods of implementation.

A.1 Recommendations to be implemented in the Near Term:

1. The SPLM should establish and encourage enterprises with Indigenous dispensation accountable only to its Economic Team, formed through a deliberate selection from the abundant national talented cadres. This mobilization effort aims to rescue the national economy from the hands of foreign entrepreneurs who have monopolized the trade in this country.

2. The Presidency is to direct the BoSS to immediately implement the resolution of the National Legislature, as contained in the FY2013/2014 Appropriation Act, concerning **SDG1.92 billion** that should have been redeemed by the BoSS when we separated from Sudan. Therefore, the equivalent **SSP1.92 billion** must be deposited into the Ministry of Finance and Economic Planning account.

3. The Minister of Finance and Economic Planning is to issue to the Governor of BoSS an **irrevocable standing order** on the payment of the salaries of the public sector on or around the 28th of every month.

4. The BoSS has to build its **international reserve** (i.e., foreign exchange reserves) equivalent to **five (5) months** of imports by buying dollars accruing to the GoSS from crude oil sales at the parallel market rate as a temporary measure until the presidency decides on a definite exchange rate policy measure.

5. However, the Taskforce recommends that the BoSS gradually **move toward unifying the exchange rates into a single**

regime. Such a move would, in turn, improve the Government of South Sudan's worsening fiscal situation.

6. The Presidency is to instruct the Minister of Finance and Economic Planning to undertake, through supplementary budget, the following allocations from **SSP1.92 billion** to:
   a. SSP288 million for jump-starting the importation of fuel by the Nilepet;
   b. SSP230 million for the rehabilitation of 1,135 km of roads given in Table 2 of this report;
   c. SSP232.8 million for the construction of storage facilities and importation of food commodities required for Phase I, as specified in the Report;
   d. SSP200 million to the DFCA for pharmaceutical supplies, laboratory, minilabs for testing drugs, testing tool kits, and drug warehouses;
   e. SSP100 million to the War Disabled, Orphans, and Widows Commission as seed funds for the importation and distribution of building materials; and
   f. SSP430 million for a salary increase of all public sector employees, including constitutional post holders, as a critical component of compensation packages, should the recommended policy of gradual realignment of exchange rates be approved.
   g. The total estimated cost of these allocations is about **SSP1.48 billion, which would still leave SSP420 million as reserves or could be used for the repayment of overdue domestic debt.**
7. The BoSS is to negotiate with the East African Central Banks on the convertibility of the SSP with their currencies, as by way of facilitating business payments using local currencies.

All financial transactions, payments, and transfers must be in Local Currency (i.e., SSP). Moreover, any transaction in the country must be in South Sudanese pounds.

8. Individual requests for hard currency should only be transferred to a **specified** account number to the **corresponding** bank abroad, including school fees payments and medical treatments abroad.

9. The BoSS supervises and regulates the financial sector to ensure its effectiveness and conformity with the country's legal framework. Moreover, the BoSS must design mechanisms to ensure the intended purposes of LCs and track money remitted into and out of the country (i.e., diaspora, NGOs, embassies, donor agencies, UN agencies, private investors, etc.).

10. The Presidency is to instruct the Minister of Finance to re-examine and, if possible, re-negotiate some of the loans (e.g., NORINCO with the Ministry of Defence and Veteran Affairs) acquired during the austerity period. In addition, it is recommended that the **undisbursed** portion of loans with Trafigura, CNPC, and Petronas be cancelled.

11. SPLM-registered companies should be empowered to participate in the importation and distribution of basic commodities (e.g., food items, fuel, pharmaceuticals, building materials, etc.) that affect the daily livelihood of ordinary South Sudanese people. However, these companies must be managed effectively with the main objective of profit-making, for they are not charity organizations. Their oversight and reorganization can, temporarily, be under the SPLM National Economic Task Force.

12. The SPLM companies and the national private sector should initiate commercial poultry production. Furthermore, the

Ministry of Finance and Economic Planning should release funds allocated in the FY2013/2014 budget for the Agricultural Bank to purchase Gum Arabic for exports, boosting non-oil exports.

A.2 Recommendations to be Implemented in the Medium–Term:

1. The Ministry of Finance, together with the BoSS, is to establish a public credit system to promote rapid growth and diversification of the economy through national financial institutions. Our public credit system would be based on our confidence in the future, especially when this country is blessed with natural resources that are mostly owned (e.g., oil) by the public sector. This credit system should focus on promoting agriculture, trade, manufacturing, and so forth.
2. The Ministry of Finance should start repaying overdue debt, especially to the domestic private sector (i.e., genuine contractual obligations).
3. The Ministry of Petroleum, through NilePet, is to construct large depots of 40-60 million liters for strategic fuel reserves in various strategic locations.
4. The Food Reserve Agency (FRA) to implement Phase II of the National Food Security Council program.
5. The Ministry of Transport, Roads, and Bridges must rehabilitate the river transport system, which requires dredging and the construction of ports. It also needs to encourage the private sector to acquire modern boats, fuel tankers, and barges for carrying passengers and goods.
6. The Ministry of Petroleum, Mining, and Industry is to expedite the completion of the two refineries and associated infrastructure for distribution to consumption areas.

7. The Ministry of Petroleum, Mining, and Industry is to initiate mining exploration and production (e.g., gold, cement, and other minerals).
8. The DFCA is to complete the construction of food and drug control testing laboratories.
9. The Ministry of Labor, Public Service, and Human Resource Development should initiate an integrated program of capacity building and institutional strengthening of the key sectors identified in this report. Moreover, the Ministry of Labor, Public Service, and Human Resource Development should ensure that NGOs and international organizations operating in South Sudan utilize national capacities.
10. The SPLM companies and other national businesses should endeavor to source construction materials directly from the international supply centers/hubs. In this regard, the Ministry of Telecommunication and Postal Services is to launch the Gateway and commence the billing system.

A.3 Recommendations to be Implemented in the Long-term:

1. The SPLM should establish a monitoring and evaluation (M&E) mechanism to ensure the smooth and effective implementation of actions recommended for the near and medium term.
2. Notwithstanding the above recommendation, the current SPLM National Economic Taskforce should continue, on a quarterly basis, to assess the economic, political, social, and security implications of the country's fiscal and monetary policies.
3. The Taskforce will continue to coordinate with the GoSS economic team through the Presidency.

4. The Taskforce recommends intensifying fishing activities, including training fish-folk, providing fishing gear, processing and refrigerating fish, and developing a transportation system to deliver fish products to the areas of consumption.
5. The livestock sector should target improving livestock, eradicating diseases, and establishing abattoirs/slaughterhouses in major livestock-consuming/production areas. This would, in turn, create an industry for tanneries.
6. The Taskforce recommends robust operations of the Agricultural Bank and Cooperative Bank, both of which should improve financial services delivery to the private sector, especially small-scale producers, to boost the production and productivity of farm produce. Additionally, agro-processing should be given priority, with agricultural products distributed to all consuming areas.

Revised National Development Strategy (R-NDS)
In his foreword to the R-NDS, Agak Achuil Lual, Minister of Finance and Planning, then stated that:

> *"Development planning in South Sudan dates back about eight years to when the South Sudan National Development Plan (SSNDP) 2011–2013 was first published. The SSNDP was extended to 2016, and then eventually was succeeded by the South Sudan National Development Strategy (SSNDS) 2018–2021, which has now been revised into this document as required by the Revitalized Agreement on the Resolution of Conflict in*

South Sudan (R-ARCSS)."[87]

The R-NDS became the analytical framework on which the annual budgets of the GoSS are formulated. This point is articulated by President Salva Kiir Mayardit in the preface of the R-NDS:

> *"I have instructed the Minister of Finance and Planning to base all future national budgets on the R-NDS. I am happy to note that deliberations on FY2022/23 budget planning have fully incorporated the priorities of the R-NDS. We must lead our own development, and this must be reflected in government expenditure. At the same time, we equally recognize the immense efforts and partnerships of our humanitarian and development partners. They have been with us throughout our journey."* [88]

Public Financial Management Reforms Strategy (PFMRS)
The third example is the Public Financial Management Reforms Strategy (PFMRS). It was formulated by the Ministry of Finance and Planning (MoFP), though with a technical backstopping from the Ebony Center for Strategic Studies. Box 1 below contains eleven priorities identified in 2020 by the MoFP. The IMF recommended two of the eleven priorities: strengthen the macro-fiscal framework, the budget process, and credibility. But the whole exercise was done by the staff of the MoFP under the able leadership of Mr. Ocum Karlo, then Undersecretary of Planning.

---

87 From the Revised National Development Strategy 2021-2024: Consolidate Peace and Stabilise the Economy. Republic of South Sudan, Juba, 2021.

88 From the *Revised National Development Strategy 2021-2024: Consolidate Peace and Stabilise the Economy.* Republic of South Sudan, Juba, 2021.

It is essential to emphasize that a Public Financial Management (PFM) system serves as a comprehensive budget-management framework. A typical PFM system is characterized by three principal components: a) control over inputs related to financial assets, human resources, and physical assets; b) a focus on annual planning and accountability; and c) centralized management practices. Collectively, these elements represent the fundamental functions of the PFM system. Within this framework, the PFM system embodies both policy-related and management-oriented objectives.

South Sudan PFMRs Priorities
1. Implement a Treasury Single Account (TSA)
2. Strengthen the cash management system
3. Relocate the Loan Committee to MoFP
4. Review, verify, and clear all arrears
5. Review and verify loans and contracts collateralized or guaranteed against crude oil
6. Strengthen the Anti-Corruption Commission (ACC) and the Audit Chamber (external auditor)
7. Establish a Public Procurement and Asset Disposal Authority (PPADA)
8. Roll out the electronic payroll for the public sector employees using a biometric system
9. Strengthen the Fiscal and Financial Allocation Monitoring Commission (FFAMC)
10. Strengthen macro-fiscal framework (recommended by the IMF)
11. Strengthen the budget process and budget credibility (recommended by the IMF)

When examining the policy formulation capacity within South Sudan, it is imperative to recognize the profound implications of effective governance on the nation's future. The three examples articulated above not only highlight the relative strength of this capacity but also underscore the urgent need for its enhancement to foster sustainable peace, economic growth, and poverty eradication.

The integration of evidence-based policymaking into the formulation process is essential for crafting effective strategies that respond to the complexities of the South Sudanese context. By leveraging data and research, policymakers can make informed decisions that are not only responsive to immediate needs but also aligned with long-term development goals. This approach not only enhances the credibility of policy initiatives but also fosters a culture of continuous improvement and adaptation.

In conclusion, the relative strength of policy formulation capacity in South Sudan holds significant promise for the nation's trajectory. However, stakeholders must prioritize initiatives that bolster this capacity, ensuring that the policies crafted are not only effective but also reflective of the diverse needs of the population. By doing so, South Sudan can pave the way for a brighter and more sustainable future. As discussed in the next section, this relative strength is undermined by a generalized weakness in implementation capacity.

2.1.4 Implementation Capacity

> *"On that glorious day, 9 July 2011, we raised our own flag high in the sky, as all our people and freedom-loving peoples around the world joined in unison to celebrate the birth of a new nation. This was achieved out of decades of struggle, death and despair. As our people gazed into*

the sky, observing the black, red and green emblem interspersed with white stripes fluttering in a freedom dance with the wind, they were teeming with hope. But since then the freedom dance has been disrupted again and again by violence and instability, mainly orchestrated by us, members of the political elite."[89]

The emergence of South Sudan as an independent nation is not merely a political event; it is a culmination of decades marked by relentless struggle, profound loss, and unparalleled despair. This point is articulated by President Salva Kiir Mayardit in the above passage. He highlights that the journey to independence was not achieved through mere aspiration but through the formidable resilience of a people determined to reclaim their sovereignty. The liberation struggle, characterized by immense sacrifices, endowed the nation with a foundational implementation capacity. This capacity, forged in the fires of conflict, was anticipated to be recalibrated toward establishing effective governance structures by the day of independence.

However, it is imperative to recognize that the potential for progress was thwarted by the political elite, who indulged in factional disputes rather than embracing the opportunity for building coherent governance. This deviation not only undermined the hard-won gains of the liberation struggle but also paved the way for a cycle of violence and instability that continues to plague the nation. The failure to adjust the institutional capacity toward coherent governance has negatively impacted the country's ability to implement its economic policy. Hence, the fragmented pursuit of power among various factions in

---

89 From the Revised National Development Strategy 2021-2024: Consolidate Peace and Stabilise the Economy. Republic of South Sudan, Juba, 2021.

South Sudan has significantly weakened the nation's ability to implement effective governance.

This deterioration hinders the vital objectives of achieving sustainable peace, fostering economic growth, and eradicating poverty. It is imperative to recognize that the establishment of robust implementation capacities is crucial for coherent governance and economic management. To address the pressing issues, one must advocate for a strategic focus on building these capacities. Coherent governance will not only enhance the implementation of policies but also provide a stable framework within which sustainable development can flourish. Without such a foundation, the aspirations for peace and prosperity will remain elusive, further perpetuating the cycle of conflict and underdevelopment.

The call to bolster governance implementation capacities in South Sudan transcends mere suggestion; it stands as an essential requirement for the nation's future. The current challenges facing South Sudan demand immediate and decisive action to ensure sustainable development and stability. Without a robust governance framework, the aspirations for peace and prosperity remain unattainable.

Stakeholders must recognize the urgency of enhancing governance implementation capabilities. This call is not simply a bureaucratic reform; it is a pivotal element that will shape the trajectory of South Sudan's socio-economic landscape. By investing in governance, we are addressing immediate concerns and laying the foundation for a resilient and thriving society. In this context, the necessity of strengthening governance implementation capabilities in South Sudan is clear. It is a critical step toward realizing the nation's potential and securing a prosperous future for all its citizens.

In light of this historical context, it is crucial for the stakeholders in South Sudan to reflect on the lessons of the past. The political elite must rise above personal interests and engage in a genuine dialogue aimed at national reconciliation and effective governance. The destiny of South Sudan hinges on the willingness of its leaders to prioritize the collective well-being of its citizens over factional gains. Only through a commitment to building inclusive and accountable institutions can the nation hope to overcome the legacy of its struggles and forge a path toward lasting peace and prosperity.

2.1.5 Monitoring and Evaluation (M&E) Capacity

South Sudan is at a critical point in its pursuit of sustainable peace, economic growth, and poverty reduction. Building strong Monitoring and Evaluation (M&E) capabilities is not just beneficial but essential to effectively achieve these interconnected goals.

M&E capabilities are the backbone for assessing the effectiveness of programs designed to foster peace and economic advancement. By implementing a structured evaluation framework, South Sudan can collect vital data, enabling stakeholders to understand what strategies yield results and which do not. This insight allows for continuous improvement, ensuring that resources are allocated efficiently and effectively, ultimately enhancing the impact of development initiatives.

Moreover, establishing M&E systems fosters a culture of accountability and transparency. In a nation where trust in institutions is paramount for stability, the ability to track progress and report findings transparently can help rebuild confidence among citizens and international partners. When the populace sees tangible evidence of progress, it cultivates a culture of purpose-driven work, a sense of ownership, and engagement in the peace and development processes, which are vital for long-term sustainability.

International partners and investors are increasingly prioritizing transparency and accountability in their funding decisions. By demonstrating a commitment to robust M&E frameworks, South Sudan can attract much-needed foreign investment and support. This influx of resources is essential for bolstering economic growth and facilitating comprehensive poverty eradication strategies.

Furthermore, M&E capabilities empower policymakers with the data necessary to make informed decisions. Evidence-based policymaking is crucial in addressing the complex challenges South Sudan faces. By utilizing data collected through M&E systems, decision-makers can identify emerging trends, assess program efficacy, and allocate resources strategically. This informed approach not only enhances the likelihood of achieving desired outcomes but also ensures that interventions are tailored to the unique socio-economic context of South Sudan.

In this context, the critical importance of M&E capabilities for South Sudan cannot be overstated. As the nation strives toward sustainable peace, economic growth, and poverty eradication, investing in M&E is essential for effective program implementation, accountability, attracting investment, and supporting evidence-based policymaking. By prioritizing these capabilities, South Sudan can lay a solid foundation for its future, ensuring that the aspirations of its people are not only met but exceeded.

2.2 The 'Resource Curse'

Many policy analysts agree that South Sudan was born on July 9, 2011, with a golden spoon in its mouth. This is because the country received a monthly amount of USD 0.5 billion from oil revenue during the first six months of independence. However, the failure to implement the SPLM Strategic Framework for War-to-Peace Transition during the Interim Period of six years (January 2005 – June 2011), in turn, led South Sudan to low investment in key areas, such as basic services, social capital, human capital, physical capital, infrastructure, and so forth. This failure, in turn, deepened the fragility of the South Sudanese state, thereby creating a vicious circle of fragility that is difficult to break.

Furthermore, the reliance on oil revenue has created a significant economic vulnerability. Oil accounts for more than 90 percent of South Sudan's Government revenue and 98 percent of exports, making the nation's economy exceptionally sensitive to fluctuations in global oil prices. The lack of diversification in the economy has left the country susceptible to crises, such as the conflict in the Sudan, and a steep decline in oil prices in recent years, which pushed the economy further into despair. This dependency, which some policy analysts have called "resource curse," highlights institutional weakness with respect to economic management and a failure to invest in other sectors, such as agriculture, which could have provided a more stable economic foundation.

The phenomenon of "resource curse" [90] has been a persistent issue in oil-rich countries, which often experience poor economic performance despite their abundant natural resources. This paradox can be attributed primarily to the lack of accountability in governance structures. Unlike non-oil-producing nations, where governments derive revenues through taxation paid by citizens, oil-rich governments receive substantial funds directly from oil companies. This direct revenue stream creates a disconnect between the government and its citizens, leading to a diminished sense of responsibility regarding the management of these resources.[91]

---

90   For more on this point see: Gelb, Alan. 1988. *Oil Windfalls: Blessing or Curse? A World Bank Research Publication.* Oxford University Press. Van der Ploeg, Rick. 2011. Natural Resources: Curse or Blessing? Journal of Economic Literature 49(2) 308-420.

91   See Devarajan, Shantayanan. 2019. *How to use oil revenues efficiently.* In

In non-oil-producing countries, the necessity to collect taxes fosters a relationship of accountability between citizens and their government. Citizens demand transparency and responsible fiscal management, as their contributions directly impact public services and infrastructure. In contrast, the absence of such a relationship in oil-rich nations allows governments to operate with limited public oversight, often resulting in mismanagement and corruption.

In light of the preceding paragraph, policymakers and stakeholders in South Sudan must advocate for systems that promote accountability in the management of oil revenues. This can be achieved through the implementation of transparent governance frameworks, citizen engagement initiatives, and robust regulatory measures that ensure oil revenues benefit the broader population. By emphasizing accountability, we can shift the narrative surrounding resource-rich South Sudan from one of stagnation to one of sustainable peace, economic growth, and poverty eradication. Only through this shift can we hope to harness the true potential of these resources for the benefit of all South Sudanese citizens as envisioned by Dr. John Garang.

In the realm of public finance, a critical challenge persists: the transparent allocation of revenues generated from natural resources, particularly oil. A significant body of evidence suggests that citizens often remain unaware of the full extent of these revenues. This lack of awareness can lead to a troubling disengagement from the scrutiny of governmental spending. When citizens disapprove of how funds are allocated, their options for recourse are limited, as they cannot refuse to pay taxes on the grounds of discontent with spending practices. This point will become clearer if we look into the findings of recent research.

Mohaddes, K., J. Nugent and H. Selim, eds., Institutions and Macroeconomic Policies in Resource-rich Arab Economies, Oxford University Press.

Research conducted by Devarajan (2019) across 115 countries over a 15-year span reveals a striking correlation between accountability and revenue types. The study indicates that accountability is negatively associated with oil rents accruing to an oil-producing state, suggesting that reliance on these revenues diminishes governmental responsibility to its constituents. Conversely, the same research highlights a positive relationship between accountability and tax revenues, which underscores the importance of diversified revenue sources in fostering governmental transparency and responsiveness.

Moreover, the implications of weak accountability are profound, leading to the misallocation of public resources. Giugale and Nguyen (2014) assert that reallocating just 30 percent of oil revenues could potentially eradicate poverty. This assertion starkly contrasts with the current reality, where actual spending has failed to mitigate the rise in poverty levels. Such data not only illustrate the necessity of improved accountability mechanisms but also serve as a clarion call for policy reform aimed at building resilient institutions for coherent governance in South Sudan.

Hence, the lesson of experience from the "resource curse" literature is that the evidence overwhelmingly supports the need for enhanced accountability in the management of public resources. By prioritizing transparency and responsible governance, South Sudan can ensure the appropriate application of John Garang's ideas and vision. But we must remove politics and bias from our decision-making processes in the service of the people of South Sudan. For instance, implementing the idea of making agriculture the engine of the economy and fueling it through oil revenues would ensure that we are on the path to sustainable peace, economic growth, and poverty eradication.

Furthermore, in assessing South Sudan's first decade of independence, it is evident that the nation has failed to utilize its oil revenues effectively to benefit its population. The challenges are multifaceted, stemming from the nature of revenues and their implications for governance. However, as we move into the mid-point of the second decade, a pressing opportunity exists to rectify these failures by adopting a more strategic approach to oil revenue management.

For instance, in an ideal world, the government would channel oil revenues toward stimulating economic growth, enhancing human capital, and diversifying the economy. Such measures would significantly alleviate poverty in the near term and improve the overall quality of life for South Sudanese citizens in the long term. Nevertheless, the reality is starkly different. Development programs are consistently undermined by ongoing conflicts and a lack of implementation capacity as we have highlighted previously.

Furthermore, the incentives for the government to allocate public expenditure toward initiatives that would yield the greatest benefit for the populace are severely lacking. High levels of corruption and captured public policies exacerbate this issue, leading to a situation where oil revenues do not translate into tangible benefits for the citizens. In this context and in order to address these challenges, several key strategies must be considered:

- **Strengthening Governance**: Establishing transparent systems for revenue management to minimize corruption and ensure that funds are allocated efficiently, effectively, and equitably.
- **Investing in Human Capital**: Prioritizing education and health sectors to build a skilled workforce that can contribute to economic diversification.
- **Encouraging Economic Diversification**: Developing sectors beyond oil, such as agriculture, tourism, and other critical minerals (e.g., gold, tin, uranium, etc.), to reduce dependency on oil revenues and create sustainable economic growth.

- **Promoting Community Engagement**: Involving local populations in the decision-making process to ensure that development projects align with their needs and priorities.

In conclusion of this subsection, while South Sudan's first decade has been characterized by missed opportunities regarding oil revenue utilization, the second decade offers a chance for transformative change. By adopting a structured approach to governance and public expenditure, the government can enhance the welfare of its citizens, ultimately fulfilling the promise of independence. The time for action is now; the future of South Sudan depends on it.

3. Future Directions in Economic Management

The future of South Sudan demands an immediate and transformative approach to economic management—one that places the well-being of its citizens above personal greed and political turmoil. This paradigm shift must be rooted in the visionary ideas of John Garang, particularly his assertion that agriculture should serve as the cornerstone of our economy, supported by oil revenues. It is imperative that we critically reassess our reliance on oil while simultaneously addressing the institutional weaknesses that have hindered our progress. By embracing Garang's vision, we can cultivate a robust economic framework that fosters sustainable peace, economic growth, and poverty eradication in South Sudan.

We are a landlocked country surrounded by six countries, but this could be turned into an advantage. Our geopolitical landscape is currently profoundly influenced by our reliance on oil production, which is a critical artery for our economic sustenance. And since our separation from Sudan in 2011, we have failed to leverage our oil reserves into sustained economic growth, with export revenues from this resource representing the lion's share of our government's revenues. We have mentioned earlier in this chapter that the oil dependency poses strategic challenges and opportunities.

Our lack of refinery capabilities necessitates the exportation of crude oil via pipelines traversing Sudan, placing a geopolitical lever in the hands of our northern neighbor. The absence of a domestic refinery also precludes the possibility of utilizing crude for local power plants, exacerbating South Sudan's energy insecurity.

Hence, the prevailing reliance on oil production as the cornerstone of South Sudan's economy has proven to be an embarrassing vulnerability amidst geopolitical and market volatilities. Thus far, we have neglected to capitalize on opportunities to diversify South Sudan's economic portfolio, which could have offered a more stable platform for resilience in the face of such crises. While the country possesses a wealth of natural resources and potential avenues for growth, such as agriculture and mining, the lack of infrastructure development for alternatives, like power plants for energy independence, is a glaring oversight.

The excessive reliance on a mono-commodity economy heightens vulnerability to external shocks and hampers our initiatives to combat poverty and a sense of marginalization in South Sudan. Therefore, economic diversification must transcend mere theoretical discussions; it necessitates the formulation of a pragmatic blueprint that champions innovation and secures national prosperity and resilience against unforeseen downturns. This strategic approach is essential not only for sustainable growth but also for safeguarding our future.

Dr. Francis Mading Deng tells us that there is always an opportunity in crisis, and we share his optimism in the face of the enormous challenges in the world. For instance, the SAF-RSF strife in Sudan creates an opportunity for South Sudan to plan for a network of pipelines to export crude oil through Djibouti and/or Somaliland and refined oil products to the neighboring countries of CAR, DR Congo, Uganda, Kenya, and Ethiopia. As global energy markets evolve, it becomes increasingly imperative for South Sudan to diversify its economy to mitigate the risks of overdependence on a volatile commodity that underpins its regional relationships and internal stability.

Central to these strategies is the optimization of our oil production capabilities. As the backbone, at this point, of the South Sudanese economy, maximizing the efficiency and output of oil production not only promises a more stable financial foundation but also positions Juba as a key player in the regional energy market. Nevertheless, Juba must use oil revenues to diversify the economy, especially ensuring transparency and accountability of the oil for roads fund. The development and maintenance of export pipelines are essential in this regard, as they provide critical conduits for the transportation of oil to international markets, thus ensuring a consistent and smooth flow of revenue.

Furthermore, the establishment or enhancement of local refinery infrastructure could significantly reduce South Sudan's reliance on imported refined oil products, fostering economic resilience through diversification. Additionally, investing in power plant projects that leverage the nation's hydrocarbon resources cannot only meet domestic energy needs but also create avenues for export to neighboring countries, generating alternative income streams for the government and mitigating the risk of an economic collapse.

On institutional weakness, the future directions are informed by analyzing the CPIA index for South Sudan across four key categories, utilizing 16 indicators as outlined in Table 7 on the following page. The Country Policy and Institutional Assessment (CPIA) index provides critical insights into the governance and policy frameworks of South Sudan over a five-year period (2020-2024). The analysis is organized into four key clusters: Economic Management, Structural Policies, Policies for Social Inclusion and Equity, and Public Sector Management and Institutions. Each cluster comprises specific indicators that reveal trends and areas for improvement.

Table 7: South Sudan's CPIA for the Period 2020 - 2024

Indicator & Cluster	2020	2021	2022	2023	2024
A. Economic Management	**1.2**	**1.5**	**1.5**	**1.7**	**1.2**
1. Monetary and Exchange Rate Policy	1.0	2.0	2.0	2.0	1.5
2. Fiscal Policy	1.0	1.0	1.0	1.5	1.0
3. Debt Policy	1.5	1.5	1.5	1.5	1.0
B. Structural Policies	**1.8**	**2.0**	**2.0**	**2.0**	**1.5**
4. Trade	2.0	2.5	2.5	2.5	2.0
5. Financial Sector	2.0	2.0	2.0	2.0	1.5
6. Business Regulatory Environment	1.5	1.5	1.5	1.5	1.0
C. Policies for Social Inclusion and Equity	**1.5**	**1.5**	**1.6**	**1.7**	**1.4**
7. Gender Equality	1.5	1.5	1.5	1.5	1.5
8. Equity of Public Resource	2.0	2.0	2.0	2.0	1.5
9. Building Human Resources	2.0	2.0	2.5	2.5	2.0
10. Social Protection and Labor	1.0	1.0	1.0	1.5	1.0
11. Policies and Institutions for. Environmental Sustainability	1.0	1.0	1.0	1.0	1.0
D. Public Sector Management and Institutions	**1.4**	**1.4**	**1.4**	**1.3**	**1.2**
12. Property Rights and Rule-Based Governance	1.5	1.5	1.5	1.5	1.0

13. Quality of Budgetary and Financial Management	1.0	1.0	1.0	1.0	1.0
14. Efficiency of Revenue Mobilization	2.0	2.0	2.0	2.0	2.1
15. Quality of Public Administration	1.0	1.0	1.0	1.0	1.0
16. Transparency, Accountability, and Corruption in the Public Sector	1.5	1.5	1.5	1.5	1.0
Overall CPI	**1.5**	**1.6**	**1.6**	**1.7**	**1.3**

Source: From CPIA Africa - Assessing Africa's Policies and Institutions. Annually Published by the World Bank

1. **Economic Management**
   a. **Overall Trend:** The CPIA score for Economic Management fluctuated, peaking at 1.8 in 2021 before declining to 1.2 in 2024.
   b. **Indicators Performance:**
      - **Monetary and Exchange Rate Policy:** A decrease from 2.0 to 1.5 suggests instability; focusing on macroeconomic stability is crucial.
      - **Fiscal Policy:** Consistent low scores (1.0) indicate a need for more robust fiscal management strategies.
      - **Debt Policy:** The score remains stable at 1.5, but future efforts should focus on sustainable debt management practices.

2. Structural Policies
   a. **Overall Trend:** The scores in this cluster also exhibit a decline, from 1.8 in 2020 to 1.5 in 2024.
   b. **Indicators Performance:**
   - **Trade:** A drop from 2.5 to 2.0 suggests stagnation; enhancing trade relations and agreements can boost this score.
   - **Financial Sector:** A decrease from 2.0 to 1.5 highlights the necessity for reforms to bolster financial inclusivity.
   - **Business Regulatory Environment:** The consistent score of 1.5 signals the need for regulatory reforms to stimulate business growth.

3. Policies for Social Inclusion and Equity
   a. **Overall Trend:** Scores remained relatively stable, with a slight decrease from 1.5 in 2020 to 1.4 in 2024.
   b. **Indicators Performance:**
   - **Gender Equality:** Consistently scored at 1.5 suggests a stable but inadequate focus on gender issues; initiatives promoting gender equity should be prioritized.
   - **Equity of Public Resources:** The drop from 2.0 to 1.5 indicates a need for more equitable resource distribution.
   - **Building Human Resources:** An increase from 2.0 to 2.5 shows promise, but further investment in education and skill development is necessary.

4. Public Sector Management and Institutions
   a. **Overall Trend:** The CPIA score declined from 1.4 in 2020 to 1.2 in 2024, indicating deteriorating governance.
   b. **Indicators Performance:**
   - **Property Rights and Rule-Based Governance**: The

scores range from 1.0 to 1.5, indicating a generally low to moderate perception of property rights and governance. This suggests ongoing challenges in establishing robust property rights, which may hinder economic growth and investment.

- **Quality of Budgetary and Financial Management**: Consistently rated at 1.0 indicates a significant area for improvement. The lack of effective budgetary management confirms inefficiencies in resource allocation and financial oversight, which is underpinning fiscal instability in the country.
- **Efficiency of Revenue Mobilization**: Scores of 2.0 to 2.1 show a more favorable view of revenue mobilization, indicating some effectiveness in tax collection and resource mobilization. However, the marginal increase to 2.1 may reflect slight improvements or reforms that are not yet fully realized.
- **Quality of Public Administration**: With all scores at 1.0, this indicates critical deficiencies in public administration practices, which are affecting service delivery and undermining citizen trust in government institutions.
- **Transparency, Accountability, and Corruption in the Public Sector**: Scores range from 1.0 to 1.5, highlighting persistent issues with transparency and accountability. The drop to 1.0 in the last measurement suggests worsening perceptions of corruption or accountability.

In conclusion, the CPIA index for South Sudan highlights significant opportunities for governance and policy enhancement. By strategically addressing the identified weaknesses, South Sudan can indeed elevate its CPIA scores and promote sustainable development. Emulating Dr. John Garang's path-goal strategy, it is both feasible and imperative for South Sudan to aim for a CPIA score of 6 across the four clusters. This ambitious goal reflects a commitment to improvement and serves as a catalyst for transformative and coherent governance that can lead to sustainable peace, economic growth, and poverty eradication in the long run.

1. Economic Management
- Implement monetary policies that stabilize inflation and exchange rates. Initiate a dialogue on the introduction of a Central Bank Digital Currency (CBDC)[92] as one strategy for ensuring price stability underpinned by economic growth in South Sudan.
- Expedite implementation of the current Public Financial Management Reforms Strategy (PFMRS) launched in May 2020.
- Strengthen debt management capabilities through training and adopting best practices.

---

92   Introducing a CBDC could be crucial in fostering economic stability in South Sudan. By providing a more secure and reliable monetary system, a digital SSP could help mitigate the issues of delay in the payment of wages and salaries of public sector employees, inflation, and currency devaluation that have plagued the economy since 2012. Furthermore, digital currency could facilitate greater financial inclusion, enabling more citizens to participate in the formal economy and decreasing reliance on cash transactions, which are often vulnerable to theft, loss, wear and tear. This move toward digital finance could lead to more resilient economic structures by promoting savings and investments within the overall framework of macroeconomic stability. This would be possible since macroeconomic policy objectives under the CBDC system are: (a) focus on real price stability by moving away from the current practice of inflation forecast targeting to aggregate price level target; and (b) full employment.

2. Structural Policies

- Foster trade partnerships and create favorable conditions for investment to stimulate economic growth.
- Reform the financial sector to improve access to banking services and credit for underserved populations.
- Simplify business regulations to encourage entrepreneurship and attract foreign direct investment.

3. Policies for Social Inclusion and Equity

- Promote initiatives that focus on gender equality, such as economic empowerment programs for women.
- Ensure equitable access to public resources through inclusive policy frameworks.
- Invest in health, education, and skill development programs to enhance human capital.

4. Public Sector Management and Institutions

- **Enhanced Governance Frameworks**: Strong rule-based governance and property rights must be pushed to encourage investment, particularly in the agricultural sector and urban developments.
- **Financial Management Reforms**: As awareness of the importance of budgetary management grows, initiatives aimed at improving the quality of financial management will emerge, which would stabilize fiscal situations.
- **Increased Revenue Efficiency**: Efforts to enhance revenue mobilization must continue, especially with the rise of technology in tax collection, potentially leading to higher efficiency scores in the future.
- **Public Administration Overhaul**: Due to the low scores, there

is an urgent need to reform public administration practices, emphasizing efficiency and service delivery.
- **Focus on Transparency and Anti-Corruption**: As citizens demand greater accountability, we must seize this opportunity to implement strict anti-corruption measures, aimed at increasing transparency and reducing corrupt practices in the public sector.

Chapter Eight

Conclusion

"The struggle for fundamental socio-economic change cannot be achieved through the mere replacement of personalities in government. Our nascent republic is under attack—both from outside our borders and from within, by traditional elites who have failed to understand the vision of the New Sudan. The historical significance of South Sudan's independence cannot be captured in a few sentences; it deserves a separate, in-depth discourse. For now, it suffices to say that independence was not an end in itself but a means to an end. If we fail to grasp this, it will be difficult for us to move forward as a nation."
(Mabior Garang 24/01/2025)

The above passage from Mabior Garang, the elder son of Dr. John Garang de Mabior, is a powerful point of entry for concluding the second edition of this book. By a curious coincidence of history, this passage is from what Mabior posted on 24 January 2025, precisely the date his father revealed the vision of New Sudan 53 years ago on 24 January 1972. We have highlighted the vision of New Sudan in Chapter Four of this book. Mabior is right: "**to say that independence was not an end in itself but a means to an end. If we fail to grasp this, it will be difficult for us to move forward as a nation**." And the end is sustainable peace, economic growth, and poverty eradication.

Indeed, the people of South Sudan must internalize John Garang's ideas and vision to be on the path to sustainable peace, economic growth, and poverty eradication. They must understand that the vision of New Sudan is underpinned by two struggles – the political struggle for independence and the struggle for "fundamental socio-economic change." The "Sunset" generation of Dr. John Garang has brought the political independence on a golden plate, but at a very high price of more than two million precious souls of our martyrs. It is the "Sunrise" generation of the "Seeds of Nation" that will bring about "fundamental socio-economic change" in South Sudan.

We want to conclude the second edition of this book with:
a. Final reflections on the enduring legacy of John Garang;
b. The importance of creative reasoning in shaping the future; and
c. Call to action for readers to engage with Garang's vision.

Final Reflections on the Enduring Legacy of John Garang
As we reflect on the enduring legacy of Dr. John Garang, we recognize that we should not be stuck in the past. We want to reflect on the fact that his vision for South Sudan transcends the mere achievement of independence. His commitment to socio-economic transformation and national unity resonates deeply in today's context, especially as we navigate the complexities of our nascent republic. Garang's principles serve as a guiding light, reminding us that true progress requires more than just a change in leadership; it necessitates a collective commitment

to the ideals of equality, justice, peace, unity, and development. His legacy is not just a historical account but a living call to action, urging us to cultivate an inclusive society that values every citizen's contribution. We summarize our reflections on the enduring legacy of Dr. John Garang in five points presented below.

1. **Vision Beyond Independence**: Dr. John Garang's legacy extends far beyond the mere act of achieving independence for South Sudan. His vision encompassed a holistic approach to nation-building, emphasizing the importance of socio-economic transformation alongside political freedom. This perspective encourages us to strive for a future that integrates governance and the people's welfare on a steady state of sustainable peace, economic growth, and poverty eradication.

2. **Commitment to National Unity**: Garang's unwavering commitment to national unity remains a cornerstone of his legacy. In a country marked by diversity, his call for inclusivity and collaboration serves as a vital reminder of the strength that lies in unity. This principle is essential as South Sudan continues to forge its identity amidst various challenges of building a viable South Sudanese state at peace within itself and with its neighbors.

3. **Guiding Principles of Justice and Equality**: At the heart of Garang's philosophy is a profound belief in equality and justice for all citizens. His teachings advocate for a society where every individual has the opportunity to contribute and thrive, emphasizing that true progress hinges upon the fair treatment of every member of the community. *Garangnomics* underpins the principles of justice and equality. These principles call for combating poverty and a sense of marginalization in South Sudan.

4. **A Call to Action**: Garang's legacy is not merely historical but a living call to action. His ideals should motivate policymakers to engage actively in the development of South Sudan, inspiring a new generation of leaders and citizens to uphold his vision and work toward the socio-economic upliftment of their communities. Here, the idea of making agriculture the economy's engine, fueled through oil revenues, is popular and will remain a solid foundation of his enduring legacy.

5. **Cultivating an Inclusive Society**: Dr. Garang's powerful message advocates for the establishment of an inclusive society that recognizes and values the contributions of every citizen. By fostering an environment where all voices are not only heard but also respected, we can create a robust and resilient nation. This commitment to inclusivity not only honors Dr. Garang's enduring legacy but also effectively addresses the diverse needs of our populace. Embracing this vision will empower communities, strengthen social cohesion, and pave the way for a brighter future for all.

The Importance of Creative Reasoning in Shaping the Future of South Sudan

In this pivotal moment, the importance of creative reasoning cannot be overstated. As we face challenges that threaten our national identity and statehood, innovative thinking becomes essential in crafting solutions that reflect the diverse voices of our people. Dr. Garang emphasized the need for a vision rooted in creativity and imagination, enabling us to envision a future where peace, prosperity, and coexistence are attainable. By embracing creative reasoning, we open ourselves to new possibilities and strategies that address the pressing socio-economic issues that have persistently plagued our nation.

Below, we summarize the importance of creative reasoning in shaping the future of South Sudan. The summary elucidates five important points that could be utilized in the service of our people.

1. **The Imperative of Creative Reasoning in Governance:** The pressing challenges of coherent governance and leadership in South Sudan underscore the necessity for innovative thinking as a pivotal strategy for navigating national identity and statehood issues. The preceding chapters of the second edition of the book have introduced various frameworks for creative reasoning, including Venn diagrams and policy matrices, which serve as powerful analytical tools. These frameworks can effectively address the complex obstacles hindering fundamental socio-economic transformation and facilitate a peaceful leadership transition to a new generation in South Sudan. Embracing these innovative methodologies, which are the foundation of creative reasoning, is essential for fostering sustainable development and achieving lasting change.

2. **Vision Rooted in Imagination**: Dr. Garang advocates for a forward-looking vision that is grounded in creativity, which is vital for conceptualizing a peaceful and prosperous future. It also has theoretical underpinnings rooted in economics, which enhances critical understanding of the interactions between proximate and fundamental causes of economic growth. In this context, the idea of making agriculture the engine of South Sudan's economy at this initial stage of our development, fueled by oil revenues, is grounded in the history of economic thought.

3. **Diverse Voices Matter**: Effective solutions must reflect the diverse perspectives and experiences of the South Sudanese people, emphasizing inclusivity in the problem-solving process.

There is a general agreement that South Sudan has 64 nationalities and ethnicities, which necessitates that whatever we do, we must ensure that it includes their varied interests. On this point, Dr. John Garang always cited the Holy Book, as stated in the Book of John (John 14:2, NIV), "**In my Father's house are many rooms; if that were not so, would I have told you that I am going there to prepare a place for you?**" This quotation underscores the importance of inclusivity and the accommodation of all voices in our endeavors. Moreover, it elucidates Dr. John Garang's call for the pay-back time for all our people as a compensation package in their unwavering commitment to the liberation struggle.

4. **Addressing Socio-Economic Issues**: Dr. John's innovative approach highlights the profound influence that societal and communal institutions exert on individual motivation within communities. By fostering an environment that encourages education, innovation, and productive contributions to the economy, we can significantly enhance the production and distribution of goods and services. Creative reasoning, grounded in a robust understanding of economic policy management, is essential for developing effective strategies that address the pressing socio-economic challenges facing our nation today. Embracing this perspective will not only empower individuals but also drive sustainable economic growth and social progress.

5. **Openness to New Possibilities**: By embracing creative reasoning as conceptualized by Dr. John Garang, South Sudan can unlock new opportunities and approaches, fostering resilience and adaptability in an evolving landscape. An example of new opportunities is the idea of introducing a Central Bank

Digital Currency (CBDC). Adopting an account-based and interest-bearing CBDC in South Sudan presents a significant opportunity for the country to leapfrog into the 21st-century digital economy. By shifting toward a digital currency, South Sudan can enhance its monetary policy implementation, improve transaction efficiency, secure the SSP as a store of value, stabilize the SSP as a unit of account, and promote financial inclusion among its citizens. A CBDC can also help resolve the problem of recurrent arrears of wages and salaries of public sector employees, combat issues related to currency counterfeiting, and facilitate easier tracking of transactions, thereby strengthening the government's ability to monitor economic activity and tax compliance.

Call to Action for Readers to Engage with Garang's Vision

As we conclude this edition, we extend a heartfelt call to action for each reader: engage with the vision of John Garang. Reflect on his teachings and how they apply to our current crises of state and identity. Let us not be passive observers but active participants in the transformation of South Sudan. Each one of us has a role to play in realizing Garang's dream of a prosperous and unified nation. It is imperative that we harness our collective energies and resources to champion the ideals of creativity and innovation, ensuring that the legacy of Dr. John Garang lives on in our actions and aspirations.

Together, let us strive to embody the principles of creative reasoning in our daily lives, fostering a culture of dialogue, collaboration, and hope. In doing so, we honor Garang's legacy and pave the way for a brighter future for South Sudan.

Bibliography

African National Congress. Ready to Govern: ANC Policy Guidelines for a Democratic South Africa, adopted at the National Conference, 1992.

Aleng, E. M. The Southern Sudan Struggle for Liberty. Nairobi: East African Publishers, 2009.

Ali, A. G., I. Elbadawi, and A. EI-Batahani. "The Sudan's Civil War: Why Has It Prevailed for So Long?" In Understanding Civil War: Evidence and Analysis, Volume 1: Africa, edited by Paul Collier and Nicholas Sambanis. Washington, DC: World Bank, 2005.

Alier, A. Southern Sudan: Too Many Agreements Dishonored. New York: Ithaca Press, 1990.

Bacevich, A. J. The Limits of Power: The End of American Exceptionalism. New York: Metropolitan Books, 2008.

Barnard, C. I. The Functions of the Executive, 3rd ed. Cambridge: Harvard University Press, 1938.

Blackings, M. J. "South Sudan One Year On: From the World's Newest State to Another African Story." A paper presented at St Antony's College, Oxford University, 2012.

Bonar Law, A. "Address to Electors of the Central Division of Glasgow." Bonar Law Papers. November. London: House of Lords' Archive, 1922.

Boswell, A. "The Failed State Lobby." Foreign Policy Magazine, July 9, 2012. www.foreignpolicy.com/articles/2012/07/09/the_failed_state_lobby.

Bowring, P. "Sudan's Chan." New York Times, January 11, 2011. www.nytimes.com/2011/01/11/opinion/11iht-edbowring11.html.

Bromley, D. W., ed. Making the Commons Work: Theory, Practice and Policy. San Francisco: Institute for Contemporary Studies Press, 1992.

Bromley, D. W. "Toward sustainable livelihoods in South Sudan: the necessary institutions of governance." Paper presented at the conference "A New Start For South Sudan: Building Resilient Institutions and Effective Governance," Juba, Republic of South Sudan, February 13-15, 2014.

Central Intelligence Agency (US). Facebook, 2012. https://www.cia.gov/library/publications/rss-updates/WFB-april-13-2012.html.

Chomsky, N. Failed States: The Abuse of Power and the Assault on Democracy. New York: Metropolitan Books, 2006.

Collier, P., and N. Sambanis, eds. Understanding Civil War: Africa. Washington, DC: The World Bank, 2005.

Commons, John R. Institutional Economics-Its Place in Political Economy. New York: Macmillan, 1934.

Deng, F. M. Africans of Two Worlds: The Dinka in Afro-Arab Sudan. New Haven: Yale University Press, 1978.

—. War of Visions: Conflict of Identities in the Sudan. Washington, DC: The Brookings Institution, 1995.

Dickens, C. A Tale of Two Cities. New York: Longman Publishers, 1910.

Dixon, R. "South Sudan's Dreams Slipping Away Already." Los Angeles Times, 2012.

Easterly, W., and R. Levine. "Africa's Growth Tragedy: Policies and Ethnic Divisions." Quarterly Journal of Economics CXII (1997): 1203–50.

Easterly, W. "Can Institutions Resolve Ethnic Conflict?" Economic Development and Cultural Change 49(4) (2001): 687–706.

Fanon, F. The Wretched of the Earth. New York: Grove Press, 1961.

Fardon, S. Southern Sudan and Its Fight for Freedom. Bloomington, IN: AuthorHouse, 2006.

Frost, G. "Officials Can't Afford to Squander Political Capital." The Aesthetic, 2003. www.theaesthetic.com/NewFiles/capital.html.

Garang, J. "Letter to the Commander in Chief Anyanya National Armed Forces Leader of the Southern Sudan Liberation Movement Members of the Anyanya SSLM Negotiation Committee." 1972. http://memberfiles.freewebs.com/34/97/92559734/documents/Garang%20Letter.pdf.

Garang, M. WhatsApp Discussion Group managed by the SPLA/SPLM Veterans' Foundation. [Exact date unknown; cited on p. 22].

Giles, L. The Art of War. English translation published by the US Military. Washington, DC: Gutenberg Project, 1910.

Gumede, W. Restless Nation: Making Sense of Troubled Times. Cape Town: Tafelbeg, 2012.

Hardy, Henry, ed. Berlin, 1 The Power of Ideas. Princeton: Princeton University Press, 1960.

House, R. J. "A Path-Goal Theory of Leader Effectiveness." Administrative Science Quarterly 16 (1971): 321–39.

Inter-Governmental Authority on Development (IGAD). The Comprehensive Peace Agreement between the Government of Sudan and the Sudan People's Liberation Movement (SPLM). Nairobi, Kenya: January 9, 2005.

International Crisis Group. South Sudan's Civil War: Petroleum, Power and Identity. Report No. 288, 2017. [Cited on p. 87].

Johansson, Patrik. "Aid and Conflict in Sudan." A Report to SIDA, Division for Humanitarian Assistance and Conflict Management, Stockholm, Sweden, 2001.

Johnson, D. H. "Editor's Introduction." In The Upper Nile Province Handbook: A Report on Peoples and Government in the Southern Sudan, 1931, by C. A. Willis, 17. Oxford: Oxford University Press, 1995.

Kelly, M. "Social Contract." American History, 2011. http://americanhistory.about.com/od/usconstitution/g/social_contract.htm.

Kennedy, J. F. Profiles in Courage. New York: HarperCollins, 1956.

Kenyi Legge, M. R., and B. A. Ogwaro. "Revitalizing Agriculture and Local Economic Integration." Paper presented to the First National Economic Conference, Juba, South Sudan, September 4–8, 2023.

Khalid, M. Nimeiri and the Revolution of Dis-May. London: Kegan Paul, 1985.

—. The Government They Deserve: The Role of the Elite in Sudan's Political Economy. London: Kegan Paul, 1990.

Kirkpatrick, S. A., and E. A. Locke. "Leadership: Do Traits Matter?" Academy of Management Executive 5 (1991): 48–60.

Kuir, G. "South Sudanese and Mr. President: Tomorrow belongs to the young." www.facebook.com/notes/kuirthiys-word/south-sudanese-and-mr-president/300066263342534.

Law, S. Philosophy: Visual Reference Guide. 2007. www.goodreads.com/author/list/17858.Stephen_Law.

Lewin, K., R. Lippitt, and R. K. White. "Patterns of Aggressive Behavior in Experimentally Created Social Climates." Journal of Social Psychology 10 (1939): 271–99.

Locke, J. An Essay Concerning Human Understanding. Abridged and edited by K. P. Winkler, Cambridge, IA: Hackett Publishing Company, Inc., 1960.

Mabior, J. G. The Vision of New Sudan: Questions of Unity and Identity. Edited by Ghamer Wathig. Cairo: Consortium for Policy and Analysis and Development Strategies (COPADES), 1998.

—. The Vision of New Sudan: Questions of Unity and Identity, 1997. [Cited on p. 50].

March, J. G., and J. P. Olsen. "The New Institutionalism: Organizational Factors in Political Life." American Political Science Review 78 (1984): 734–49.

Maxwell, J.C. The 17 Indisputable Laws of Teamwork: Embrace Them and Empower Your Team. Nashville, TN: Thomas Nelson Publishers, 2001.

Morrison, D. "Merowe, Sudan." National Geographic News, June 18, 2007.

Mukhtar, Al-Baqir al-Afif. "The Crisis of Identity in Northern Sudan: A Dilemma of a Black People with a White Culture." A paper presented at the CODESRIA African Humanities Institute, 1999.

Nyaba, P. A. The Politics of Liberation in South Sudan: An Insider's View. Kampala: Fountain Publishers, 1997.

Nyerere, J. K. "The Arusha Declaration." Freedom and Socialism. Dares Salaam, Oxford University Press, 1968.

—. *Freedom and Socialism: A Selection from Writings and Speeches 1965-1976*. Dares Salaam: Oxford University Press, 1968.

Oduho, J., and W. Deng. The Problem of the Southern Sudan. London: Oxford University Press, 1963.

Omer, I. "The Kushite Conquest of Palestine and the 'Assyro-Kushite Wars.'" 2008. http://www.ancientsudan.org/history_07_assyro.htm.

Putnam, R. Making Democracy Work: Civic Traditions in Modern Italy. Princeton: Princeton University Press, 1993.

—. "Bowling Alone: America's Declining Social Capital." Journal of Democracy 6 (1995): 65–78.

—. Bowling Alone: The Collapse and Revival of American Community. New York: Simon & Schuster, 2000.

Rawls, J. A Theory of Justice. Cambridge, MA: Harvard University Press, 1971. [Cited on p. 55].

Revitalized Agreement on the Resolution of the Conflict in South Sudan (R-ARCSS). Addis Ababa, Ethiopia, September 12, 2018.

Rodney, W. How Europe Underdeveloped Africa. Washington, DC: Howard University Press, 1974.

Sambanis, N. "Conclusion" in Understanding Civil War: Africa, edited by P. Collier and N. Sambanis. Washington, DC: World Bank, 2005.

Smith, A. An Inquiry into the Nature and Causes of the Wealth of Nations, 1755. [Quoted on p. 77].

South Sudan National Bureau of Statistics. Population and Housing Census. NBS Publication, 2008.

—. Statistical Yearbook for Southern Sudan (2010). NBS Publication.

Sudan People's Liberation Movement (SPLM). The Manifesto of the Sudan People's Liberation Movement. 1983.

—. Peace through Development: Perspectives and Prospects in the Sudan. Nairobi: SPLM, 2000.

—. SPLM Strategic Framework for War-to-Peace Transition. New Site,

South Sudan: The SPLM Economic Commission, 2004.

Sun Tzu. The Art of War. Translated by Lionel Giles, 1910. [Cited on pp. 64, 140].

Turner, R., and R. Muller. "The Project Manager's Leadership Style as a Success Factor on Projects: A Literature Review." Project Management Journal 36 (2005): 49–61.

Vall elle, D., and C. Bonnet. The Nubian Pharaohs: Black Kings on the Nile. Cairo: AUC Press, 2007.

Versi, A. "Let Us Harness Our Wounded Pride." IC Publication, 2006. http://www.africasia.com/services/opinions/versi.php.

Welsby, D. A. The Kingdom of Kush: The Napatan and Meroitic Empires. London: British Museum Press, 1996.

—. The Kingdom of Kush: The Napatan and Meroitic Empires, 1998. [Cited on p. 55].

Wikipedia. "Kingdom of Kush." http://en.wikipedia.org/wiki/kingdom_of_kush#cre_note-Welsby.2c_DerekA1998-1. [Cited on p. 55].

World Bank. Building Institutions for Markets. World Development Report 2002. New York: Oxford University Press, 2002.

—. Managing Development: The Governance Dimension. Discussion paper. Washington, DC: The World Bank, 1991.

—. Interim Strategy Note (FY 2013–2014) for the Republic of South Sudan. Report No: 74767-SS.

Wysinger, M. "Nubians." wysinger.homestead.com/Nubians.html. [Cited on pp. 49, 54].

Index

Ababa 22
Abdalla 94
Abdel 94, 126
Abdul 30
Abdurohman 188, 190
Abdurrahman 148
Abel 122-123
Abiol 44-45
Absorptive 158
Abyei 44, 84, 101, 103, 110, 141, 176, 260
Acemglou 219
Acemoglu 201-202, 207-7, 210-212, 215, 218-9
Achan 87
Achuil 267
Acuil 128
Adam 70-71, 197
Adams 51
Addis 22

Addis Ababa 33, 56, 74, 114, 130, 303
Aden 176
Adherence 214
Afghanistan 192, 226
Africa 4, 7-8, 29, 42-3, 46, 64, 86, 93-4, 105, 121, 132, 140-3, 159, 168, 174, 177, 192, 226, 246, 256, 259, 284, 298-8, 303
African 29, 31, 33, 43-4, 48, 80, 102, 111-2, 140, 143, 145, 159, 169, 188, 190, 203, 226-6, 229-9, 248, 263, 298, 302
Africans 44, 299
Agak 267
Agencies 165
Agricultural 88, 91, 265, 267
Ajak 132
Ajawin 242
Akol 242

Akot 186
Akuein 244
Alan 63, 275
Alemayehu 196
Aleng, E. M. 58, 298
Alfred 220
Ali, A. G. 59, 94, 123, 126, 188, 190, 298
Aliab 15
Alier, A. 122-123, 298
Aljazeera 4, 173
Allison 157, 165
Ambiguity 174
American 26, 49, 82, 298, 301-2
Amid 20, 23
Amidst v
Andrew 51, 57
Angeles 139, 300
Anton 41-42
Anver 93
Anyanya 300
Apayi 185-187
Arab 44, 94, 101-2, 111, 132, 174, 276
Arabia 174
Arabic 26, 44, 131, 265
Aristotle 38
Arop 58
Arthur 205, 244
Arts 82

Arusha 19, 136, 177-8, 302
Arvanitidis 201
Asia 29
Asian 205
Athenian 51-52, 127
Athor 147
Augustino 188, 190
Austerity 140
Australia 244
Authority 71, 147, 175, 269, 301
Autonomy 113
Awan 22
Awet 186
Awut 128
Ayahu 256
Babo 107
Bacevich, A. J. 57, 298
Bahr 87, 103-4, 239
Banfield 219
Bannon 158
Bapiny 148
Barkal 44
Barnard, C. I. 38, 133, 298
Barro 207
Bates 220
Battalion 33
Belt 87
Benjamin 166, 185, 187
Berkeley 33
Berlin 300

Bermuda 228
Besley 217
Besouw 192-193, 195-5
Betty 87
Blackings 298
Bloomington 300
Blue 26, 103-4, 141, 260
Bob 208
Bol 166, 185, 187
Boma 100
Bomas 97-98
Bona 16, 58
Bonar 56, 299
Books 220, 298-8
Bor 45
Borders 101
Boswell, A. 299
Bosworth 205
Bowring, P. 26, 299
Brady 216-217
British 15, 63, 307
Broadly 218
Bromley, D. W. 86, 115-6, 161, 194, 299
Brookings 299
Burkina 226
California 33
Cambridge 302-303
Canada 227
Capabilities 251

Capital 107, 214, 223-3, 226-6, 229-9, 300, 303
Carville 26
Catholicism 219
Cdr 18, 251
Census 303
Ceremony 141
Chad 226-227
Chan 299
Chand 208
Charismatic 36
Charles 193
Chekhov 41
Chester 133
Chicago 46
China 174
Chinese 29-30, 38
Chol 244
Chomsky, N. 139, 299
Christian 114
Christianity 114
Christians 26
Christmas 244
Cirino 121
Clinton 174
Cohesive 65
Collins 205
Commons, John R. 38, 56, 129, 161, 299
Complementing 213

Confucius 38
Congo 43, 139, 175, 192, 230, 281
Consortium 188, 190, 302
Cooperation 142
Counterterrorism 176
Creation 110
Crisis 31, 64, 80, 176, 254, 301-1
Cush 46
Dak 68
Dam 174
Dan 46, 115-6
Dani 205
Daniel 86, 96, 115, 151, 161, 186
Darfur 104, 237, 240
Daron 201-202, 210, 212
David 68, 147
Debt 110, 283-3
Deloitte 244
Demarcation 110
Democracy 121, 299, 303
Deng, F. M. 3, 5, 7, 9, 11, 13, 15, 17, 19, 21, 23, 25, 27, 29, 31, 33, 35, 37, 39, 43-5, 47, 49, 51, 53, 55, 57, 59, 61, 63, 65, 67, 69, 71-3, 75, 77, 79, 81, 83, 85, 87, 89, 91, 93, 95, 97, 99, 101, 103, 105, 107, 109, 111, 115, 117, 119, 121, 123, 125, 127-9, 131-3, 135, 137, 139, 141, 143, 145, 147, 149, 151, 153, 155, 157, 159, 161, 163, 165, 167, 172, 174, 176, 178, 180, 182, 184, 186, 188, 190, 192, 194, 196, 198, 200, 202, 204, 206, 208, 210, 212, 214, 216, 218, 220, 222, 224, 226, 228, 230, 232, 234, 238, 240, 242, 244, 246, 248, 250, 252, 254, 256, 258, 260, 262, 264, 266, 268, 270, 272, 274, 276, 278, 280, 282, 284, 286, 288, 292, 294, 296, 299-9, 302, 304, 308, 310, 312, 314, 316, 318, 320, 322, 324, 326, 328, 330, 332, 334, 336, 338, 340, 342, 344, 346, 348

Derek 3-4, 48
Dessalegn 148
Devarajan 275, 277
Diaspora 130
Dickens, C. 299
Digital 173, 287, 296
Dinka 15, 58, 60, 71, 299
Diplomacy 8
Dixon, R. 139, 300
Domar 202, 204
Douglas 161-162
Early 48

East 4, 7-8, 205, 227, 229-9, 263, 298
Easterly, W. 300
Eastern 7, 82, 87, 237
Ebony 86, 169, 173, 184-4, 268
Economic 65, 87, 131, 142-3, 168, 175, 188, 190-191, 205, 210, 213, 220, 230, 233, 237, 242-2, 247-8, 255-6, 261-5, 275, 278-8, 282-3, 287, 300-301, 307
Economics 43, 94, 106, 130-1, 191, 220, 300
Edwin 39
Egypt 8, 47-8, 174
Egyptian 48
Egyptians 3
Elbadawi, I. 94, 123, 298
Electors 299
Electricity 231
Elijah 58
Embeling 46
Energy 125, 127
England 58
English 57, 131, 219, 300
Equality 283
Equally 181
Equatoria 64, 82, 87, 131, 186, 239
Equity 168, 247-7, 282-2, 285, 288
Ernst 244
Ethnic 173, 300
Europe 49-50, 80, 303
Evanston 31
Evsey 202
Exiting 168
Facebook 299
Factbook 43
Fanon, F. 300
Fardon, S. 300
Faso 226
Fatih 59
Feudalism 49
Finland 227, 229
Foremost 180
Fragile 143, 168
Fragility 142, 144-6, 168
France 142
Francis 72, 280
Fundamentally 17
Funj 84
Gabriel 148
Gadet 148
Gadir 94, 126
Garang, M. vi, 1-5, 10, 12-8, 23-4, 32-3, 38-44, 51-3, 56, 58, 60, 62, 64-5, 70-2, 76-9, 82, 84, 113-7, 124, 126, 131, 134, 141, 147, 170, 184, 187-7, 194, 198, 211, 234, 237-241, 244, 276, 279, 290-296, 300

Garangism v, 2, 5, 43, 45, 50, 53, 114, 187
Garangnomics 94, 189-191, 202, 207, 211, 223, 225, 234-4, 292
Geda 196-197
Gelb 275
Gelweng 68, 72
Gender 283, 285
Genesis 46
Geoff 46
Geopolitical 174
George 26, 147
Ghamer 302
Ghana 29
Ghazel 103
Giles, L. 57, 300, 307
Giugale 277
Glasgow 299
Globalization 199
God 219
Goulty 63-64
Governance 64, 94, 122, 150, 152, 155, 160, 165, 222, 240, 283, 288, 299, 307
Graham 157, 165
Greek 3
Greeks 3
Grier 207
Grinnell 33
Guek 15
Gulf 111, 174, 176
Gum 265
Gumede, W. 300
Gutenberg 300
Hackett 302
Hailemariam 148
Ham 46
Hamduk 94
Harrod 202
Harvard 298, 303
Hassan 94, 114
Hayami 161
Health 99, 214, 226, 230
Heglig 19
Hemedti 174
Henry 300
Hiteng 121
Hoeffler 126
Hofara 176
Hon 256
Hong 227, 229
Housing 303
Howard 303
Humanities 302
Hussien 188, 190
Ian 158
Ibid 46, 209-9
Ibrahim 94
Igga 147, 186
Illinois 31

Imatong 87
Indians 29-30
Indices 152
Indigenous 262
Insecure 67
Institutionalism 129
Intergovernmental 175
Internalizing 63
Interstate 173
Iowa 33
Iran 174
Iraq 184
Ireland 228
Ironstone 87
Irvine 133
Islam 114
Islamist 26
Islamization 114
Israel 174
Italy 303
Ithaca 298
Jamal 26
James 26, 186
Janjaweed 170
Japan 227
Jebel 44
Johansson, Patrik. 301
Johnson, D. H. 161, 301
Jones 215-217
Jonglei 71

Juba 5, 31, 86-7, 102-3, 108-9, 111, 124, 140, 147, 169, 174-4, 184, 253, 257, 268, 271, 281, 299, 301
Julius 82
Justin 58
Kafumann 96
Kapoeta 82, 237
Karlo 268
Kaufmann 151
Kegan 301
Kelly, M. 301
Kendall 47
Kennedy, J. F. 51, 57, 301
Kenya 18, 43, 121, 141, 145, 174, 227, 230, 281
Kenyi 87, 301
Kerma 48
Ketting 94
Keynesian 202
Khalid, M. Nimeiri. 301
Khartoum 15, 17, 26, 33, 52-3, 59, 94, 101-3, 108-9, 111, 124, 134, 140, 175
Kiir 5, 14, 16, 18-23, 40, 127-8, 134-5, 140, 145-6, 166, 172, 177, 185, 251, 268, 271
Kirkpatrick, S. A. 39, 301
Klaus 161, 166
Kong 227, 229

Kordofan 104
Korea 227
Kostner 158
Kraay 151
Kremendi 207
Kuan 157, 164-5
Kuir, G. 301
Kun 185-187
Kuol 166, 186
Kurt 34
Kush 3-4, 6-7, 9, 42-50, 105-6, 109, 115, 307
Kushite 6, 8, 48-50, 303
Kushites 3-4, 6-8, 45, 47
Kuznets 199, 203, 219
Kwaje 134
Laches 51-52, 127
Lam 242
Lastly 37, 135, 137
Law, S. 117-122, 299, 301
Lazaros 251
Lee 157, 164-5
Legge 87, 301
Lends 213
Leone 226, 228
Levine 300
Lewin, K. 34, 302
Lewis 202, 204-6
Libya 192
Libyaization 173

Liliir 71
Lionel 57, 307
Lippitt, R. 302
Locke, J. 39, 117, 301-1
Longman 299
Los 139, 300
Lou 15
Lucas 207
Mabior, J. G. vi, 12, 16, 32, 56, 60, 82, 113, 124, 126, 147, 237, 244, 290-291, 302
Macao 228
Macedonian 3
Machakos 115, 251-1, 260
Machar 20-21, 124-5, 140, 147, 172, 179, 183, 242
Macmillan 299
Maddison 200
Mading 72, 280
Madison 44
Madut 16, 58
Mahathir 30
Majak 134, 176
Majok 107
Majur 68
Malak 58
Malanima 200
Malays 29-30
Malaysia 29-30
Malaysian 29-30

Mali 226
Malong 22, 176
Malwal 16, 58
Manchester 205
Mandela 140
Manyang 186
Marginalization 55, 92, 222
Marginalized 233
Marine 134
Maritime 176
Markus 158
Marshall 80, 220
Mary 185-187
Massimo 151
Mastruzzi 151
Matrix 96, 101, 168
Max 219
Maxwell, J.C. 63, 302
Mayai 188, 190
Mayardit 5, 14, 128, 134, 140, 166, 172, 177, 185, 251, 268, 271
Maynard 252
Medani 173
Medeni 4
Mediterranean 7
Mel 166, 185, 187
Mequire 207
Meroitic 47, 307
Merowe 44

Midwest 82
Military 33, 91, 176, 300
Millennium 94
Minkaman 15
Mizrhai 157
Mobilization 213, 284
Mohaddes 276
Mohamad 30
Mohamed 59
Monaco 229
Monday 134
Morality 116
Morrison, D. 46, 302
Mukhtar, Al-31, 302
Muller, R. 32, 38, 307
Museerya 101
Museveni 64
Muslims 26
Musserya 107
Nairobi 18, 121, 141, 145, 244, 301
Naivasha 60, 115
Namibia 228
Napatan 307
Nashville 302
Nasir 68, 71-2
Nelson 52, 140, 302
Netherlands 228, 243
Ngok Dinka 44, 101, 107
Nguyen 277

Nicholas 298
Nielsen 161, 166
Niger 226-227
Nile 26, 46, 68, 71, 87, 103-5, 141, 239, 260, 301, 307
Nilotic 105
Nimeiri 301
Nimir 107
Nimule 147
Nkurunziza 205
Noah 46
Noam 139
Nobel 193, 199, 205
Nonetheless 29, 161, 201, 237
Northeast 7
Northwestern 31
Norwegian 251
Notwithstanding 266
Nuba 84, 141, 260
Nubia 8, 42, 47
Nubian 44, 307
Nuer 15, 71
Nugent 276
Nur 94
Nyaba, P. A. 302
Nyandeng 82
Nyerere, J. K. 82, 302
Ochang 242
Ocum 268
Odongi 256
Oduho, J. 302
Ogwaro, B. A. 301
Olken 215-217
Olsen, J. P. 129, 302
Oluny 148
Omar 79, 170, 240
Omer, I. 239, 242, 303
Ordinary 26
Osman 59
Oxford 49, 58, 275-5, 298, 302, 307
Oyai 176
Oyay 132
Palestine 3, 303
Panthou 19, 57, 176
Paris 142
Patrik 301
Paul 22, 298, 301
Payam 83, 100
Payams 84, 98-100
Perotti 221
Peter 148
Petrakos 201
Petrodar 134
Petroleum 265-266, 301
Petronas 264
Ploeg 275
Polanyi 220
Policymakers 178, 182, 232
Powersharing 260

Presidency 55, 73-4, 257, 262-3, 266
Pretoria 22, 94
Priorities 269
Prioritize 193
Prioritizing 278
Prometheus 220
Protestantism 219
Psychology 302
Putnam, R. 107, 129, 219, 303
Quarterly 300
Rahman 30
Ralf 32
Rashid 94
Rawls, J. A 48-49, 303
Rebecca 82
Regulatory 152, 283, 285
Renaissance 174
Reshuffle 177
Reunification 19, 136, 177-7
Revitalized 22, 73-4, 85, 136, 177, 182, 267, 303
Revitalizing 87
Rick 275
Riek 20, 124-5, 134, 140, 147, 172, 179, 183, 242
Robert 56-57, 107, 129
Roberto 87
Robyn 139
Rodney, W. 32, 303

Rodrik 162, 205, 207, 220
Romer 207
Rostow 205
Roundtable 31
Roy 202
Rumbek 12, 18, 33
Russia 174
Russian 41
Ruttan 161
Rwanda 80, 174-4, 230
Rwandan 80
Sachs 220
Salaam 302
Salva 5, 14, 16, 18-20, 22-3, 40, 127-8, 134-5, 140, 166, 172, 177, 185, 251, 268, 271
Sambanis, N. 126, 298-8, 303
Samson 134
San 299
Saudi 174
Savvy 7
Schultz 194
Schuster 303
Secretariat 245, 255
Selim 276
Sennar 103-104
Shantayanan 275
Shelley 39
Siddig 59
Simon 176, 185-6, 199, 303

Singapore 157, 227-7
Skaperdas 221
Smith, A. 70-71, 197, 303
Smriti 208
Sobat 87
Socialism 302
Socrates 51-52, 127
Solow 201, 208, 210
Somalia 139, 192
Somaliland 281
Somalization 173
Southerners 113-114
Spence 216-218
Stakeholders 272
Starlink 84
Stephen 200
Steve 196
Stockholm 301
Sudanism 42, 44-5
Sudd 87
Sulu 148
Sumbeiywo 251
Sun Tzu. 57, 132-3, 307
Sweden 228, 301
Tafelbeg 300
Taginyang 148
Taha 59
Tahir 94
Tale 299
Tamazuj 55, 101-110

Tanzania 33, 82, 230
Tapoza 82
Taskforce 256-257, 261-1, 266-6
Telecommunication 266
Teny 124
Tharjath 107
Thel 68
Theoplus 242
Thirdly 211
Tiber 3
Timothy 47
Ting 188, 190
Tomorrow 301
Torit 15, 124
Tornell 221
Trafigura 264
Troika 111
Tulio 256
Tulock 207
Tunku 30
Turner, R. 32-33, 38, 307
Tzu 57, 132, 307
Uganda 43, 87, 174-4, 230, 281
Ujamaa 83
Undersecretary 268
Unemployment 69
Unity 18, 43, 74, 85, 103-4, 136, 149, 240, 302
Uprising 15
Ustaz 59

Vall 307
Velasco 221
Venn 251, 254, 294
Verdier 221
Vernon 161
Versi, A. 93, 307
Vice 20, 59, 74, 101, 110, 134, 147, 183
Violence 143, 168, 191, 196
Violent 177
Waat 71
Wad 173
Walt 204-205
Wani 134, 186
Warlordism 173
Warrap 103-104
Washington 64, 132, 142, 216, 298-9, 303, 307
Wathig 302
Wealth 197-198, 201, 303
Weber 219
Welsby, D. A. 3-4, 48, 307
Wikipedia 48, 307
Willis 301
Wilson 64
Windsor 145
Winkler 302
Wisconsin 44
Woodrow 64
Wunlit 71

Wysinger, M. 307
Yac 58
Yale 299
Yambio 131
Yau 147
Yei 18, 64
Yemen 174
Yemenization 173
Yew 157, 164
Yirol 15
Yujiro 161
Zanden 200

www.ingramcontent.com/pod-product-compliance
Lightning Source LLC
Chambersburg PA
CBHW010824070526
44583CB00022B/2925